D1558738

Straight Through Processing for Financial Services

Complete Technology Guides for Financial Services Series

Series Editors

Ayesha Khanna

Jürgen Kaljuvee

Series Description

Industry pressures to shorten trading cycles and provide information-on-demand are forcing firms to re-evaluate and re-engineer all operations. Shortened trading cycles will put additional emphasis on improving risk management through front-, middle-, and back-office operations. Both business and IT managers need to effectively translate these requirements into systems using the latest technologies and the best frameworks.

The books in the **Complete Technology Guides for Financial Services Series** outline the way to create and judge technology solutions that meet business requirements through a robust decision-making process. Whether your focus is technical or operational, internal or external, front, middle, or back office, or buy vs. build, these books provide the framework for designing a cutting-edge technology solution to fit your needs.

We welcome proposals for books for the series. Readers interested in learning more about the series and Elsevier books in finance, including how to submit proposals for books in the series, can go to: http://www.books.elsevier.com/finance

Other Titles in the Series

Introduction to Financial Technology by Roy S. Freedman

Electronic and Algorithmic Trading Technology by Kendall Kim

Straight Through Processing for Financial Services by Ayesha Khanna

Straight Through Processing for Financial Services

The Complete Guide

Ayesha Khanna

AMSTERDAM • BOSTON • HEIDELBERG • LONDON
NEW YORK • OXFORD • PARIS • SAN DIEGO
SAN FRANCISCO • SINGAPORE • SYDNEY • TOKYO

ELSEVIER

Academic Press is an imprint of Elsevier

HG
1616
.S36
K53
2008

Academic Press is an imprint of Elsevier
30 Corporate Drive, Suite 400, Burlington, MA 01803, USA
525 B Street, Suite 1900, San Diego, California 92101-4495, USA
84 Theobald's Road, London WC1X 8RR, UK

Library of Congress Cataloging-in-Publication Data
Khanna, Ayesha.
    Straight through processing for financial services : the complete guide /
Ayesha Khanna.
        p.   cm.
    Includes bibliographical references and index.
    ISBN-13: 978-0-12-466470-8 (alk. paper)   1. Banks and banking—Securities
processing.   2. Clearing of securities.   3. Financial services industry—Technological
innovations.   I. Title.
    HG1616.S36K35 2008
    332.10285—dc22
                                                                                2007024525

British Library Cataloguing-in-Publication Data
A catalogue record for this book is available from the British Library.

ISBN: 978-0-12-466470-8

For information on all Academic Press publications
visit our Web site at www.books.elsevier.com

Printed in the United States of America
07 08 09 10 11   9 8 7 6 5 4 3 2 1

For My Parents, Javed and Farida Malik

Contents

Preface

Straight through processing (STP) is a concept that has matured over the last few years from a hyped buzzword to a fundamental goal of the securities industry. It originally entered the limelight as the name given to initiatives that would result in a shortened settlement cycle of securities—from T+3 to T+1 (where T stands for trade date). A shorter time to settlement would lower counterparty and liquidity risks significantly, a benefit that the Securities Industry Association (SIA) cited when it pushed the industry to meet a deadline for achieving T+1.

The industry's inability to meet the 2004 deadline highlighted the many roadblocks—inefficiencies due to manual processes, data inconsistencies, lack of connectivity, and mismatched records—that lay in the way of achieving this goal. The SIA dropped its insistence on T+1, advocating instead a focus on incremental steps, such as matching and confirmation of trades, as necessary milestones on the way to achieving a faster settlement cycle.[1] STP began to be associated with a far bigger goal, which was the automation of all processes related to the trade lifecycle of financial securities, including equities, fixed income, and derivatives.

Today, STP stands for complete automation of trade-related processes in the securities industry. It constitutes an end-to-end streamlining of operations within and across firms, from trade initiation to settlement, and inclusive of auxiliary processes, such as risk management and accounting. STP is therefore the set of operations and technology solutions that entirely replaces manual processes with system communication of transaction details between the parties involved in processing a trade. It requires all market participants, such as exchanges, clearinghouses, vendors, and broker-dealers, that play a role in the trade lifecycle to improve their IT systems within their firms and to standardize their communication with each other. Thus, STP must be understood as a two-pronged strategy, involving system improvements for both internal and external transaction processing.

▌ The Drive Toward STP

The pressure to achieve STP has never been greater. In the current market environment, participants retain their competitive edge only by enhancing their ability to

---

[1]"Industry Drops Push for T+1 Settlement," *On Wall Street*, September 2004.

partake in industrywide STP. Business success is increasingly difficult without the benefits of IT systems that ensure accuracy, speed, and secure connectivity at all stages. This is as relevant to broker-dealers who are providing trade execution services, as to marketplaces that are creating electronic interfaces for clients, and to buy-side institutions that are searching for ways to improve returns on their portfolios: all players are affected one way or another by the drive toward increased automation and scalability in a global 24/7 trading environment.

Several factors are particularly motivating senior management to expand their efforts to improve their STP implementation. More people are trading securities than ever before, and they are also trading these securities more often. In other words, both trading volume and trading frequency have risen significantly in recent years. The ability to trade electronically and the commoditization of financial securities have contributed to this surge in volume. However, these very factors have also shrunk profit margins as the spread between bid and ask prices have become thinner as markets have become more liquid. Buy-side institutions are putting increasing pressure on their broker-dealers to provide them best execution prices for their orders, and are even beginning to access the market directly to trade (as is often the case with hedge funds that use prime brokerage facilities). Couple these changing market conditions with regulations, such as Reg NMS and MiFID, which call for more transparent and efficient markets, and the securities industry suddenly finds itself in a landscape that has changed drastically. The new mantra is to have faster access to market, quicker decisions on how to find the best price for a trade, and ability to store and analyze vast amounts of data for risk management. And all this must be done within the confines of a regulatory environment that is becoming stricter across the globe as governments strive to protect investor interests.

The only way to be competitive and succeed in such an environment is to have high-speed, scalable, and reliable systems that can communicate transaction information to each other securely. Operations and IT systems need to be set up in such a way that the trade lifecycle moves seamlessly and quickly from one phase to another—from pre-analytics to trade order, from trade execution to trade matching, from trade settlement to account allocation, and so on. Streamlining the trade lifecycle is not an easy undertaking. It requires a deep understanding of the financial processes involved, and a framework in which to make decisions on which technologies will be best suited to improve these processes.

The Need for a Framework

Market participants are faced with a plethora of technology options to choose from, each advocated by a different group of enthusiastic supporters in the industry. More often than not, senior management finds itself overwhelmed by questions on how to move from their legacy environments, in which applications and data are stuck in silos and updated by processes that are manual and redundant, to a streamlined STP environment that will result in lower business risk and operational costs. There is no comprehensive guide in the market that gives answers to the question of how to automate the trade lifecycle and all its associated processes. This book was written to address precisely these needs by answering the questions: What are the current trends in the market and how is the trade lifecycle affected by these trends? What are the key technology solutions available to solve business requirements, and how can one choose the best solution given a particular problem? What are the laws and regulations that are relevant to implementing an STP environment for the securities industry?

Straight Through Processing for Financial Services provides a foundation for thinking about how the trade lifecycle can be automated in the light of current trends in the industry. It starts with a description of how the market is evolving today, explaining the main business drivers for STP in the industry. Readers are given a detailed overview of the trade lifecycle as it pertains to broker-to-broker and institutional investor-to-broker transactions for equities, fixed income, and derivatives products. The automation of the stages of the trade lifecycle explained in this overview constitutes the business goal of an STP system.

After having laid out the business foundations of the STP environment, the book proceeds to build a framework and strategy for choosing particular technology solutions. At every stage, readers are given a basic introduction to the kind of technologies that address a fundamental part of STP, such as connectivity or machine-to-machine communication. Each chapter addresses one important pillar of achieving automation in the industry, and directs the reader to solutions that are cutting-edge and have been received positively by leading market players.

For instance, there are many software architectures that can be employed when designing a large-scale complex system. In this book, Service-Oriented Architecture (SOA) is recommended because it is increasingly the most highly valued software architecture for financial systems. There are many ways to connect systems internally and between market partners. The book recommends using a high-speed message bus for internal communication and advocates choosing an external connection—direct, an extranet, or industry messaging provider—depending on the particular needs of the business. For example, if the need is lightning-speed connectivity and the company can afford it, then connecting directly to an exchange or marketplace is a very expensive but viable option; if the need is high-speed connectivity but the allocated budget is medium, using an extranet such as Radianz is recommended. One other common problem that technologists often face is how to deal with databases that are stuck in silos and carry inconsistent information about the same reference entities. This book recommends creating data warehouses for read-only reference data, such as historical prices, and then propagating this data through a high-speed message bus across the enterprise. For quick access to data stored in local databases, using virtualization in the form of an enterprise data fabric is presented as a solution that has recently been met with considerable success.

These are just a few examples showing the complexity of problems and variety of choices facing technologists today. The needs of the financial services industry are particular, and the demands of the business are aggressive; in order to successfully compete, a holistic understanding of how to automate transaction-related processes as they occur within the firm and in partnership with other firms is required. This book provides the strategy that can be used to effectively leverage technology to give an organization the competitive edge it needs to be successful in today's market environment.

Constructing a Strategy

The first step to creating a strategy is to understand the business requirements in detail. The book, therefore, begins with two chapters that discuss the trends in the securities industry today, and the key phases of the trade lifecycle that will be automated. The remainder of the book devotes each chapter to a technology solution for a particular business need of implementing STP. Together, these chapters form a comprehensive guide on how to achieve STP of securities processing.

CHAPTER 1: THE BUSINESS CASE FOR STP

Any technology initiative must be undertaken based on a thorough analysis that shows there are significant advantages to investing in a particular IT project. Although it is difficult to put a precise dollar value on the increases in profits due to expanded and improved IT systems, it is possible to make a case for an implementation based on a review of the business requirements of today's markets. The financial landscape is changing rapidly with the ability to trade electronically, manage risk effectively, and comply with stringent laws becoming the most prominent drivers of automating trade processing and settlement.

CHAPTER 2: THE TRADE LIFECYCLE

STP revolves around the efficient and timely processing of trade-related activities, from trade initiation to settlement and then on to position monitoring and risk management. The trade lifecycle for all security types can be divided into four main phases: pre-trade (analytics and price discovery), trade (order creation and execution), post-trade (clearing, allocation, and settlement), and post-settlement (risk management, profit and loss accounting, and position monitoring). During the course of one lifecycle, many different systems are used within a firm, and data is exchanged with multiple systems outside the firm. The ability to transmit and confirm accurate and complete transaction-related information results in lower risk and operational costs.

CHAPTER 3: SERVICE-ORIENTED ARCHITECTURE

Deciding on a sound architecture is the first foundational step to building and extending software systems. Service-Oriented Architecture (SOA) is advocated by this book as the technology architecture of choice to use for implementing an STP infrastructure. Most of the solutions in this book are presented under the SOA paradigm— a framework for representing software modules as loosely-coupled services that can be invoked individually or together to execute a business process. SOA enables a flexible and scalable architecture in which even legacy components can be seamlessly reused by wrapping them as services.

CHAPTER 4: INDUSTRY STANDARDS

Machine-to-machine communication constitutes the core of STP; it eliminates the time delays and errors caused by manual processes. However, it cannot be achieved unless the securities industry chooses standards for exchanging financial data, both in terms of message format and message language. Currently, three languages dominate system communication—FIX, FpML, and SWIFT—and it is imperative for firms that want to connect electronically to industry partners to use one or more of these standards. The code delimited FIX is the most popular industry standard for electronic trading, particularly for equity trading in which it has been credited for revolutionizing the efficiency of the market.

CHAPTER 5: CONNECTIVITY

Systems connected over networks transmit transaction-related information both within the firm and to partners in the industry. Trade messages travel from broker-dealers to exchanges, from exchanges to clearinghouses, and from clearinghouses to custodians, to name just a few of the connections that must be made to ensure STP. Within the firm, the front, middle, and back offices continually send information back and forth for risk calculations, profit and loss accounting, and reporting purposes. While an enterprise message bus is the SOA prescribed connectivity paradigm internally, firms have the option of direct connectivity, using an extranet, or an industry messaging provider such as SWIFT for external connectivity. The choice of network is determined by the speed, budget, and specific requirements of the business unit using the network.

CHAPTER 6: DATA MANAGEMENT

The need for effective data management has risen in the priority ladder of resource allocation with a C-level officer, the Chief Data Officer (CDO), joining the ranks of the top management of companies for the first time. Firms are inundated by high-frequency, high-volume data coming from multiple sources that must be funneled at tremendous speed to various applications across the enterprise. Having a centralized data management strategy that consists of data warehouses for reference data, and an SOA-based data architecture for accessing local databases through data access layers, is the most cost-effective way of accommodating the needs of modern enterprise data management.

CHAPTER 7: RECONCILIATION AND EXCEPTION HANDLING

Reconciliation and exception handling are usually considered second-tier topics of interest when discussing how STP makes the trade lifecycle more efficient. However, this book considers the checks and balances of continual reconciliation between systems throughout the trade lifecycle as a key enabler of STP. Without proper matching of transaction details, the trade will fail to settle or risk will be miscalculated post-settlement, both of which are costly and time-consuming errors. The ability to handle events that are not part of the normal functioning of a system, including those that occur when reconciliation errors occur, is known as exception handling. Firms should have a central exception-handling platform that uses a combination of system validations and operations personnel investigations to identify and resolve exceptions.

CHAPTER 8: REGULATORY COMPLIANCE

As market innovation increases the complexity and variety of financial services and products, governments are also increasing their surveillance of the securities industry. In a global economy, market players often operate in more than one country, and they must constantly keep abreast of regulations if they are to avoid heavy fines and government lawsuits. Regulations primarily aim to improve market transparency and efficiency and to protect the interests of the small investor. Five major regulations are currently affecting firms in the US and the EU—Sarbanes-Oxley, Basel II, MiFID, Reg NMS, and the Patriot Act. All STP systems must be implemented in compliance with these regulations.

CHAPTER 9: BUSINESS CONTINUITY

The terrorist attacks of September 11, 2001 on New York City highlighted the vulnerabilities of the financial sector in coping with unexpected disasters. Business continuity or disaster recovery has since 2001 become a priority for firms that saw disruption in business operations and devastating loss of personnel, systems, and information. A business continuity plan is a cohesive set of procedures that will be carried out in case of an emergency event, such as an earthquake, a terrorist attack, or a pandemic. Business continuity is a concern for the entire industry; regulatory authorities across the globe are working in partnership with industry members to test the ability of the entire industry to recover from disaster scenarios.

CHAPTER 10: VIRTUALIZATION AND GRID COMPUTING

Virtualization extends the SOA approach by making even the physical infrastructure used by software services virtual, thereby allowing a grid of resources across the firm to be utilized on demand. This greatly enhances the computing power available to applications such as risk analytics and algorithmic trading applications, which require massive amounts of power to process high-volume high-frequency data. The twin technologies of virtualization and grid computing have therefore become some of the most highly coveted technologies on Wall Street.

APPENDIX: THE SECURITIES INDUSTRY

The securities industry is one of the most important contributors to the economy of developed countries. It provides a forum for bringing together investors and those looking for capital—businesses and governments—through the issuance and exchange of financial securities. This chapter provides an overview of major players and products in the market and serves as background material for the book, and a refresher course for those familiar with the industry.

Who Will Benefit?

This book will be useful to senior management responsible for trading, risk management, and technology operations, financial analysts, technology managers, strategy consultants, IT developers, and students interested in the industry. It provides a framework for choosing technology solutions for automating and streamlining operations when trading financial securities. Whether you are a technology manager looking for cost-effective solutions to implement STP in your firm, a trader or risk manager keen to improve profits and reduce risks, or an interested industry observer, I hope you find reading this book as educational and enjoyable as I found the process of writing it.

Ayesha Khanna
October 2007, New York

Acknowledgments

I would like to express my appreciation for the excellent support provided by Elsevier, especially Karen Maloney, whose vision and leadership for the series have been exemplary. Jürgen Kaljuvee as co-editor of this series gave key insights throughout the writing process. In addition, Assistant Editor Roxana Boboc and Project Manager Jeff Freeland did wonderful work in helping me get the book into the form it is in today.

Straight Through Processing for Financial Services has benefited enormously from the numerous discussions I have had with colleagues in all sectors of the industry over the last 10 years. I would like to thank Andrew Bartlett who has helped facilitate many of my varied consulting projects, thereby allowing me to examine the industry in depth and breadth.

Every book is ultimately written with the invaluable help of friends and family. I would like to thank Sonia Mansoor and Charles Peterson for their love and support, and especially my wonderful husband Parag Khanna for providing sunshine, inspiration, and encouragement.

Chapter 1

The Business Case for STP

▍ 1.1 Introduction

The straight through processing (STP) paradigm is a set of business processes and technologies that can be used to create an infrastructure for automated real-time transaction processing. In an industry that has STP, systems at every stage of the trade lifecycle, from pre-trade analytics to order creation, routing, and execution, to post-trade settlement would be seamlessly connected. Manual rekeying of data and information would become unnecessary, reducing trade failures caused by human error; in fact, human intervention would be minimal, and required mainly for exception handling and investigation. The creation of such an industrywide environment would require participants, such as sell-side broker-dealers, buy-side institutional investors, exchanges, and clearinghouses, to make investments equal to millions of dollars in their internal technology infrastructures, and in their external connectivity with each other. This book is a guide to choosing the appropriate technologies when building this STP system. But first, it must be proved that there is a valid business case for undertaking the time, resources, and financial investment such an implementation requires. The US securities industry is the largest such industry in the world, and is exponentially growing in size and simultaneously undergoing rapid change. Its contribution to the US economy is significant, with nearly half of all households in the country holding some of their investments in the stock market, and both businesses and the government relying on it to raise capital. To keep this industry efficient and globally competitive is so important that the US government regularly mandates policies to stimulate growth and manage risks in the industry. Section 2 provides an overview of the trends in the US securities industry that will dominate the market over the coming years. The purpose of this section is to show how every indicator of the future of securities services is pointing to the trend of increased automation of trade-related processes. The business case for STP can be made by examining what the market views as current and future goals of the industry, and how closely these goals are linked to technology improvements.

Technology solutions are always formulated *after* articulating the business requirements. The discussion on business goals and directions is the perfect segue to an examination of the technologies that would be necessary to achieve them. Section 3 introduces the concept of straight through processing, and the main concepts that define it. Coupled with the trade lifecycle outlined in Chapter 2, this chapter provides the business and operations foundation for an STP world.

1.2 Trends in the Securities Industry

The securities industry is experiencing dramatic growth in products, services, and markets. Technology and business process improvement have become the need of the hour as firms struggle to meet the demands of an exploding market and its risk management. Changes are driven by many factors, including globalization, new technologies, and transformation of marketplaces. This section summarizes the seven main trends in the US securities industry, showing that each trend underscores the business need for better technology and STP (see Figure 1-1). These are:

- Exploding volumes
- Shrinking margins
- Evolving marketplaces

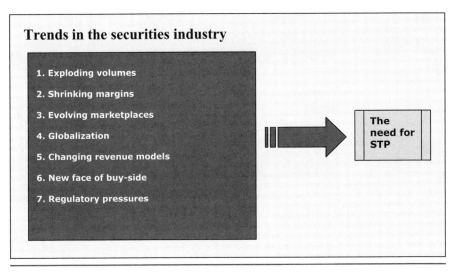

Trends in the securities industry

1. Exploding volumes

2. Shrinking margins

3. Evolving marketplaces

4. Globalization

5. Changing revenue models

6. New face of buy-side

7. Regulatory pressures

The need for STP

Figure 1-1   Trends in US securities industry.

- Globalization
- Changing revenue models
- New face of buy-side
- Regulatory pressures

1.2.1   EXPLODING VOLUMES

The industry is globally growing both in terms of sheer size and also in terms of the volume of trading that occurs daily. That is, not only are more securities being issued, but they are being traded more frequently as well. According to a report published by the SIFMA (Securities Industry and Financial Markets Association), the total market capitalization of equity, debt, and derivatives instruments outstanding increased from $71.1 trillion in 2000 to an estimated $120 trillion in 2006.[1] See Figure 1-2. The total number of shares traded daily has also simultaneously risen in all categories and marketplaces. One example of this explosion in trading volume is the growth in the daily share volume at the NYSE, which more than doubled from 1 billion a day in 1997 to 3 billion a day in 2005, a span shorter than a decade.[2] See Figure 1-3.

---

[1]SIFMA, Research Report, November 2006. Securities Industry & Financial Markets Fact Book Global Addendum 2006.
[2]NYSE website.

Global Securities Markets ($ trillions)							
	2000	**2001**	**2002**	**2003**	**2004**	**2005**	**2006**
Equity market capitalization	32.2	27.9	23.5	32.1	39.1	43.6	49.2
Debt securities outstanding	35.3	36.8	42.1	20.0	57.0	58.3	60.0
Derivatives market value	3.6	4.5	7.3	8.1	10.7	10.8	11.5
Securities industry total	71.1	69.2	72.9	90.2	106.9	112.8	120.7

Figure 1-2 Global securities gross market value. Source: SIFMA, Research Report, November 2006, Securities Industry and Financial Markets Fact Book Global Addendum 2006.

Daily share volume	Year	New York Stock Exchange (NYSE)
1 million	1886	
5 million	1928	**Highest volume day:**
10 million	1929	**3,115,805,723 shares**
50 million	1978	**June 24, 2005**
100 million	1982	
500 million	1987	**Lowest volume day:**
1 billion	1997	**31 shares**
2 billion	2001	**March 16, 1830**
3 billion	2005	

Figure 1-3 Steady rise in daily volume share at the New York Stock Exchange. Source: NYSE website.

With trade volumes rising at an accelerating pace, the market settlement exposure also rises because more transactions now have to be processed and settled daily. *Settlement exposure* is the risk of counterparty default between the time a trade agreement is made and the time the payments are made. It can be divided into two types of risk: credit risk and liquidity risk. *Credit risk* is the risk that the party defaults on its obligations, whereas *liquidity risk* is the risk that the counterparty can meet only partial obligation. The longer the time between trade date and settlement date, the greater the settlement exposure. According to the Securities Industry Association T+1 Business Case report, in 2000 the total dollar value of T+3 trades awaiting settlement on a daily average basis was about $125 billion.[3] Shortening the

---

[3]*SIA T+1 Business Case.* Final Report. Release 1.2. August 2000.

settlement cycle by two days, that is, moving to T+1, would have reduced daily settlement exposure by $250 billion. The same report then predicted that given rising trade volumes, the reduction in this exposure would have been about $750 billion in 2004. Obviously, this risk exposure is even more now. STP of the clearing and settlement of transactions mitigates this risk, and is the primary function of central clearinghouses such as DTCC and the central multi-currency settlement bank CLS (Continuous Linked Settlement).

1.2.2 SHRINKING MARGINS

Interestingly, even though the industry is experiencing a boom in volumes, this is not translating into greater profits for everyone. In fact, quite the opposite is happening for the sales and trading departments in some products. The buy- and sell-sides make revenues and profits in the following way:

1. *Buy-side*—The buy-side manages financial assets for investors, either institutional investors such as pension funds or high-net-worth private clients of the kind that hedge funds manage. Investors entrust their money to these managers because they value the business expertise of these managers, and believe they can earn a higher return on their money this way rather than by investing it themselves. Managers charge investors a management fee for assets under their management. *Assets under management (AUM)* is the total market value of assets that an institutional investor manages and administers for itself and its customers. A mutual fund can charge about 0.5–1% annually on AUM as a management fee. Sometimes, buy-side managers also charge a commission on the profits. For instance, hedge funds charge on average 1–2% of net assets, plus 20% of profits. In addition, hedge funds may also put in extra charges such as account administration. Since the returns on their investments are high (hedge funds returned an average of 11.6% a year after fees to investors from the period of January 1990 to April 2005; note that the S&P 500 stock index returned an average of 10.6% over this same time period), investors don't mind paying these high fees.[4]

2. *Sell-side*—The sell-side acts primarily as broker-dealers, that is, people who execute trades on behalf of the buy-side, matching buyers and sellers. For this service, they charge a fee or commission per trade executed. In addition to intermediation fees, the sell-side may also add research costs for the advice provided to investors. These are known as *soft-dollar commissions* as they are implicitly added into the service fee. If a buy-side firm, such as a hedge fund,

---

[4]*A Fee Frenzy at Hedge Funds,* Business Week, June 6, 2005.

wants to only use the technology and operations infrastructure to execute these trades, the sell-side is acting only as a *prime broker*, and charges fees solely related to these services. Note that sell-side fees include the money it pays to the stock exchange and other utilities to execute the trades.

Thus, the buy-side makes its revenue by charging for its portfolio management capabilities to generate returns on investment, while the sell-side provides research and the infrastructure to access markets and execute trades related to this asset management. Of course, the sell-side also trades with its own money, known as *proprietary trading*, and on behalf of high-net-worth individuals, and in this capacity, acts like a buy-side institution itself at times. In this book, sell-side firms are viewed in their traditional role of broker-dealers who provide research services as well.

Three developments in the securities industry are adversely affecting profit margins, which are affecting the sell-side, the buy-side, and both in varying degrees:

(i) evolution of marketplaces to include electronic trading and after-hours trading;

(ii) increased commoditization of financial products, which makes it easier to trade them electronically;

(iii) regulatory laws such as decimalization of stock prices that have allowed investors to negotiate smaller commissions.

1.2.2.1 Electronic Trading

Quite simply, electronic trading is the ability to use IT systems to buy and sell securities. This means that brokers shouting prices to each other in the middle of a stock exchange have been replaced with the quiet hum of computers being used by brokers to negotiate trades, or even by just the computers themselves matching up buyers and sellers. This poses a huge problem for broker-dealers who made commissions based on their ability to match buyers and sellers.

Sell-side firms employed the floor brokers who represented them in stock exchanges; now their services can be completely replaced by computers. In 1996, in what has come to be known as The Big Bang, the UK government deregulated financial markets in one swift move. One of the big changes was the change from open outcry in the London Stock Exchange (LSE) to electronic screen-based trading. Within six months, a significant number of the floor traders had lost their jobs.

Now the NYSE has also unveiled what it calls the NYSE Hybrid Market, partly an automated trading system, which will allow buy-side firms such as hedge funds and mutual funds to bypass floor brokers and connect directly the NYSE computers for trade execution. Under this system, most of the liquid stocks will be traded automatically, moving to floor traders at the specific request of clients. The total share volume handled by trading-floor specialists and floor brokers fell from 86% in the beginning of the 2006 to just 18% by mid-2007.[5] The brokerage firm Van der Moolen, one of five specialist firms that handled the bulk of NYSE-listed stocks, cut 30% of its US trading operations a day before the NYSE Hybrid Market went live on January 24, 2007 in anticipation of floor traders becoming redundant. Goldman Sachs and Bank of America, among others, also have been cutting down on their floor brokerage business.[6] In May 2007, Bear Stearns announced that it was writing down the value of its specialist division and taking a $225 million charge on its balance sheet for this write-down, making it the latest casualty to succumb to the "death of the floor trader" syndrome.[7]

1.2.2.2 Commoditization

Commoditization refers to the *standardization* of financial products, which in turn makes them easier to understand and to trade electronically. For instance, credit derivatives were financial contracts that were negotiated privately between two parties, and the terms and conditions were unique to each contract. However, as the market realized their value in hedging credit risk and raised its demand for them, the International Swaps and Derivatives Association (ISDA) began working on formulating an industry standard for credit derivatives. Now credit default swaps (CDS) are a standard contract, allowing more people to engage in CDS trades, making the market more liquid. When the *liquidity* for a product rises, that is, there are more buyers and sellers in the market, the spread between bid and ask prices falls. This directly translates into lower commissions for broker-dealers who charge a commission on the price that is finally agreed upon for a trade. In addition, standardization opens the door for automation of the trade lifecycle, thus leading to a decrease in the need for staff to support these functions, including front-office traders and middle-office risk support teams. Only more complicated structured derivatives require a large staff of traders, quantitative analysts (so-called quants) and other support staff. In particular, this trend was seen in the equities industry, where equity trading personnel in the US were laid off, even though trade volume on both the NYSE and the NASDAQ was increasing. In 2005, for example, Goldman Sachs fired 30 equity traders in response to electronic trading and shrinking margins.[8]

---

[5]Matthew Kirdahy, *NYSE Turns Profit, Looks to Hybrid Market,* Forbes.com, February 2, 2007.
[6]Liz Moyer, *Hybrid Trading Costs Jobs,* Forbes.com, January 23, 2007.
[7]Yalman Onaran, *Bear Stearns to Take Write-off on Specialist Unit,* Bloomberg, May 14, 2007.
[8]*Icap Eyes Acquisitions to Boost e-Trading,* Finextra, November 22, 2005. Also, *Goldman Fires 30 Equities Traders as Electronic Volumes Rise,* Finextra, June 29, 2005.

1.2.2.3 Regulation

The SEC regularly mandates changes by the securities industry aimed at protecting the interests of investors; sometimes, these regulations directly translate into lower profit margins. Two examples illustrate this point. First, take the SEC order in 2000 to all US stock markets to convert stock prices from the 200-year-old system of quoting in sixteenths of a dollar to pennies. This decimalization of the markets finally put the US exchanges at par with foreign exchanges, which had all converted to decimal quotes before 1997. The impetus was to make stock prices more easily understandable by small investors and to bring the US stock markets more in conformity with their foreign counterparts. However, it also had the effect of shrinking the spread between bid and ask prices; now the minimum spread could be a penny ($0.01) and not a sixteenth of a dollar ($0.0625). Since commissions are often based on the price of a share, trading commissions shrank when the bid-ask spread shrank. While investors benefited, the margins of dealers and stock brokers fell significantly. In fact, a report by the NASDAQ stock market in June 2001 showed that the quoted and effective spreads fell for most stocks by an average of about 50% since the introduction of decimalization.[9]

Another instance in which regulatory orders led to shrinking margins was when the SEC mandated the capture of all fixed income prices to make markets more transparent. This was important since fixed income prices were always difficult to gauge because bonds are traded OTC and negotiated privately between two parties. In compliance with this law, in 2002 NASD (National Association of Securities Dealers), the primary private-sector regulator of America's securities industry, installed a system that posts prices of all registered corporate bonds 15 minutes after they occur. This system, known as TRACE (trade reporting and compliance engine), facilitates the mandatory reporting of OTC secondary market transactions in TRACE-eligible corporate bonds via a website. All broker-dealers who are NASD member firms have an obligation to report transactions to TRACE, which then publishes this information on its website. Buy-side buyers now no longer have to call several dealers to find the best price for a bond; instead they can check latest prices on the TRACE website. As a result, many corporate bond salesman and traders who benefited from market opacity have found their margins dwindle and their jobs disappear.[10]

---

[9]NASDAQ Stock Market, Inc. *The Impact of Decimalization on the NASDAQ Stock Market, Final Report to the SEC,* June 11, 2001.

[10]Mark Pittman and Caroline Salas, *Bond Traders Lose $1 Million Incomes as Transparency Cuts Jobs,* BondsOnline, Oct 24, 2006.

1.2.3 EVOLVING MARKETPLACES AND DIRECT MARKET ACCESS

A desirable market structure is usually characterized by three things: transparency, access, and competition. The first characteristic means that information regarding prices should be available to all participants so that they can make an informed decision; the second means that access to markets should be easy and not fragmented; and lastly, there should be a large volume of buyers and sellers so that a fair value price is reached because of high liquidity. Traditionally, the marketplaces that provided this structure were stock exchanges, and the way to access these exchanges was to communicate instructions via phone or fax to a broker who was a member of the exchange. For instruments such as bonds that only traded on OTC markets, an investor might have to call several dealers to get an idea of the price range in the market for his or her security.

Now everything about marketplaces is changing: government regulations are forcing traditional marketplaces to display prices, but in response, broker-dealers have set up dark pools of liquidity where prices are hidden; even as these pools fragment the market, traditional marketplaces such as exchanges are merging across the globe, consolidating the old-school marketplace, and incorporating new technologies to counter business flowing away from them; and whatever the market type may be—exchange, Electronic Communication Network (ECN) dark books—market access has become increasingly electronic with the buy-side demanding direct execution and order management connectivity to every pool. In addition, though liquidity pools have been asset-specific up to the present, multi-asset marketplaces will likely emerge over the next few years.

1.2.3.1 Mergers and Acquisitions

In the last couple of years, there has been incredible consolidation in the world of exchanges. The year 2006 saw the acquisition of the Chicago Board of Trade (CBOT) by the Chicago Mercantile Exchange (CME) for $8 billion, effectively creating the world's largest derivatives exchange. Both exchanges are over 70% electronic with only 25% open outcry, and have seen a rise in trading volume in recent years primarily boosted by surges in electronic trading volume.[11] Together, the newly formed entity will trade approximately 9 million contracts per day with an underlying value of $4.6 trillion.[12]

Meanwhile, stock markets have not strayed far behind in this merger mania. In order to pull order flow toward them, the two major US exchanges, NYSE

---

[11]*Electronic Trading Propels CME Earnings,* Finextra, January 31, 2006.
[12]Aaron Lucchetti, Alistair MacDonald, and Edward Taylor, *Chicago Merc to Buy Board of Trade,* Wall Street Journal, October 18, 2006.

and NASDAQ, have merged with ECNs, giving them an immediate technological edge over their competitors. In 2005, the NYSE announced that it would merge with ECN Archipelago to form a new for-profit enterprise known as NYSE Group. Following a time of integration, the NYSE Group finally launched its resulting NYSE Hybrid Market, a combination of electronic and floor trading, in early 2007. Meanwhile, NASDAQ had announced around the same time that it would purchase Instinet Group, another leading ECN. Interestingly, before merging with the stock exchanges, these ECNs were becoming significant competitors to them, taking away market share through their innovative electronic trading platforms. However, the newly consolidated exchanges are now so strong that regional exchanges, such as Philadelphia, Boston, and Chicago, have been steadily losing liquidity and money, with many questioning their viability.

The drive to become leading marketplaces has not been confined to the US; the NYSE offered to buy the largest European exchange, Euronext, in 2006 for $10.2 billion, which was overwhelmingly approved by Euronext's shareholders, in effect making the new merged entity not only the largest stock exchange, but also the first global exchange in the world. Euronext itself was formed in 2000 after a merger of the Amsterdam, Brussels, and Paris Stock Exchanges to create a more pan-European exchange, making it the first cross-border exchange in Europe. While the NYSE Euronext merger would have been the biggest bull in the glass house of both stocks and derivatives, the CBOT-CME merger means that they will get a run for their money in the coming years. Spreading its wings further globally, the NYSE announced a strategic alliance with the Tokyo Stock Exchange in early 2007. Further highlighting the trend toward consolidation and globalization in marketplaces, another major headline-grabbing story in 2007 was NASDAQ's failed bid for a hostile takeover of the London Stock Exchange, as the battle for global dominance raged on. See Figure 1-4.

1.2.3.2   Fragmentation

When buyers have to go to several different markets to determine the price for their trades, it is indicative of a fragmented market. Fragmented markets have many problems including lack of price dissemination and low liquidity due to market dispersion. The US markets had been fairly fragmented, with liquidity dispersed across major and regional exchanges, ECNs, and broker-dealer networks. As discussed in the last section, the consolidation of marketplaces both within and across countries in recent times has been a big coup for efficient market advocates. However, countering this trend is the fragmentation brought by dark books or dark pools of liquidity. While dark books have responded to a market need by buy-side firms, their presence has also had the negative externality of making markets more fragmented.

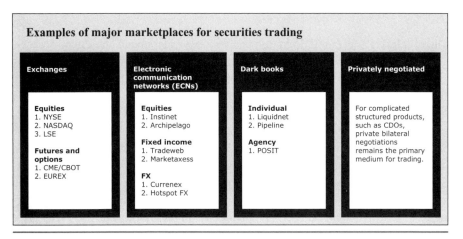

Exchanges	Electronic communication networks (ECNs)	Dark books	Privately negotiated
Equities 1. NYSE 2. NASDAQ 3. LSE **Futures and options** 1. CME/CBOT 2. EUREX	**Equities** 1. Instinet 2. Archipelago **Fixed income** 1. Tradeweb 2. Marketaxess **FX** 1. Currenex 2. Hotspot FX	**Individual** 1. Liquidnet 2. Pipeline **Agency** 1. POSIT	For complicated structured products, such as CDOs, private bilateral negotiations remains the primary medium for trading.

Examples of major marketplaces for securities trading

Figure 1-4   Major marketplaces in securities trading.

Dark books or internal pools of liquidity have several advantages for both the buy-side and the sell-side. On the one hand, prices and orders are not made public in pools, which is clearly the antithesis of the traditional efficient market paradigm. However, buy-side firms don't mind this situation because when it comes to placing large blocks of trade, they prefer to minimize market impact by hiding the size of their orders. Sell-side firms prefer it because they can match order flow internally and save on exchange and ECN commissions. There are four main liquidity pools for block trading in the market, POSIT, Liquidnet, Instinet, and Pipeline, with more being created as an increasing number of sell-side firms want to take advantage of the opportunity. Ironically, what started out as a good idea is turning sour as buy-side firms find themselves having to visit several dark liquidity pools to find a good price for their trades. In response to this concern, JP Morgan subsidiary Neovest announced in February 2007 that it would provide connectivity to 15 different dark pools of liquidity, providing simultaneous access to multiple sources.[13] Meanwhile, in September 2006, six of the industry's leading players including Citigroup, Merrill Lynch, and Goldman Sachs said they planned to launch an electronic block trading service called BIDS (block interest discovery service). BIDS is going to address the fundamental need of buy-side investors to execute large blocks of trades without prematurely revealing their intentions, and inadvertently affecting the market price. BIDS will compete with NYSE and NASDAQ; however, it will let parties remain anonymous and only reveal order size when a suitable counterparty is identified. Thus, marketplaces continue to evolve through several stages as market participants try to balance needs with efficiency.

---

[13]*Neovest Provides Access to 15 "Dark Liquidity" Pools,* Finextra, February 16, 2007.

1.2.3.3 Direct Market Access

Direct Market Access (DMA) tools allow buy-side clients to directly access electronic exchanges, liquidity pools, and ECNs without having to go through the broker's trading desk. DMA demand is directly correlated with the buy-side desire to have more control over the execution of their trades. Often, the DMA tool may be the trading infrastructure provided by the broker-dealer, but because the buy-side is taking control of the order management, the commissions on using the DMA are far lower than on using the broker-dealer's trading desk. In general, DMA commissions are about one cent per share, while program trading commissions are two cents a share and block trading commissions are four cents a share.[14] Given that trading volume runs into the hundreds of thousands, it is obvious that the buy-side prefers to save on what would be substantial commission fees. Hedge funds, which pride themselves on their superior staff, use DMAs aggressively; in general, over 30% of buy-side orders are routed through DMAs, a number which is only likely to increase. Examples of DMAs are Citigroup's Lava Trading, Goldman Sachs' REDIPlus, and Morgan Stanley's Passport. Bells and whistles such as algorithmic trading and smart order routing are being offered as add-on features to DMAs, and providers are rapidly trying to expand the asset class base from just equities to FX, options, and futures. Some people believe that the incorporation of order routing into DMA tools, also sometimes known as *execution management systems (EMS)*, will make them direct competitors to the order management systems (OMS) that vendors currently provide clients to route orders to liquidity pools.[15] See Figure 1-5.

1.2.4 CHANGING REVENUE MODELS

Given the increasing automation and commoditization in the markets, profit margins are shrinking. There are only two ways to make high profit margins: create and offer very sophisticated electronic and algorithmic trading infrastructures to clients for liquid standardized products; or create and offer complex financial products that meet the specialized financial needs of some clients and that require significant human expertise. The former is referred to as a low-touch, high-frequency revenue-generating model, while the latter is known as a high-touch, low-frequency revenue-generating model. Of course, the amount of human supervision required is what determines the level of touch in this categorization.

    Low-touch models imply that the execution is automated as far as possible, with minimum human intervention. Usually, high volume goes hand-in-hand with auto-

---

[14]Ivy Schmerken, *Direct Market Access Trading,* Wall Street & Technology, February 4, 2005.
[15]Daniel Safarik, *Execution Management Systems: From the Street and on the Block,* FinanceTech, September 26, 2006.

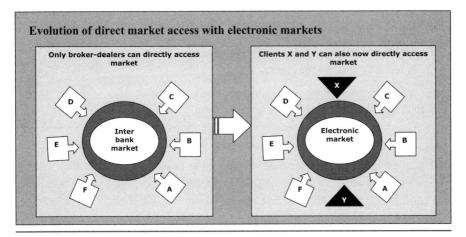

Figure 1-5 Evolution of Direct Market Access with electronic markets.

mation and electronic trading, because trades can be executed in seconds and players can therefore take advantage of the slightest profit opportunities in the market. Hedge funds have led the way by using sophisticated mathematical algorithms such as statistical arbitrage (StatArb) for equity trading, which identifies mispricing in asset values by using statistical indicators. Whereas buy-side firms such as hedge funds are out specifically to earn high returns on their portfolios, sell-side firms which provide brokerage services are more interested in making sure that buy-side trades are executed at the best speed, price, and transaction cost. They do this by providing algorithms that minimize the market impact of block trades (1 block can equal 10,000 shares) sent by buy-side firms. Buy-side firms can access these algorithms as part of the prime brokerage agreement that they have with their broker-dealers. Packaged with the algorithms are pre-trade analytics, which allow the buy-side manager to simulate market impact and make decisions regarding which algorithm he or she prefers to use. The whole package leverages sophisticated analytics and fast access to electronic markets; for this infrastructure, the sell-side charges a fee to its buy-side clients. These are just two examples of how complex trading strategies executed electronically at high speed are generating revenue for buy and sell-side firms; even though each trade may be low margin, substantial revenues can be generated because they are high volume.

At the other end of the revenue-generating spectrum lie highly complex structured products, components of the *high-touch model*, which are made specific to the needs of particular clients and require a great deal of expertise. These deals occur infrequently, but when they do, they carry very high-margin profits for the sell-side brokers that offer these services. Examples of these structured products are collateralized debt obligations and structured equity derivatives, also known as exotic products. They are tailor-made structured solutions for equities, hybrids, and funds that can be used by clients to hedge their portfolio risks and diversify exposure. All major broker-dealers offer these advisory services and charge high fees for creating these structured products for clients.

1.2.5 NEW FACE OF BUY-SIDE

Recent years have seen buy-side institutions change in their composition, in the demands they make on broker-dealers, and in the products they offer their clients. Overall, the buy-side has become a savvier player in the industry, who wants more control in trade execution. The first major change that happened was the entrance of hedge funds, institutional investors that have experienced an explosive growth in recent years. Hedge funds now hold $1.2 trillion in assets, which is double what they had five years ago.[16] It is estimated that there were over 9,000 hedge funds in the US as of early 2007. As high volume traders, their presence has been a driver for increased automation and STP in the industry, especially in the area of prime brokerage. Hedge funds license the brokerage infrastructure of broker-dealers to route and execute their trades; they have provided the sell-side with increased revenues because of this, but they have also imposed costs on the sell-side by demanding faster electronic trading platforms.

More traditional buy-side firms like mutual funds and pension funds have also relied on sell-side firms for research and advice. They have paid brokers for this advice in the form of *soft dollars* or additional payment wrapped in the commission they give for trade execution services. Recently, the buy-side has begun to question the value of this research, demanding that broker-dealers unbundle research fees from commission fees so that institutional investors can better gauge the value-added quality of the research. This is the first time that buy-side firms have asserted that they may choose research from one broker-dealer and use another for best execution.[17]

Finally, the buy-side is itself under pressure from its own clients to give a more unified multi-asset portfolio management offering. In this vein, funds have started presenting multi-strategy portfolio options to customers, where customers have a choice of optimizing over investments in equity, fixed income, and alternative investments. Known as *Unified Managed Accounts (UMA)*, their implementation requires investment in IT infrastructure by funds. Over time, the buy-side demand to have market access that provides a single access point to multiple liquidity pools across asset classes will spur further evolution in the market.

---

[16]Susan Pulliam, *The Hedge-Fund King Is Getting Nervous,* Wall Street Journal, September 16, 2006.
[17]Ivy Schmerken, *The Buy-Side Dilemma: Research vs Execution,* Advanced Trading, November 28, 2006.

1.2.6   GLOBALIZATION

The global securities industry has seen capital markets evolve both within countries and in connectivity between countries, a trend that will only increase over the coming years. Market participants benefit from access to customers across the globe, while investors appreciate the benefits of greater choice in assets and service providers, and the ability to diversify portfolios over a whole range of risk profiles around the globe. The most obvious example of integration across markets is the formation of a pan-European financial market. The *Markets in Financial Instruments Directive* (MiFID) is a regulatory law that aims to set up a single market for securities services across the 25 member states of the European Union. Firms that meet the transparency and audit requirements of the law will be given a financial passport allowing them to work with customers across the EU regardless of their country of incorporation.

Cross-border exchange mergers are another premier example of globalization and the opportunity it provides investors in terms of lower costs, access to deeper pools of liquidity, a more diversified set of financial assets, and the possibility of 24/7 global trading. The merger between Euronext and NYSE makes it the first transatlantic merger of its kind among securities exchanges, and results in the world's largest and most global marketplace for securities. According to an article in *Financial News*, the merger would result in "projected pre-tax annual cost savings and revenue synergies of $375 m (€297 m), including $250 m from streamlined technology."[18] The NYSE has already penned a strategic alliance with the Tokyo Stock Exchange, and expressed interest in expanding its operations to China in addition to looking into buying a stake in the National Stock Exchange of India.[19] In fact, some believe that eventually all markets will run on the same technology and share data centers. This will require systems to communicate using industry standards for financial products and transactions, such as SWIFT, FIX, and FpML, in order to reduce failure when clearing and settling cross-border trades.

1.2.7   REGULATORY PRESSURES

The primary goal of regulations imposed on the securities industry is to protect the interest of the investors, ensuring a fair, transparent, and efficient market for all. Five

---

[18]Isabelle Clary, *NYSE and Euronext Likely to Merge Technology, Not Platforms,* Financial News, June 19, 2006.
[19]Anuj Gangahar and David Turner, *Tokyo Joins NYSE in Strategy for a Global Market,* Financial Times, January 31, 2007.

major regulations continue to affect the securities industry: Sarbanes-Oxley, Basel II, MiFID, Reg NMS, and the Patriot Act, each of which requires improvement and enhancement of technology infrastructure. This section examines regulatory pressures in light of Sarbanes-Oxley and Reg NMS. Chapter 8, Regulatory Compliance, examines all five regulations in detail.

The *Sarbanes-Oxley (Sarbox) Act* of 2000 was the first major regulatory law to hit the securities industry in many decades. Created after the collapse of Enron and the consequent disclosure of its accounting fraud, Sarbox was instituted to return investor confidence in the stock market. The government mandated that detailed audit trails be kept regarding the calculation and reporting of financial accounts, including documentation of internal IT controls that would supervise the systems that created these reports. The CFO of each firm was to sign the final report on compliance to Sarbanes-Oxley, in effect making him or her directly liable for false representation of facts. This heavy regulation of the industry eventually led to the flight of IPOs overseas to London and Hong Kong, as companies found it stressful to comply with the stringent demands. In retrospect, most would agree that the Act represented an instance of over-regulation. However, it is the nature of regulations that companies *must* comply with them if they are mandated. Thus their impact cannot be underestimated, whether it is positive or negative.

Regulation National Market System (Reg NMS) is a significant set of rules mandated by the US government to modernize equities markets in the country. Reg NMS, with a deadline of fall 2007 for full implementation, aims at increasing market transparency, the use of electronic trading to access markets, and the guarantee that investors will always get the best price in the market. For starters, the rule makes it mandatory for exchanges to guarantee investors the best available price and requires them to automatically execute this price. For market centers, this translates into having to upgrade their IT infrastructure to accommodate automated quotation of prices and electronic execution of prices. For brokers, it means that they must connect to multiple marketplaces so that they can view the prices displayed across all markets, and choose the best price for their investors. These are just a few of the significant changes that this regulation will have on the US securities industry.

1.2.8 RACING TO THE FUTURE

Each of the market trends identified and discussed in this section highlights the industry's race to the future in terms of trading securities in as efficient a manner as possible. Winners and losers are determined by their ability to adapt to market changes and their capability to meet the technology standards of connectivity, data processing, and automation set by market leaders. Some have called the current era equivalent to a veritable arms race with sophisticated technology as the primary means of achieving a competitive edge in the battle for market share and supremacy. Not only are business paradigms shifting, creating the need for better technology infrastructures, but technology itself is driving business change in the industry. Without STP of the trade lifecycle, the rapidly evolving business goals of the securities industry will be impossible to achieve.

1.3   Straight Through Processing

Traditionally, STP is the general name given to the creation of an infrastructure that allows automated workflow of trade lifecycle events. The original impetus for STP came from the push by the SEC (Securities and Exchange Commission) and the SIA (Securities Industry Association) to shorten the trade settlement time from three days to one day. However, the T+1 goal expanded slowly into a more holistic approach of improving, streamlining, and automating all operations related to the trade lifecycle both within a firm and between market participants. In this book, it is stressed that a true STP solution is more than just the infrastructure required for a shortened settlement cycle; STP comprises all aspects of securities operations, both from a business process perspective and from a technology infrastructure perspective.

The ultimate goal of STP is to replace the traditional phone and fax confirmations with a completely automated loop, from pre-trade communication and trade deal capture through post-trade clearing and settlement. One ramification of this goal is automating all processes and communications between market participants, such as investment managers, broker-dealers, clearing agencies, and custodians. Overall, in every aspect, STP puts significant pressure on industry participants to make their operations more technology-dependent, and less personnel-dependent, thereby benefiting from faster, more reliable, and less error-prone financial transactions.

The key pillars of STP can be outlined broadly as follows:

1. *Seamless communication between parties*—The STP environment will contain all the necessary infrastructure and communication protocols that will make it possible for the participants in the trade lifecycle to link seamlessly to each other. Parties include sell-side and buy-side firms, exchanges, clearinghouses, and custodians.

2. *Significant real-time processing, less batch processing*—Participants will have to create systems that process information in real-time or near real-time. This naturally necessitates that manual entry of data or other functions performed by personnel be replaced by software and other technologies.

3. *Electronic, not physical, processing*—Physical processing or the use of physical checks and securities will be reduced dramatically. Contracts will be declared

legal if messages are exchanged confirming the details of the trade by both counterparties.

4. *Concurrent, not sequential, exchange of information*—Several steps in the trade lifecycle will occur concurrently, not sequentially, in an almost real-time automated environment.

There are several metrics along which the success of these objectives of STP can be measured. At the most obvious level, once the settlement period is effectively shortened to T+1, the industry will have achieved STP in some sense between all the major players. In general, the strength of an STP implementation can be evaluated across the following dimensions:

■ *Connectivity*—The foremost concept for the STP infrastructure is connectivity between the systems, both within the firm and between firms involved in the trade execution and post-trade monitoring, risk management, and reporting activities.

■ *Speed*—All the phases of the trade lifecycle must be processed as close to real-time as possible, eventually compressing even the T+1 settlement time into a shorter span. The speed to market execution also depends on computing power and requires firms to use their resources as efficiently and intelligently as possible.

■ *Accuracy*—The accuracy and integrity of financial data is the most fundamental requirement for reducing settlement failures.

■ *Standardization*—Industry standards for system communication are the only way that industry participants will be able to effectively and seamlessly exchange transaction-related information with each other.

■ *Extensibility*—Any STP solution should be flexible and extensible in order to accommodate new products and services.

■ *Scalability*—Since the financial landscape has expanded to cover larger and larger parts of the globe, the ability to scale as new markets are entered is a necessary requirement when designing STP systems.

■ *Reliability*—The infrastructure must have failover and disaster recovery mechanisms to make sure the system is always stable and reliable.

■ *Security*—Since securities processes involve the transfer of large amounts of money, participants must be assured that the systems involved are completely secure.

The good news is that technology spending is witnessing another boom for the first time after seeing a decrease in the years between 2000 and 2005. More and more, technology is being recognized by market participants as a way to help them gain advantage in a world of shrinking margins. According to the report *IT Spending Trends: A Global Financial Services Review* by the market research firm Celent, financial services firms in North America, Europe, and Asia-Pacific will spend approximately $320 billion on information technology, an increase of 8% over the amount spent in 2005.[20] The important decisions lie in choosing the technology solutions that will eventually enable firms to become more competitive given trends in the market. It is the purpose of this book to explain high-level technological solutions for achieving an STP infrastructure.

∎ 1.5 Summary

In summary, this chapter has made a business case for undertaking an STP implementation by highlighting the business goals that are fundamentally dependent on improved and automated processes. STP is a framework precisely for the automation of trade-related processes, and its technology solutions significantly expand an organization's ability to compete in a global highly-tech savvy market environment. The next chapter gives a detailed overview of the different phases of the trade life-cycle, which will benefit in terms of efficiency, lower operational costs, and lower risks when STP is implemented.

---

[20]*Celent: IT Spending Soars*, Waters, November 14, 2006.

Chapter 2

The Trade Lifecycle

▮ 2.1 Introduction

From the moment a trader or investor decides to buy or sell a security in the market, the trade lifecycle is kicked off. It includes every step the trade follows from the time a security is chosen to when it is matched with a counterparty, to the time it is settled; in fact, several other auxiliary steps, such as accounting and reporting, are also a result of the trade transaction. Multiple personnel, aided by sophisticated software systems both within and outside a firm, work together to make sure that the execution of the financial transaction is accurate and efficient. Straight through processing (STP) aims to automate as much of this lifecycle as possible, making systems confirm and match a trade, ensure that the correct amount of money is exchanged, run risk analytics, and generate accounts of the transaction. Today, the securities industry loses millions of dollars because of the inefficiencies in the trade lifecycle, due primarily to human error and lack of connectivity and effective electronic communication between systems. The goal of this chapter is to step through all the processes that make up a trade lifecycle in the US, including the lifecycle of the transaction and the post-settlement processes that follow. Only by understanding this information and the operation flows can the foundation for an STP infrastructure be laid.

The trade lifecycle follows three transaction-related phases: pre-trade, trade, and post-trade, as well as several post-settlement processes. The *pre-trade phase* is the stage at which the trader researches and chooses a security to buy or sell. This entails having easy access to current market price information for securities and a set of analytics tools that can simulate the impact of the proposed trade on the value of the trader's portfolio. But the trader is not at complete liberty to trade as he or she wishes; there are limits set by banks on how much of a risky asset a trader can buy, and the government or the trader's clients may also put limits on certain actions. The final component of the pre-trade phase is, therefore, the satisfaction of the limit and compliance rules provided to the trader.

The *trade phase* is the stage at which the order is created and routed to an exchange or such a marketplace where it can find the best counterparty and price. This is known as order routing and execution, and the industry has seen the development of several "smart" order management systems (OMS), which search financial markets to find the best possible execution venue for a particular transaction. If the trader finds a suitable party to trade with, he or she now exchanges the details of the trade with that counterparty to ensure that everyone is in agreement on key points, such as price and quantity. This matching and confirmation begins the post-trade pre-settlement part of the trade lifecycle. Once all concerned parties have agreed on the terms and conditions of the trade, it is ready to be settled.

In the *post-trade phase*, the obligations of each party are calculated, and the money and securities exchanged. The calculation of obligations is known as clearing, whereas the final step of handing over the required obligations is known as settlement. As part of the settlement process, buy-side firms also inform their custodians to allocate money and securities appropriately between the individual accounts under their management. If the securities involved in the transaction are derivatives such as in the case of a credit default swap, then periodic payments are exchanged between the participants of the trade. Cash flows that occur after the settlement of a trade are known as post-trade events. Other post-trade events include changing either the details of the trade (amendments, terminations) or one of the parties in the trade (assignments). All post-trade events require continual reconciliation between the systems of the parties that are affected by the event.

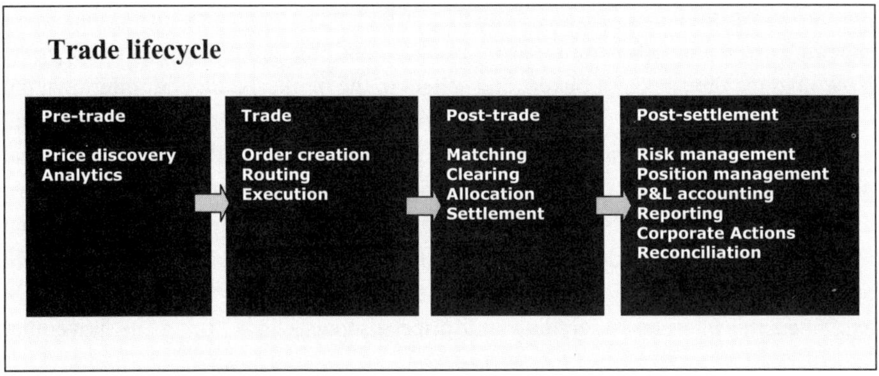

Trade lifecycle

Pre-trade	Trade	Post-trade	Post-settlement
Price discovery Analytics	Order creation Routing Execution	Matching Clearing Allocation Settlement	Risk management Position management P&L accounting Reporting Corporate Actions Reconciliation

Figure 2-1 Phases of a trade lifecycle.

While the transaction lifecycle may have ended with the post-trade phase, this chapter proffers that the trade lifecycle includes more than just the execution and settlement of the transaction; it also includes all the auxiliary steps in the *post-settlement phase* that are triggered by the transaction. Essentially, these are the monitoring and reporting processes, such as cash and collateral management, risk management, profit and loss accounting, compliance, credit event monitoring, and reporting. A truly efficient STP infrastructure has to take into account the technological requirements of these processes as well. See Figure 2-1.

2.2 Pre-Trade

The pre-trade phase includes all the steps that a trader takes before he or she creates an order for the trade. Traders at buy-side firms usually direct their orders to a broker-dealer who then executes the trade in the marketplace. There are three main aspects to pre-trade processes: researching a security to trade, which involves looking at real-time market data for prices; running analytics to determine the best way to execute the transaction, and to analyze various scenarios to see its impact on the trader's portfolio; and finally, checking business rules, including risk limits, client requests, and government regulations.

2.2.1 PRICE DISCOVERY

Price discovery occurs when buyers and sellers together set the price of a security; that is, the price is determined by demand and supply in the market. A seller has an ideal specific price that he or she wants to achieve for a particular transaction, and this is known as the *ask price*; similarly, a buyer has a specific price that he or she wants to achieve for the same transaction, and this is known as the *bid price*. Now imagine thousands of buyers and sellers in the market, each with their own bid and ask prices. In some cases, the price will be negotiated between the buyer and the seller, and in other cases, either the buyer or the seller will get his or her ideal price. The average price of thousands of these transactions in the market is known as the *market price,* and in large markets this is referred to as *price discovery*; that is, the market has "discovered" the price through trading the security. Chester S. Spatt, Chief Economist of the US Securities and Exchange Commission (SEC), explained the interplay of trading and price discovery in a speech in November 2006.

A crucial aspect of the role of trading is the generation and discovery of asset values through the marketplace. While specific identifiable announcements are the trigger for some valuation changes, much of the valuation changes in the marketplace just emerge as a consequence of trading. Though the release of public information and the immediate reaction to those releases are important, much of the information generated in the marketplace occurs through the trading process, reflecting not only the market's reaction to various public announcements, but also the transmission of private information to the capital market.[1]

Traders always want to find a marketplace where they have access to large numbers of buyers and sellers; this increases the possibility of finding a counterparty who will meet their desired price. In addition, marketplaces should preferably be transparent; that is, traders should be able to view the whole gamut of price options available to them. Exchanges are marketplaces that pride themselves on providing superior price; discovery and transparency; they do so by having wide dissemination of bid and ask prices, hosting many buyers and sellers, and allowing large volumes of trades. All these features are invaluable to traders who are always looking for the best price and the lowest trading cost.

2.2.1.1 Price Transparency

Price transparency dictates that information on all orders for a particular security should be publicly available, including the volumes and bid and ask prices on each of them. If deals are not privately negotiated, then they occur in a marketplace and

---

[1]Chester S. Spat, Keynote Address at the Wilton Park Conference on Capital Flows and the Safety of Markets, Wilton Park, England, November 10, 2006.

varying levels of price disclosure are available to the public depending on the opacity of the market. Prices are usually announced by order or by quote, depending on the marketplace.

In an *order driven market* such as the New York Stock Exchange (NYSE), bids, offers, and prices are determined by orders arriving at a central marketplace. All the orders of both buyers and sellers are displayed in the market, including details of the price and quantity at which they are willing to buy or sell a security. For example, if you place an order to buy 500 shares of Google stock at $480/share, your order will be displayed in the market. The advantage of this system is that prices are completely transparent; however, there is no guarantee of order execution at any price, as prices could change between the time you placed an order and the time it was executed.

In a *quote driven market*, such as the London Stock Exchange (LSE), only prices that are determined by dealers' bid/offer quotes are displayed. *Dealers* are individuals who hold securities in their own inventory and have been assigned particular securities in which they are marketmakers or specialists. A *marketmaker* or *specialist* for a security is someone who is always available to either buy or sell that security at a publicly quoted bid and ask price. While order execution would be assured given guaranteed liquidity offered by dealers, there is no transparency for investors in this kind of market. See Figure 2-2.

2.2.1.2 Price Discovery

Price discovery, or the setting of the price of a transaction, can happen in three ways: through private negotiation in OTC markets; through continuous auction in a formal centralized exchange; through dealers in a dealer network.

In *dealer markets*, investors (represented by their brokers) don't buy and sell securities directly to each other; instead, a dealer is the counterparty to all deals. As

Order driven market			
Buy orders		**Sell orders**	
Shares	**Price**	**Shares**	**Price**
134,084	42.64	59,100	42.65
477,634	42.63	184,969	42.66
387,190	42.62	195,682	42.67
190,780	42.61	372,964	42.68
250,441	42.60	300,630	42.69
252,286	42.59	162,506	42.70
526 Buy orders		**445 Sell orders**	

Figure 2-2   Example of buy and sell orders in an order driven market. Source: Investopedia.

mentioned above, dealers are individuals who hold securities in their own inventory and have been assigned particular securities in which they are marketmakers. Note that many marketmakers can represent the same security in a dealer market and compete with each other to provide the best price for that security. In this way, a marketmaker creates a liquid market for the security. A good example of a dealer market is NASDAQ, the largest electronic stock exchange in the US, where dealers competitively advertise their bid and ask prices for investors. Some financial securities such as derivatives and bonds can only be traded in dealer markets.

In *continuous auction markets*, buyers and sellers can buy directly from each other via their brokers. In a continuous auction, orders are continually checked for possible matches when they are received by the market and are executed at whichever price is available. This means that the highest bidding price is matched with the lowest asking price, effectively leading to the market price for that trade. Just as marketmakers exist in dealer markets, other marketplaces have *specialists* who stand ready to always buy and sell a security at a publicly quoted price. Like marketmakers, specialists also add liquidity to the market for that security; however, whereas several marketmakers can represent one security, specialists are the sole representative of a security in a particular marketplace. The NYSE, the largest stock exchange by dollar volume in the world, has assigned specialists for different securities. These specialists stand at a specific location of the floor (the NYSE is driven partially by floor traders) and manage an open outcry auction for brokers and traders on the floor.

2.2.1.3   Types of Price Orders

When an investor places a price request with a broker, he or she can also provide further instructions regarding the price he or she is willing to accept. In fast-moving markets, the price that the investor was quoted by a broker or saw on a real-time quote service may change by the time his or her order is executed in the market. Given the changing nature of prices, it is imperative for investors to tell their brokers how they want to proceed in case the price is different. If investors are cautious, they will put a limit to the price at which they are willing to sell or buy. In this way, they protect themselves against potentially heavy losses due to market movements. In some cases, the broker may be asked to sell the security immediately at the best available price in the market. This is known as a *market order*. Or if the investor is risk-averse, the broker may be asked to put a maximum or minimum price threshold on the trade in a type of order known as a *limit order*. A limit order prevents the investor from committing to a trade when the price has moved significantly away from what is acceptable to him or her.

Investors also carefully assess implicit costs of a transaction that go beyond the price of the security, but that are eventually incurred as part of the price by the buyer. There are two kinds of costs: explicit and implicit. *Explicit costs* include brokerage fees, exchange fees, and any taxes levied on the transaction, while *implicit costs* include loss of price advantage due to market impact and timing. The difference between the price of the security and what it ends up costing the buyer, due to these additional costs, is known as *implementation shortfall*. Calculating these extra costs is called *transaction cost analysis (TCA)*, which has become an integral part of trading these days and is discussed in the next section.

2.2.2   PRE-TRADE ANALYTICS

Before a trader commits to a transaction, he or she wants to analyze the impact of this transaction on his or her portfolio, and ensure that he or she is getting the best price for the trade. The first goal is called portfolio analysis, and the second is called best execution. Pre-trade analytic tools provide sophisticated decision support features, which help traders with this kind of analysis.

Portfolio analysis allows traders to see the impact of buying or selling a security on the value of their holdings. Say a trader has a $200 million portfolio divided between Treasury bills and different stocks. If the trader decides to sell some Treasury bills and invest that money in stocks, he or she needs to simulate the impact this will have on his or her portfolio in the long run. Taking current market prices for the bills and the stocks, he or she inputs them into an analytics tool, and with the aid of trends distilled from historical market data, forecasts whether this trade will be beneficial or not. If the trader realizes that while investing in Company A stock looks like a good bet right now, Company A stock has historically been very volatile and this puts the portfolio at great risk in the future, he or she may decide not to undertake this trade at all. Portfolio optimization is the process of optimizing the dollar value of a portfolio while keeping its risk exposure at a selected minimum threshold. There is little point in investing in a stock that increases in price one month, raising the value of the portfolio, but then plummets even below the price at which it was bought, thus resulting in a net loss in the value of the portfolio.

Best execution is the goal of finding the best price, fastest execution speed, and lowest transaction cost for a particular trade. TCA is conducted as part of pre-trade analysis to compare different trading scenarios and gauge which trade is as close to best execution as possible. The first step is having direct market access to all major electronic marketplaces so traders have real-time quotes on market prices and superior connectivity to ensure that the speed of execution is fast. The industry has recently seen the emergence of sophisticated tools that not only find the best venue of the execution, but also calculate the opportunity cost of not using price information at a particular period in time to trade. In addition, the tool recommends strategies on how to spread out the trade over time so that the transaction has minimum *market impact*. All three of these functions help minimize implementation shortfall or the difference between the quoted price of a security and the price at the time of execution.

Market impact occurs when a large order for buy or sell negatively affects the price of the market, raising it when it's a buy order and reducing it when it's a sell order. The logic is simple supply and demand: whenever the supply of a particular security suddenly goes up, its price falls because supply has outstripped demand; the converse occurs when the demand for a particular security suddenly spikes. Market impact is especially a concern for institutional investors who regularly buy and sell large volumes of securities. As soon as a mutual fund manager places millions of stocks of a company for sale, its supply in the market increases, leading to a steep decline in its price.

Several algorithms can be utilized for spreading out large orders over time and markets to reduce market impact. Using computer programs or algorithms to trade in the market is popularly known as *algorithmic trading*. One algorithm for minimizing market impact utilizes the concept of the *volume-weighted average price (VWAP)*. The VWAP of a stock over a specific period is simply the weighted average price by volume during that period. For example, say that the mutual fund manager wanted to sell $50 million of Company A stock. If this order were released to the market as a whole, the explosion in the supply of Company A stock would make its price plummet. However, if there were a way that the order could be released in small blocks of a few million dollars each, over the course of a day, then it might be possible to reduce the negative market impact of this order. There are several strategies of how to release the order slowly into the market. The trader could sell the shares uniformly from 8–4 pm throughout the day. This would not be advisable since the market will immediately notice that the shares are being sold even during hours that traditionally have been quiet for this stock. Another option would be to apply an algorithm that matches the volume of trades executed for that share so that it follows the surges and lulls in trading, thereby hiding the fact that the supply of shares is increasing in the market. This algorithm would make sure that the price received for each block of trade is as close as possible to the VWAP.

Analytics software uses intraday historical data to simulate the volume of trades that a particular stock has over the course of a day. By mimicking the volume trend, that is, by trading large amounts of the security when the market is already trading large volumes, and by trading small amounts when the market is relatively quiet, the trader is able to slice up the buy or sell order of his or her client and slip it into the market "under the radar," so to speak. By sending the orders to the market in blocks dictated by the algorithm, the orders never overwhelm the market with sheer volume and the price never deviates from the average price for the day. Many clients now insist that the bank meet at least the VWAP for the day.

Traditionally, buy-side firms relied wholly on the brokers that represented them for best execution efforts, which were mostly opaque to them. However, with the introduction of pre-analytics tools in the market, investment managers can compare and contrast the entire universe of brokers and prices, and simulate the market impact of various trading strategies themselves. This has empowered the buy-side trader who is now not completely at the mercy of the broker-dealer. Adjusting to the times, broker-dealers now offer pre-analytics tools themselves to their buy-side clients, to prove that they are making best efforts to keep transaction costs to a minimum. In November 2006, Goldman Sachs announced that, under pressure from clients, it was going to give them access to algorithms from multiple brokers over REDIPlus, its front-end trading system. This would allow clients to have one system on their desktops from which they can compare and choose to route orders to any number of different brokers. This is just one example of how buy-side clients are ramping up their demand for a more transparent and efficient routing of their orders.

2.2.3 LIMIT/COMPLIANCE CHECKS

Before a trader presses the button to generate and send a trade order to a marketplace for execution, he or she must ensure that he or she is not exceeding bank risk limits, or violating any compliance regulations. Limit thresholds are instituted by a desk to prevent a particular trade from jeopardizing the overall risk profile of the desk. In other words, the trader cannot undertake such a risky position that the resulting market or credit risk exposure goes over the limits extended to him or her by the manager. Traders' bonuses are driven by the profit that they make on their trades. This money is either that of the bank's clients or of the bank itself (since sometimes banks engage in proprietary trading, which means they trade with their own money). Thus, the downside of taking on a particular trade for a trader is limited to the size of his or her bonus, leaving a great deal of incentive for traders to take on risky trades that could potentially make far more money than cautious trades. In economics, when incentives are skewed like this, it is referred to as *moral hazard*.

Moral hazard occurs when a person is insured against the risks he or she may be taking, thus making him or her immune to risky situations. For instance, a trader could invest clients' money in junk bonds, betting on the hypothesis that these bonds will rise in value in the future. Junk bonds have below investment grade credit ratings, meaning that the market expects there is a high chance of the issuer defaulting on its obligations, making the bonds worthless. On the other hand, if the issuer recovers from its financial troubles, the bonds' price would rise, in turn giving the trader very high returns. This is exactly the kind of situation that would be attractive to a trader, but very unpalatable for a risk-averse client who has trusted the bank with his or her money.

Credit exposure limits are therefore set by the bank's senior management by counterparty, industry sector, and country to ensure that the interests of clients are protected. Usually, the trader is required to run a potential order through a limit check, which automatically alerts the trader if he or she is straying beyond bank risk limits.

Compliance checks are the other kind of pre-trade checks that are conducted just before creating the trade order. Traders must comply with restrictions placed by their clients and those placed by the government. Often, if a trader is representing a buy-side firm that has individual clients, he or she will be given a list of restrictions on the kinds of securities that some clients want to hold. One example of a security restriction is when a client specifically informs the trader that he or she never wants to buy what some people consider "sin" stocks, such as tobacco and adult entertainment company stocks.

The government also places all kinds of restrictions on the sale or purchase of securities. For instance, selling and repurchasing an asset within 30 days is considered an illegal purchase, because the usual impetus for such a *wash sale* is to manipulate taxes. In the past, such pre-trade compliance checks were done in Excel spreadsheets or the trader had broad restrictions memorized. However, given that the complexity and volume of portfolios have increased significantly, it is easier to violate regulations, which can be extremely costly. Making a mistake, either in relation to a regulatory guideline or specific to a client's portfolio, can lead to both a government investigation and hefty fines, not to mention loss of current and future business.

2.3 Trade

After pre-trade analysis and limit and compliance checks have been run, the trader is now ready to create a trade ticket and route it to a marketplace for execution. These two steps comprise the trade phase of the lifecycle. See Figure 2-3.

2.3.1 ORDER CREATION

An order is created when the trader chooses a security to trade, and inputs details such as the type of price order and quantity. The system then automatically generates a trade ticket, which contains all the basic description of the trade. Usually, a trade ticket includes the following pieces of information:

1. Security identifier, such as the symbol GOOG for Google stock.
2. Buy or sell flag.

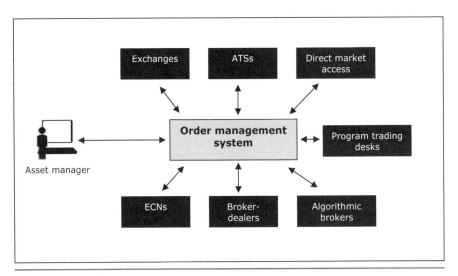

Figure 2-3 Buy-side trades using an order management system.

3. Type of price order, such as limit order.
4. Quantity to be traded.
5. Trade date.
6. Marketplace where the trade will be executed, such as the NYSE. If the trader is using a smart order routing system, then the system itself searches for the best execution venue for the trade. Order management, routing, and execution are discussed in the next section.

This trade ticket is now ready for routing and execution at a marketplace.

2.3.2 ORDER ROUTING AND EXECUTION

Every investor wants the best price for a trade. Competitive prices are available only where there are deep pools of liquidity, that is, where a great deal of trading in that security is happening. Broker-dealers who represent investors, whether private or institutional, are on the constant lookout for best execution venues where there is liquidity and transaction costs are low. Note that although individual investors who trade through online brokerage accounts think that they have a direct connection to the securities market, in fact, their orders are sent to a broker who decides where to execute the order.

A broker has several execution options when he or she receives a trade order. The broker may route the order to an exchange such as the NYSE, if the stock is listed on an exchange, or direct it to an OTC market such as the NASDAQ, asking a marketmaker to fill the requested order. The broker may also route it to an alternative trading system such as an Electronic Communication Network (ECN) that automatically matches buy and sell orders at specified prices. If the broker finds that his or her firm carries an inventory of that security, he or she may fill out the order from the firm's own repository, a process called *internalization*. Note that most equities, exchange-traded funds, and exchange-traded derivatives are routed to exchanges and ECNs; most corporate bonds and fixed income products are traded OTC and through broker-dealers directly; and many OTC derivatives are so unique and specific that they are traded bilaterally.

Brokers make money in several ways apart from the commission that they earn from the investor on the trade. If they direct the orders to a marketmaker, they may receive a fee for generating this order flow for the marketmaker; if they use their own firm's inventories to execute the trade, they might make money on the spread between the bid and ask prices on a particular transaction. Institutional investors or buy-side firms have recently begun monitoring and putting pressure on their brokers to give them the best price. This prevents brokers from executing for personal gain, or resisting searching for "best execution" of client orders.

In response to the need to have efficient order routing and execution, brokers build or buy order management and routing systems, which automatically search for and direct orders to the best price. This requires electronic connectivity to broker-dealer networks, dark books, exchanges, and ECNs. *Order management systems (OMSs)* take in data feeds from marketplaces, providing real-time price information to traders. Orders can then be routed to any marketplace of which the broker is a member. If software intelligence is added to the OMS, the system dynamically sends orders to the marketplaces that can fill the order most quickly and at the best price. Due to the uncertainty that the execution price will be the same as the quoted price on the order, speed to market is very important. Usually, the best order routing systems are those that have high speed direct connectivity to marketplaces.

In order to assess the average quality of their order execution, brokers gather statistics on four key variables: execution price, price improvement, execution speed, and effective spread. The SEC requires that all brokers guarantee their clients the best available ask and sell price, also called the *national best bid or offer (NBBO)*. The NBBO is a consolidated quote calculated from the highest bid and lowest offer prices of a security across all exchanges and marketmakers. By showing that most of their trades fall at or very close to the NBBO, brokers can prove that they give their clients a good execution price. If, in fact, they show that in a significant number of trades, their price was better than the NBBO, then this means that they showed price improvement. Execution speed, as mentioned before, is particularly important due to the vicissitudes of price levels. Execution speed is the time that elapses between the time the broker receives an order to the time the order is executed. Finally, the effective spread is how often, and by how much, the broker improves the price of a trade over what was in the price order. Many brokers publish these statistics periodically to satisfy customer expectations.

2.4   Post-Trade

Once the trade has been executed, that is, a counterparty has been matched with the order, the trade lifecycle enters the post-trade phase. This phase consists of three stages: first, the trade details from both parties are matched to confirm that they have the same understanding on the details of the transaction; second, the trade is cleared and settled; and lastly, potential post-trade events such as coupon payments, credit events, and any amendments to the trade are processed. At each point of the cycle, reconciliation between the systems of the different participants, such as utility providers, custodians, and counterparties, occurs to identify mismatches as quickly as possible, and preclude settlement delays.

Common steps of all transaction lifecycles

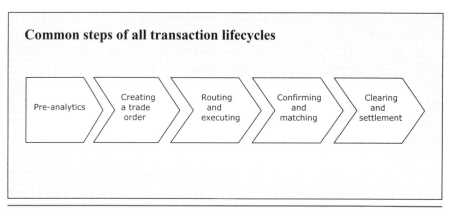

Figure 2-4 Common steps of all transaction lifecycles.

2.4.1 MATCHING, CLEARING, AND SETTLEMENT

Depending on whether it is a broker-to-broker or an institutional trade, the trade lifecycle can differ in some ways. However, each trade follows the same basic few steps: pre-analytics; order creation, routing, and execution; trade matching; and clearing and settlement. In the case of a privately negotiated derivatives contract, it is difficult to automate these processes given the complexity and unique features of each contract. However, with the standardization of derivatives contracts by the ISDA (International Swaps and Derivatives Association), STP attempts for these products have also become possible. The Depositury of Trust and Clearing Corporation (DTCC) is leading the efforts with its Deriv/SERV post-trade management service for derivatives. See Figure 2-4.

2.4.1.1 Institutional Trade

In an institutional trade, an investment manager, such as a mutual funds manager, contacts a broker-dealer to make a trade in a marketplace. The sell-side trader creates an order and routes it to a best execution venue. Recall that each investment manager, in fact, represents many private clients. Any trade that is made by a mutual fund manager, for instance, has to be distributed or allocated among all his or her clients' accounts. The money and securities of each client are kept in safekeeping at a custodian bank. This necessitates sending details of the trade to the custodian after settlement, so that the money made from the sale of securities or payment owed due to the purchase of securities can be credited and debited, respectively, from client accounts. This adds a layer of complexity to an institutional trade. In general, such considerations make the steps of matching, clearing, and settling an institutional trade a fairly involved process. The lifecycle of an institutional trade is depicted in Figure 2-5.

An institutional trade

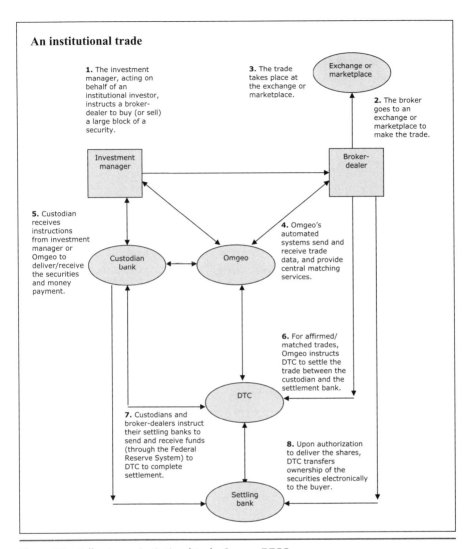

1. The investment manager, acting on behalf of an institutional investor, instructs a broker-dealer to buy (or sell) a large block of a security.

3. The trade takes place at the exchange or marketplace.

Exchange or marketplace

2. The broker goes to an exchange or marketplace to make the trade.

Investment manager

Broker-dealer

5. Custodian receives instructions from investment manager or Omgeo to deliver/receive the securities and money payment.

Custodian bank

Omgeo

4. Omgeo's automated systems send and receive trade data, and provide central matching services.

6. For affirmed/matched trades, Omgeo instructs DTC to settle the trade between the custodian and the settlement bank.

DTC

7. Custodians and broker-dealers instruct their settling banks to send and receive funds (through the Federal Reserve System) to DTC to complete settlement.

8. Upon authorization to deliver the shares, DTC transfers ownership of the securities electronically to the buyer.

Settling bank

Figure 2-5   Following an institutional trade. Source: DTCC.

2.4.1.1.1   Confirm/Affirm

After the broker-dealer executes the trade, it sends the investment manager a notice of execution (NOE), which contains the details of trade. The investment manager then sends the broker the allocation details that associate the account numbers of clients with the trade. The broker sends back a confirmation for each allocation; if the manager finds that the broker has correctly allocated the trade to the clients, an affirmation is sent back. This is commonly known as the confirm/affirm process in the industry.

The SEC requires that all broker-dealers who extend RVP/DVP privileges to their institutional clients must first have their clients agree that they will affirm trades promptly upon receiving confirmation from broker-dealers. RVP and DVP are two ways to accept payment in a transaction. *Receive-versus-payment (RVP)* is an instruction that accompanies sell orders, which states that only cash will be accepted when securities are delivered. In general, most institutions are required by law to only accept cash as payment. *Delivery-versus-payment (DVP)* is when cash from the buyer is due exactly at the time of delivery of securities. By making the two occur simultaneously, any credit risk that one of the parties will default on its obligations is eliminated. The SEC law for RVP/DVP privileges was instituted to force reconciliation of account allocation details as early as possible in the trade lifecycle, thereby reducing the potential for error and giving institutional clients confidence in the system. In addition, the SEC requires that this process occur through a registered depository or qualified vendor.

In the US, the vendor Omgeo is used as a communications hub to process and forward these messages between all involved parties. Omgeo is the leading provider of post-trade pre-settlement trade management solutions and processes over one million trades per day serving 6,000 investment managers, broker-dealers, and custodians. Generally, Omgeo confirms most of the trade allocations it receives by T+0; however, many of the affirmations do not come until T+3 (affirmation rates were approximately 23% on T+0, 85% on T+1, and 88.5% on T+2), which delays settlement and STP. There is therefore increasing pressure on buy-side firms to improve their timing of affirmation so that allocation can be verified quickly, thus leading to fewer settlement failures due to errors in recording trades. In fact, the SEC is considering reducing the time limit on affirmations to same-day affirmations only.

2.4.1.1.2 Trade Matching
Omgeo falls under a category of industry utility vendors called a Virtual Matching Utility (VMU). Omgeo's Central Trade Manager is one example of a trade matching utility that is used extensively for matching institutional trades. Omgeo receives trade details from both the buying broker and the selling broker, and matches the trade by comparing the trade details given by each. If the trade details are the same, Omgeo passes on the trade information to the custodians and the clearinghouse DTC (Depository Trust Company).

2.4.1.1.3 Clearing, Allocation, and Settlement
For affirmed and matched trades, Omgeo tells DTC to settle the trade between the custodian and the settlement banks of the two counterparties. DTC is the central clearinghouse for processing institutional trades. Clearinghouses facilitate the final

settlement of trades between parties by mitigating credit risk through a process called *novation* (see box below). Usually, FedWire is used to take money out of the buyer's account and to put it in the seller's account. FedWire is run by the Federal Reserve and enables institutions to electronically transfer funds among themselves. Along with CHIPS (Clearinghouse Interbank Payments System), FedWire forms the primary US network for large value domestic and international payments. Securities are transferred into the buyer's account by DTC using electronic book entry. If the account is held by a custodian, it is *allocated* to the client's account. Book entry allows share ownership without stock certificates; that is, electronic certificates of authorization are kept instead of physical copies of the security certificates.

ROLE OF CENTRAL COUNTERPARTY CLEARING

Clearing and settlement have become crucial in the efficient working of financial markets. Chicago Federal Reserve Bank President Michael Moskow summed it up well when he said:

Post-trade clearing and settlement are sometimes referred to as the plumbing *of the financial system. This term may suggest that clearing and settlement systems are of secondary importance. In fact, however, they are more like the* central nervous system *of the financial system. Clearing and settlement systems provide vital linkages among components of the system, enabling them to work together smoothly. As such, clearing and settlement systems are critical for the performance of the economy.*[2]

Michael H. Moskow

The Central Counterparty (CCP) plays an important role in mitigating risk management in the trade lifecycle. It achieves this by replacing the contract between counterparties with two new contracts, in each of which it becomes the counterparty. In other words, it becomes the buyer to every seller and the seller to every buyer, or the central counterparty which guarantees that it will meet its obligations. In this way, the counterparty credit risk that is often inherent in all financial transactions is removed. This process of transferring obligations to a CCP is known as *novation* and leaves only the CCP holding the credit risk if one of the parties defaults on its obligations. CCP mitigates the credit risk it carries through restricting dealing with

---

[2]Michael H. Moskow, 2006, *Public Policy and Central Counterparty Clearing,* speech delivered at the European Central Bank and Federal Reserve Bank of Chicago Joint Conference, "Issues Related to Central Counterparty Clearing," Frankfurt, Germany, April 4, 2006.

parties that are not creditworthy, and by making some parties keep collateral with the CPP for insurance.

The CCP is also crucial for operational efficiency in the markets. It provides pre-settlement clearing functions such as trade confirmation, matching, and netting. Payment netting is the process by which the CCP calculates the net cash and securities position of parties, since parties conduct so many different trades in any given day. This streamlines the payment process and reduces the number of instructions sent to settling banks, thus significantly decreasing the potential for error.

In the US, the largest CCP is the Depository of Trust and Clearing Corporation (DTCC), which in 2006 processed over $1.4 quadrillion worth of securities transactions. DTCC works through four main subsidiaries: NSCC (National Securities Clearing Corporation), which provides clearing, settlement, netting, risk management, central counterparty services, and a guarantee of completion for all street-side trades involving equities, corporate, and municipal debt; DTC, which provides settlement services for all NSCC trades and for institutional trades, which typically involve money and securities transfers between custodian banks and broker/dealers; FICC (Fixed Income Clearing Corporation), which provides clearing and settlement services for government securities and mortgage backed securities; and Deriv/SERV, which is developing automation in the clearing and settlement of over-the-counter derivatives products. All DTCC activities are regulated by the SEC.

2.4.1.2   Broker-to-Broker Trade

A broker-to-broker trade differs from an institutional trade in two main aspects: first, there is no role for a custodian; and second, the NSCC is the equivalent of Omgeo as a matching service utility. The NSCC provides centralized clearance, settlement, and information services for virtually all broker-to-broker equity, corporate bond, municipal bond, and ETF trades in the US. It eliminates market uncertainty by providing automation and central counterparty guarantees on all trades that have been confirmed and matched. In addition, it has a continuous net settlement (CNS) system, which continually nets the obligations of parties, thereby reducing the total number of financial obligations requiring settlement at any given time. According the NCSS website,[3] the system accomplishes this "for each brokerage firm by netting the total buy (receive) and sell (deliver) obligations for a given security into one net position. We then simultaneously consolidate all debits and credits from these net positions in all securities into one final net money position for each firm. On a peak day, CNS

---

[3]NSCC Clearing and Settlement, http://www.nscc.com/clearandset.html.

can reduce total dollars requiring payment by more than 95 percent." The lifecycle of the trade is depicted in Figure 2-6.

2.4.1.2.1 Trade Matching and Confirmation
NSCC generally clears and settles trades within three days or, as they say in the industry jargon, on a T+3 basis, which is the time that elapses between the trade date and the settlement date. On T+0, the trade is executed at a marketplace between two brokers, and trade details are electronically sent by the marketplace to NSCC to start clearance and settlement. If it is an equity transaction, it is almost always the case that the matching of trade details between the buying broker and selling broker is done by the marketplace at the time the trade is executed. Such trades are referred to as locked-in trades, and the NSCC sends automated reports to the two parties. These confirmations inform the parties that the trade has entered the clearance and settlement cycle and that the trade is now legally binding.

2.4.1.2.2 Novation
NSCC takes on the role of central counterparty around midnight on T+1, stepping between the two parties and taking on the counterparty credit risk of each side. This, in effect, gives both parties the insurance that the NSCC will meet the obligations due to it by the other party. Central counterparty features such as these give the public confidence in the vitality and viability of the securities market. On T+2, after novation has taken place, the NSCC sends all broker-dealers reports on their trades and their net obligations, both cash and securities.

2.4.1.2.3 Settlement
Finally, on T+3, all the trades that were executed and sent to the NSCC on T+0 are settled; that is, securities are delivered to net buyers and cash is delivered to net sellers. The DTC acts as NSCC's agent, becoming the settling authority that transfers ownership of securities via book-entry electronic movements, and transfer of funds between the settling banks via FedWire. Broker-dealers who are buyers inform their settling banks upon receipt of NSCC clearing calculations to send funds to the DTC, which the DTC then passes on to the seller's settling bank.

FROM T+3 TO T+1

It is now a well-established fact that the longer the time between trade and settlement date, the greater the uncertainty and risk trade participants face, be it credit risk, processing error, or a change in prices. The more transactions that are outstanding, the more money needs to be collected, and this adds a lot of uncertainty to the market.

While central counterparties eliminate the credit risk that individual parties take on, the other two risks still remain on the minds of market participants. Before June 1995, financial markets operated on a T+5 settlement cycle, but the SEC reduced the settlement cycle from five to three business days to reduce the operational and financial risk inherent in securities transactions processing. This means the securities must reach the buyer, and the money the seller, no later than three business days after the trade date. The T+3 rule applies to all stocks, bonds, municipal securities, and mutual funds traded through a broker. In general, government securities are settled the next day. In recent years, the SEC has been pushing a reduction in the settlement cycle to T+1. In fact, this was the first time the phrase "straight through processing" became prominent in the industry, because it was seen as imperative for achieving settlement within one business day. Originally, the T+1 goal was supposed to have been achieved by 2005, but the SEC extended it as the industry began to focus not just on meeting the deadline, but on setting up the infrastructure for STP throughout the entire industry.

2.4.1.3   Derivatives Clearing and Settlement

As derivatives continue to explode in volume, the importance of their clearing and settlement has now become an issue of major concern. The International Swaps and Derivatives Association (ISDA) reported that the notional outstanding of credit derivatives grew 52% to $26 trillion, interest rate derivatives grew 18% to $250 trillion, and equity derivatives grew 15% to $6 trillion in the first half of 2006. In fact, the sector has doubled in size every year since 2002. This exponential growth in volume resulted in enormous backlogs of unconfirmed trades, especially in the credit derivatives market. In September 2005, the Federal Reserve called a meeting of 14 leading broker-dealers to emphasize the importance of clearing this backlog and improving their post-trade processing procedures. A survey conducted by the ISDA showed that one in five derivatives trades contained mistakes and suffered settlement delays in 2005. The processing delays with derivatives are further complicated by the fact that most derivatives contracts involve the exchange of cash flows between the participating parties throughout the life of the contract. This is unlike a security such as an equity, which only has one exchange between buyer and seller. In general, one finds that the more complex a product, the less automation exists in its trade processing. See Figure 2-7.

Derivatives contracts exist in two flavors: exchange-traded and over-the-counter, the former being standardized or vanilla contracts and the latter being more structured and unique products. Clearing and settlement of derivatives depend on what kind of derivatives contract is in question. Most exchange-traded and some OTC

A broker-to-broker trade

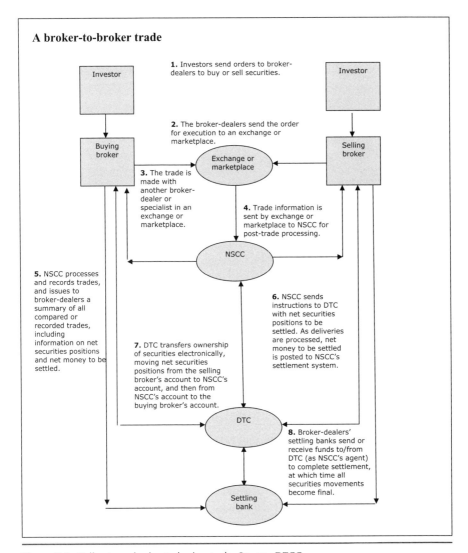

Figure 2-6 Following a broker-to-broker trade. Source: DTCC.

derivatives are cleared through a central clearinghouse such as DTCC. Most OTC derivatives are settled bilaterally.

As explained in the discussion on the important role of clearinghouses, the use of a clearinghouse plays an invaluable role in minimizing credit risk by taking on the role of CCP. This means that through novation, the clearinghouse becomes the counterparty to both buyer and seller, thus removing the counterparty risk that is a

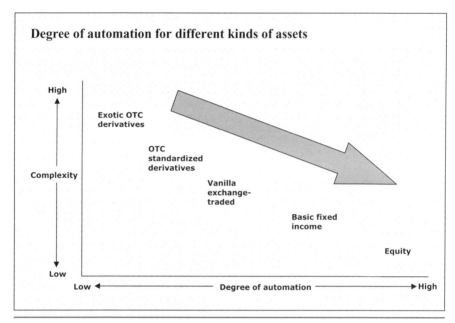

Figure 2-7 Degree of automation for different kinds of assets.

big problem in bilateral contracts. But to automate post-trade processing and introduce a CCP requires that contracts be fairly standard. ISDA has been working diligently to standardize contract features for derivatives such as credit default swaps and equity derivatives. This has allowed DTCC's Deriv/SERV to start a matching service for those OTC derivatives that have standard contracts. Deriv/SERV also processes matching and confirming post-trade events such as amendments and terminations of trades. In the future, it aims to add clearing and settlement, including all the payments that must be exchanged between the parties throughout the life of the contract. Of course, this still leaves the issue of post-trade processing of privately negotiated bilateral derivatives contracts, but with their standardization over time, these too should benefit from service providers such as Deriv/SERV. Figure 2-9 shows the trade lifecycle of a credit default swap, including those parts that are slated as part of future releases of Deriv/SERV.

2.4.1.3.1 Matching and Confirmation
Deriv/SERV began its first year in operation in 2004 with the automation of matching service for credit default swaps. It was the first utility provider in the market to provide this service. Brokers submit their trade details to Deriv/SERV, which compares key details and confirms the trade if the details match. Trade details can be submitted through three methods: back-end messages using MQ Series, uploading

an Excel spreadsheet, or inputting the details via a web interface. Once the trade is confirmed, it becomes legally binding on both parties. Before such a trade matching system was available, broker-dealers were using fax, phone, and email to match and confirm their trades, a practice that would sometimes take weeks. With Deriv/SERV, matching can be done in close to real-time, with confirmation able to take place within minutes. As mentioned earlier, Deriv/SERV also matches and confirms, using the same method, amendments to trades, such as partial terminations and increases in notional amounts. Another prominent player that has entered this arena and also provides OTC derivatives matching and confirmation service is SwapsWire.

2.4.1.3.2 Clearing and Settlement

In order to provide clearing and settlement services for OTC derivatives, a service provider such as Deriv/SERV would have to calculate the payments participants owe each other at the time of trade settlement, and at the time of all future payments that will be exchanged between the two parties. The very nature of derivatives contracts, as explained in the box on credit default swaps below, is an exchange of cash flows in the future based on the occurrence of some events. Given the complexity of the structure of these derivatives, the computation of these payments and automated generation of payment notifications and their settlement is a difficult undertaking. In addition, as in exchange-traded transactions, Deriv/SERV would have to create connectivity and messaging between the settling banks of these brokers so that cash can be exchanged at the correct time. At the time of publication, Deriv/SERV is working to set up these services.

CREDIT DEFAULT SWAPS

A credit derivative is an OTC derivative that is used as insurance against credit risk. It is one of the fastest growing derivative markets in the world, doubling in volume every year since 2002. The simplest credit derivative is a credit default swap (CDS). A CDS is structured as follows: Say Party A owns $200 million of Company X bonds. Party A is afraid that Company X will default on its coupon and principal payment, and wants to get some insurance against this risk. Party B agrees to give this insurance to Party A for a premium, say some percentage of notional ($200 million). In exchange for this insurance premium, Party B commits to covering any losses incurred on the bond if Company X defaults. This is analogous to health insurance: you make monthly health insurance payments to cover the risk of falling seriously sick and being left with a large hospital bill. In exchange for your health insurance payments, your insurer commits to covering your hospital bills.

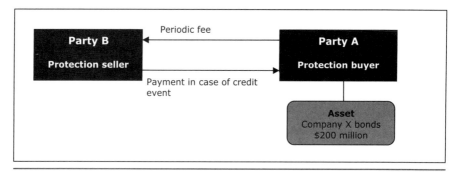

Figure 2-8 Reallocating credit risk with credit derivatives.

On the trade date, Party A and Party B enter this contract, and the contract itself is the derivatives security. Every quarter, Party A pays Party B its agreed insurance premium until the maturity of the contract. If a credit event such as Company X's bankruptcy occurs, which leads to it defaulting on its bond obligations, Party B pays Party A the equivalent of the amount of money it has lost by Company X's default. Thus, during the life of the contract, a number of cash flows can potentially be exchanged between the two parties. See Figure 2-8.

The automation of post-trade processing of credit default swaps would include the matching and subsequent confirmation of trade details, and the calculation, notification, and settlement of all cash flow exchanges between the two parties. See Figure 2-9.

2.5   Post-Settlement

There are several processes that happen after the transaction part of the trade cycle is finished. These processes can be grouped under the general heading of post-settlement monitoring and reporting operations. They comprise systems that evaluate the risk exposure of holding the security, generate profit and loss numbers as market prices change, and produce reports for senior management and the government. An STP infrastructure includes streamlining the information flows to and from these systems, by seamlessly connecting them to each other and to the transaction and market data systems outside the firm.

2.5.1   COLLATERAL MANAGEMENT

Collateral management consists of evaluating the credit risk of a counterparty and requiring it to provide collateral to engage in trades. Whenever parties trade directly

An OTC derivative trade

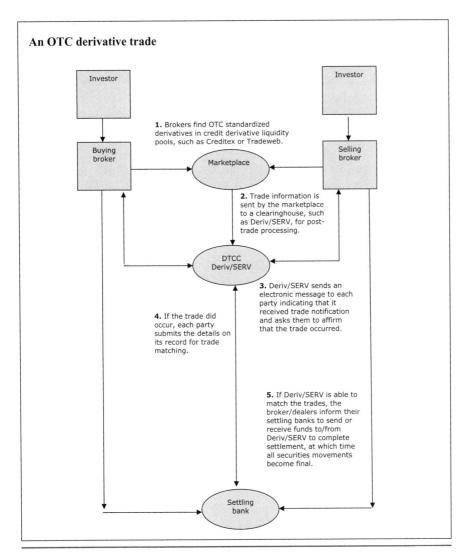

Figure 2-9   Following an OTC derivative trade.

with each other they expose themselves to what is known as counterparty risk. This means that if the counterparty were to default on payment or delivery of securities, then the trader would incur a loss proportional to the money expected from the trade. When the security is not an OTC security, the clearinghouse acts as insurance against counterparty risk through novation. In bilateral trades, however, a collateral management system automatically and continually updates the collateral required for a counterparty based on its changing credit risk assessment and the net position of trades associated with it.

2.5.2 POSITION MANAGEMENT

A real-time position management system that shows all the current positions and position orders is an integral part of most trading systems. Traders can view all the securities that they have brought or sold, and their net position in each of them. A *position* is how much of a security a trader holds. For instance, if a trader represents a client that owns 10,000 shares of Microsoft, then the client's position in Microsoft is equal to 10,000. Since traders are continually placing buy and sell orders for their clients, it is important for them to be able to view all their current positions and outstanding orders at any time in order to calculate the portfolio impact of potential trade orders.

2.5.3 RISK MANAGEMENT

After the Enron scandal, risk management has taken on an increasingly prominent role in financial services institutions. There are three types of risk that are related to any kind of institution that buys and sells securities: market risk, credit risk, and operational risk. *Market risk* is the risk associated with a portfolio of securities that are subject to changing market conditions, such as interest rate fluctuations. *Credit risk* is based on two things: counterparty risk and issuer risk. The former is the risk that the counterparty may default on any trade agreement, and the latter is the risk that the issuer of the security may default on its obligations, such as regular coupon payments for a bond. Finally, *operational risk* is the risk of errors that may occur when processing and monitoring the trade from a technology and operations perspective. Ideally, all three kinds of risk would be monitored using an integrated risk management system that is connected to real-time market and position data.

2.5.4 PROFIT AND LOSS ACCOUNTING

Accounting systems continually calculate the profit and loss associated with a position in a security based on its current market price. This is known as *marking a position to market*. It is the only way that an organization can gauge whether the trade was profitable and whether certain measures need to be taken to save a loss taking position. A position management system connected to a real-time market data feed would be necessary to continually calculate profit and loss (P&L). Reports are often generated from the P&L system and presented to senior management, which then not only has an overview of the entire assets in the firm, but also uses the data at year's end to determine the bonuses of traders.

2.5.5 CORPORATE ACTION MONITORING

A *corporate action* is any change that happens in a corporation that would affect its stock price and dividend flows. Timely reporting and capture of corporate action information is imperative for assessing risk and for determining the value of any stock held. Today, corporate actions processing is a highly manual process, with operations personnel receiving information from automated feeds, market news sources, and their custodian networks. This information is then entered into an in-house corporate actions system, such as JPMorgan's Corporate Actions system, which comes with a 24-hour customer service center to answer client inquiries on active corporate events. Some organizations use licensed vendor products such as CheckFree's eVent system for corporate actions automation. Still, most traders routinely complain about losses suffered from tardy alert notifications about a corporate action.

Examples of corporate actions include mergers and acquisitions, rights issues, stock splits, and dividends. Usually corporate actions are taken by the company's board of directors after being approved by the shareholders. A brief description of the main kinds of corporate actions is given below:

1. *Stock Split*—A stock split occurs when a company divides each of its outstanding shares into additional shares. For example, if a company announces a 2-for-1 stock split, it means that an investor who owns one share of the company now owns 2 shares of it. The price of the share is also now cut in half; so if the pre-split price were $100 per share, the new price would be $50 per share. The value of the investor's equity does not change nor does the total market capitalization of the company. Usually, the company takes such an action to increase the number of shares, also known as liquidity, in the market while causing a drop in price per share, therefore making the outstanding shares more attractive to investors. In turn, the company hopes that with time the greater liquidity and higher demand for the cheaper shares will drive the price of company shares up.

2. *Rights issues*—A rights issue is when a company offers additional shares at a discount price to existing shareholders before they are sold to the public. Usually, these additional shares are issued to fund new development. The company offers them to these shareholders because it believes that they have a stake in the company already and therefore would be more likely to take up this offer.

3. *Mergers and acquisitions*—A merger occurs when two companies combine into one. An acquisition occurs when one company buys the majority stake of a target

company's shares. In the case of an acquisition, the acquiring company may either offer to buy the shares held by investors with cash or offer its own shares in exchange for the target company's shares.

4. *Dividends*—There are two kinds of dividends that a company can issue. *Cash dividends* are distributed among the shareholders as a form of profitsharing when the company has substantial retained earnings. Usually, dividends are issued at regular intervals (quarterly, biannually, or yearly). If a new dividend is declared, it signals that the company has reached a sustainable level of growth. The second type of dividend is called a stock dividend. A *stock dividend* means that shareholders will receive additional shares, which results in an overall increase in outstanding shares and decrease in per share price.

2.5.6   RECONCILIATION

Sensitive information regarding financial transactions is exchanged back and forth between systems throughout the entire trade lifecycle. Reconciliation between these systems to ensure that there is one "golden" copy of the transaction that is consistent across all the systems is essential in the process. Traditionally, reconciliation was only performed at the tail end of the trade lifecycle after settlement. However, technologists have realized that the earlier in the process trade mismatches can be identified, the faster they can be corrected. Thus, firms have begun to reconcile data in the pre-settlement stages, comparing data held both within different systems in the firm and in the systems of all the other participants in the transaction. Trade discrepancies and exceptions bring added cost and risk into financial technology operations, which makes the monitoring and reconciliation of information crucial to STP.

2.5.7   REPORTING

There are four kinds of reports regularly produced in a financial services institution. The first is accounting reports that are provided to senior management internally to assess the asset management of its employees. The second includes annual or quarterly reports that are presented to shareholders of the institution if it is a publicly held company. The third consists of the reports sent to clients on the returns of their assets that are managed by the institution, especially if it is a buy-side firm. Finally, reports are also sent to federal government agencies such as the SEC, which mandate regular disclosure of accounts and risk management. Apart from these reports, there are others that are continually generated on everything from custody reports to risk management metrics.

■ 2.6 Mapping to Technology Operations

The chapter so far has looked at the information flows during a trade lifecycle from a business perspective and highlighted the role of industry utilities such as exchanges and clearinghouses. This section maps the departments within a bank that are responsible for these processes. In general, the technology operations of a bank can be divided along front office, middle office, and back office operations. See Figure 2-10.

The *front office* is responsible for the pre-analytics, trade routing, and execution functions. The traders and quants who work with the traders to construct trading strategies, and the sales personnel who speak to clients, all sit in the front office. The front office is where the revenues are generated, and risks are taken as part of the firm's trading strategy. This is also where the trade confirmation staff sits, especially for derivatives contracts that are not standard, and exchanges faxes and phone calls with their counterparties to iron out the legal details of each transaction. Technical support staff for analytics and trading systems used by the traders and quants also sit close by.

The *middle office* is responsible for P&L accounting and risk management. Middle office personnel make sure that trades are correctly input into the system, sometimes manually keying in details if the process is not automated. These days, it is becoming more common to get up-to-date market information through a data vendor such as Bloomberg, with the middle office monitoring and managing the banks' risk exposure by running P&L and market and credit risk metrics. In general, the middle office is considered the backbone of the information technology systems used in securities processing, and is integrated with the front and back office systems.

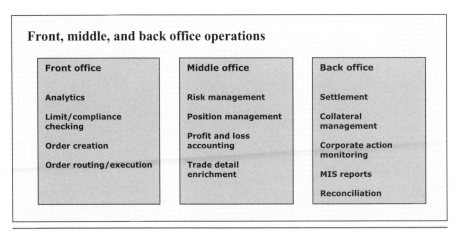

Figure 2-10   Front, middle, and back office operations.

The *back office* handles the administration related to settling trades, monitoring credit events such as corporate actions, collateral management, and report generation for government compliance. All the information related to trades is kept in databases in the back office, and a large number of the back office administration members are database personnel. Together, the front, middle, and back office work with the systems of the rest of the industry to execute and settle trades as seamlessly as possible. STP for trade transactions is as relevant in connecting business processes within a firm as it is between firms in the industry.

2.7   Summary

The trade lifecycle is the sequence of events that is triggered by the pre-trade phase of research and price discovery for a particular transaction. It involves several market participants, who each contribute to moving the transaction from inception to settlement, ending at post-settlement risk and monitoring activities. Understanding the details of the trade lifecycle is crucial when attempting to streamline the current processes, which are inefficient and costly. Starting in the next chapter, the remainder of this book will review the main technology solutions that are necessary to enable STP in all stages of the trade lifecycle.

Chapter 3

Service-Oriented Architecture

▊ 3.1 Introduction

The last three chapters highlighted how competition, regulation, and new business models are driving firms to upgrade their IT systems for industrywide straight through processing (STP). This chapter marks the part of the book that recommends technologies for implementing this STP infrastructure. It is always better for technology managers to have a *strategic* rather than a *tactical* approach when investigating technology solutions for business requirements. The tactical approach is to immediately start drawing up business requirements and then mapping out system developments. Faulty as this course of action is, it has too often been used by managers who have impatiently dived into projects without consideration of the firm's overall IT architecture. Most times, this philosophy has resulted in failed projects, with senior management shaking their heads at yet another project that went over time and over budget. The strategic approach is to stand back and evaluate the holistic technology needs of the enterprise, and to identify points where a particular technology can be leveraged across different departments. By reusing software modules across lines of business in this manner, both resources and time can be saved. Otherwise, a firm is left with legacy systems that live in silos, completely disconnected from each other, and linked only with patches of last-minute code. Unfortunately, this scenario is quite common in most financial institutions, especially those that are very large and have been around for a long time.

This book advocates spending time to ensure that systems are built using the best framework for technology development. Software architecture is equivalent to a 50,000 foot view of the entire IT infrastructure and models how software modules exchange and process information to achieve business objectives. In light of this framework, resources such as IT staff, technologies (hardware, software, programming languages), and vendors are chosen, and budgets and timelines are estimated. In recent years, the architecture of choice has been service-oriented architecture (SOA). The technology research firm Gartner called SOA one of the five hottest IT trends in 2005 and projected that "by 2008, SOA will provide the basis for 80 percent of development projects."[1]

SOA is a service-based framework for designing IT systems: it advocates the creation of software modules called services that can be reused across the enterprise, communicating with each other via messages that travel back and forth on a message bus. SOA is the culmination of a series of architectural paradigms over the years and has won the support of the software community. Section 3.2 introduces the basic concepts of SOA and traces its evolution from monolithic architecture frameworks. Coupled with the well-received technologies XML and Web Services, the SOA framework has been adopted with great success by companies as wide-ranging as eBay, Amazon, IBM, Hewlett-Packard, and DreamWorks Animation.[2] In the securities industry, the poster child for SOA implementation and success has been Wachovia, the fourth largest bank in the US. Section 3.3 discusses the increasing use and popularity of SOA in financial services, providing the Wachovia implementation as a case study. The role of enterprise architects in choosing, evangelizing, and proving the efficacy of a new architectural model such as SOA cannot be underestimated. Senior management relies on software architects to make

---

[1] David W. Cearley, Jackie Fenn, and Daryl C. Plummer, "Gartner's Positions on the Five Hottest IT Topics and Trends in 2005," May 12, 2005.
[2] Joe McKendrick, "Ten companies where SOA made a difference in 2006," ZDNet Blog, December 17, 2006.

recommendations on the choice of which architecture to employ when building a software system. Section 3.4 examines the role of the enterprise software architect in the lifecycle of a technology project.

3.2 Service-Oriented Architecture (SOA)

SOA is an architecture framework that views software as discrete services that can be reused to serve a variety of needs across the firm. For example, a software program called Calculator may be built in such a way that it can accommodate all the pricing needs of both bonds and equities. In layman's terms, traders from both the fixed income and equity desks can launch the Calculator application on their personal computers and use its features to price various securities. In SOA terms, a software *service* called Calculator is available, whose pricing functions can be utilized by sending it commands in the form of *messages* over a *message bus*. Immediately, the firm benefits from reduced costs in terms of time, money, and human resources because one software application is able to serve more than one line of business. It sounds simple and perhaps even obvious, but SOA is actually the result of a long line of architecture paradigms that have evolved, been improved, and been tried and tested over time. A brief step back into history helps shed light on how SOA came into being. See Figure 3-1.

3.2.1   EVOLUTION OF ARCHITECTURE MODELS

One of the first kinds of software architecture was the *monolithic architecture*, also known as *1-tier architecture*. In the monolithic framework, all software components reside on one machine. In the example, the graphical user interface (GUI) and the software application code for Calculator would both reside on one machine. The only way to access Calculator would be to connect a keyboard to it. Different traders would have to walk over to a machine in one corner of the trading floor every time they had to price an instrument and then come back to their desks with the output printed on a sheet of paper. This was essentially how mainframe computers worked. The model is problematic because features (GUI) and functionality (software code) share memory and processing, and end up interfering with one another. This leads to very slow processing of funtions. In addition, adding new features becomes a tedious task as everything is *tightly coupled*; that is, all the different parts of the application—its functions, its display—are closely connected to each other. In such a system, each time one part of the application is changed, all the other parts are affected as well; this makes it difficult to expand features with ease. See Figure 3-1.

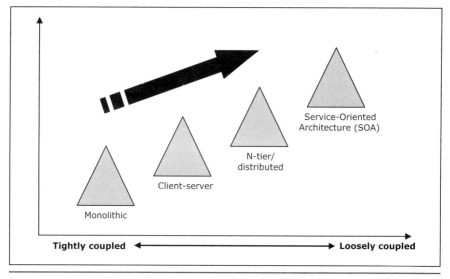

Figure 3-1   Evolution of software architecture.

In *multi-tier architectures*, the different parts of an application are separated and often kept on different machines. The philosophical basis of this separation is something known as object-oriented design. In *object-oriented design* (OOD), programs are separated into different modules based on their functionality. Each module has a standard *Application Programming Interface* (API) or set of instructions through which it can be invoked. Encoding functionality in a discrete component is known as *encapsulation*. In the example, the user interface of Calculator and its application code can be separated in two modules, as the former renders the display on the scene while the latter encapsulates the pricing functions. See Figure 3-2.

Taking this approach further, a *client-server architecture* can be built in which the GUI resides on the client and the code on the server. A client is any program that requests a service from a server. By separating the client and server, the architecture allows several clients to access one server, thereby creating a scalable architecture. Now several traders can access the Calculator from their desktops via a GUI client. While clients usually exist on the user's desktop, server software runs on powerful backend computers. The client-server architecture is also known as *2-tier architecture* because the presentation tier (the client) is separated from the application or logic tier (the server).

The client-server architecture was found to be incredibly useful, and was built upon to create more tiers of separation as systems became more complex. In *3-tier architecture*, the GUI, the application code, and the database are separated. Adding the database layer was crucial as systems became bigger and many business pro-

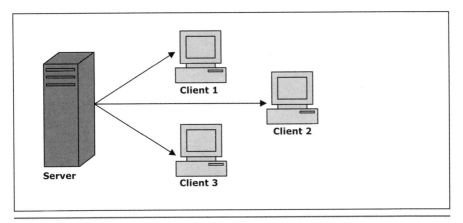

Figure 3-2   Client–Server architecture—One server can serve several clients.

cesses required the same information. Both the Calculator and the Value-at-Risk engine use current and historical market data. The separation of database management functionality ensures that data can be consistently and easily accessed by a variety of applications. In the example, the same database is used by both the pricing and risk management applications. The *N-tier architecture* was a natural extension of the 3-tier version and consisted of separating even the application tier into several tiers, each one representing distinct business functionality. When programs work together but reside in disparate physical locations, this is also referred to as *distributed architecture*. See Figure 3-3.

The most recent evolution of distributed systems is *service-oriented architecture* (SOA). SOA builds upon the notion of modular software programs and extends the idea by exposing them through standard interfaces as discrete *services*. Services can be accessed only through a published interface (API), which makes the public face of the service *loosely coupled* with its implementation code. The Calculator application may publish an interface that specifies the functions Price Bond and Price Equity that can be invoked when a client wants to price these securities. The programming language in which these functions are written, the platform the server uses, and other such details are completely hidden from the client. This abstraction of service implementation details through *interfaces* insulates clients from having to change their own code whenever any changes occur in the service implementation. Note that this was not the case in a monolithic architecture.

Several services can be composed to form a business process. For example, calculating the market risk of a portfolio of securities may use a Calculator service to first mark the securities to market, followed by a Value-at-Risk service that calculates the market risk of the whole portfolio. Thus, services can be strung together in any

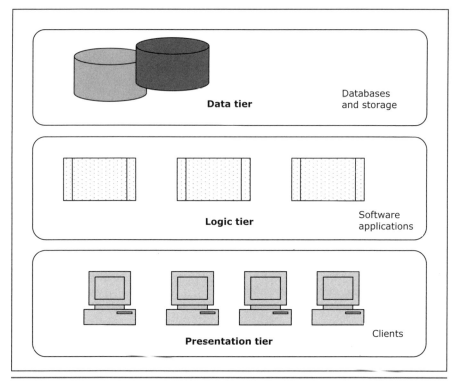

Figure 3-3 3-Tier architecture.

fashion to imitate a business flow (see Figure 3-4). This alignment of IT services to business processes is considered one of the main advantages of using SOA. It is a direct result of the fact that services are not considered particular to one line of business, but are made available to the whole enterprise. The next two sections explain the drivers for choosing SOA and its basic concepts.

3.2.2 BUSINESS DRIVERS FOR SOA

Software architectures have evolved over time to meet greater complexity and scale. Senior management is constantly looking not just to build integrated systems that are flexible and extensible, but also to manage costs and find solutions with the highest return on investment (ROI). It wants software components to mirror business processes as closely as possible, and it increasingly expects the capability to assemble these components for dynamic delivery of solutions in real time. Add to that the

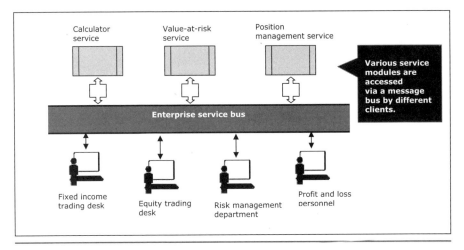

Figure 3-4   Service-Oriented Architecture.

specific pressures of an industry in which the ability to trade faster using complex algorithms directly translates into millions of dollars worth of profit, and the need for a more scalable, flexible, and powerful IT infrastructure becomes far greater. More than in any other industry, the saying "time is money" holds true in the securities industry.

3.2.2.1   Breaking Free of Silos

The way current IT systems have been built and deployed has made expansion and interoperability very difficult. The crux of the problem lies in the fact that IT systems have traditionally been built in silos. For example, the equity trading division might have a system that includes a trading application, order management system, database, and analytics module. The exact same application would be built from scratch for the fixed income trading division, when in fact some of the market data, order management, and analytics functionality could easily have been shared between the two applications. This kind of redundancy can be found repeatedly in different applications across firms in the securities industry, as applications are built independently of each other and don't leverage the data and functionality that is already available. Applications with similar business requirements are often built using different technologies and vendor products, thus tightly coupling the application with the particular business operation. The overall enterprise system as a result is reduced to an aggregate of disconnected fragmented software applications locked in silos. In such a situation, accommodating new business requirements essentially always means new technology development. Breaking software applications free

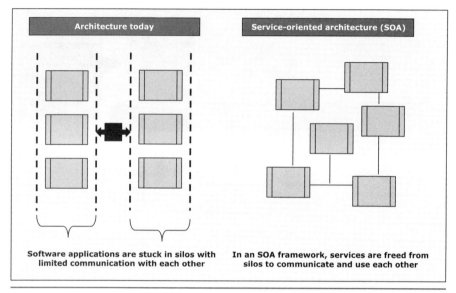

Figure 3-5   Service-Oriented Architecture simplifies integration and interoperability.

from silos is one of the primary ways to build a more flexible scalable architecture. See Figure 3-5.

3.2.2.2   Simplifying Interoperability and Integration

As firms expand and enter new markets, they not only want to reuse existing applications to save development costs, but also want to be able to link different kinds of applications for more complex product and service offerings. Integration and interoperability between applications has been another source of dissatisfaction among business users. For instance, when firmwide risk management became a concern for CEOs because of the Basel II regulation, information on positions had to be retrieved from the databases in different silos across the firm. Given that there was no standardization in data storage and representation, and no consistency in choosing vendor products or platforms, this undertaking became a long and costly process. Having an architecture that makes it easy to connect applications and integrate them into new workflows has recently become a top priority for top management.

The goal in the securities industry is therefore to build *agile* software systems that work together and can quickly take advantage of new market opportunities by plugging in additional functionality. As the next section demonstrates, SOA provides precisely this agility by freeing software components from silos and allowing them to be composed in different sequences to execute various business flows.

3.2.3 MAIN CONCEPTS OF SOA

This section outlines the main concepts of SOA. It does not give detailed implementation options so as to emphasize that SOA is a blueprint that is independent of implementation. Technologies evolve all the time: the key is to have the correct architecture whether software modules are bought off the shelf or built by the firm itself. That said, some technologies such as XML and Web Services are particularly suited to SOA implementation, and these will be highlighted appropriately in the following sections.

3.2.3.1 Services

The core of SOA is a library of services. A service is functionality that is *encapsulated* in a software program. A federation of loosely coupled services sits on a distributed network and can work alone or together to execute a business process. Services can be invoked via a public interface, which describes exactly how the service can be invoked, what parameters it will accept, and what it can be expected to return to the client. The specification of what functions the service will provide is known as its *service level agreement* (SLA). The internal workings of each service are hidden behind the interface, making it appear as a black box to the client.

3.2.3.1.1 Modular Components with Interfaces

Having such an *interface* through which the service can be easily accessed is very useful. For starters, the client is always insulated from the changes in specific implementations in hardware and software. The service can switch the program language it is coded in from Java to C#, and this change will be completely invisible to the client who will still access the service with the same command. For example, regardless of how the Calculator is implemented, the command for invoking its function for pricing a bond will always be Price Bond. Firms can easily improve, scale, and factor their code base, and yet at no time will the client be exposed to any of these changes. The system's various parts maintain complete interoperability with each other through their *implementation-agnostic* access layers. In other words, system agility is facilitated because the public interface and the implementation of each service are loosely coupled.

3.2.3.1.2 Leveraging Existing Assets

The creation of an interface to each service is also incredibly useful when integrating it with legacy systems. Under the SOA framework, the old system does not have to be replaced with a new set of services; instead, a wrapper interface around the existing module can be built making it into a reusable and interoperable service as well. This means that transition to an SOA infrastructure can be fairly smooth as the enterprise moves one by one towards wrapping old system components into distinct service modules, and builds new services as business needs expand.

3.2.3.1.3 Using Web Services

SOA is a proponent of adhering to industry standards for design and implementation. Interoperability is far easier when everyone uses the same protocol; it would be very difficult if a firm had to code to a different proprietary interface each time it engaged with another firm. Web Services are a set of standard technologies that facilitate the creation of services that can be invoked over a distributed network using messages. Protocols for Web Services are defined by the W3C (World Wide Web Consortium) and they are, in fact, completely in line with the doctrine of SOA. However, Web Services are just one way that the SOA service paradigm can be implemented. The industry standard for writing an interface to a Web Service is WSDL (Web Service Description Language). It provides a structure that can be used to define the service and state a security policy outlining who can access it, how it can be used, and what information must be provided to it for it to function. WSDL is an excellent choice when deciding on an interface language. It is an industry standard, which means that trading partners and industry utilities will most likely be employing the same language to define access to their services.

3.2.3.2 Service Communication

Clients and other services use *messages* to invoke a service's functionality. These messages can be written in a number of formats, but the most popular language for SOA implementation until now has been Extensible Markup Language (XML). XML, developed by the W3C, is a platform independent language that has become the lingua franca of system communication. In the Web Services world, the structure of this XML message is outlined in a standard called SOAP (Simple Object Access Protocol). It is analogous to choosing a plain manila envelope versus the standard FedEx envelope when sending something via FedEx. While using the FedEx envelope is not necessary, it is preferred because it has a standard format that everyone else recognizes and this reduces human error and increases efficiency.

Messages travel over a connectivity medium called an enterprise service bus. *Message-oriented middleware* (MOM) is a type of message bus that is commonly associated with the SOA framework. MOM usually resides in both the client and the server, and supports *asynchronous* messaging between the two. Asynchronous messaging implies that the client can send a message to the server and does not have to wait for a reply to continue its other functions. The response may come back at some later point in time (asynchronously). The message queue stores the message if the receiver is busy or offline; it only passes the message when the recipient is ready and connected.

Using middleware offers several advantages. It greatly simplifies the number of connections that applications must have with each other. Applications now communicate over a message bus, instead of directly with each other, which lowers the number of connectivity points for any business flow remarkably. It also insulates both the sender and receiver from each other's platform specifications as all parties only directly interact with the middleware and use its standard protocols (see Figure 3-6). Firms have generally relied on vendors to provide middleware technology, because like databases and application servers, these products are so complex and specialized that it is too much a task for an in-house development to undertake. TIBCO and MQ Series are two of the most popular middleware products in financial services.

3.2.3.3 The Dilemma over XML

Architects often face a dilemma when deciding whether to use XML as the messaging protocol. The reason is that XML messages can be quite large in size, because data written in XML is surrounded by self-describing tags (see Chapter 4 for more detail on XML). Financial protocols in the securities industry are written either in delimited format or in XML. FIX (Financial Information Exchange) is a communications protocol for exchanging trade-related information, which is currently the most popular communication method in the industry. For

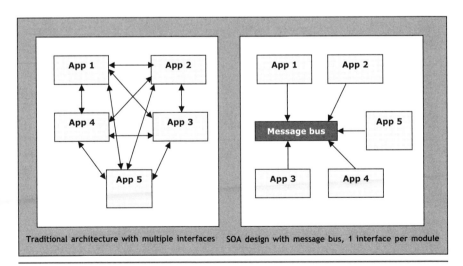

Traditional architecture with multiple interfaces   SOA design with message bus, 1 interface per module

Figure 3-6   Creating a consistent interface between modules with SOA.

high-throughput real-time requirements, such as those in algorithmic trading, FIX (which carries information using delimiters) is usually considered more appropriate than XML. The decision of whether or not to use XML depends on the service level agreement of the service, that is, whether or not it promises to provide high-speed functionality.

3.2.3.4 Service Registration and Discovery

Once services are created, they must be advertised at a central location so that they can be dynamically *discovered* by any client looking for that particular service. This central location is also known as a registry and is similar to the online yellow pages directory. Clients can look up the availability of a service by keyword and find out how to access that service. Most registries are written using the UDDI (Universal Description, Discovery, and Integration) standard, but again there are a number of other ways to write descriptions of services as well. The important thing is that the language should be as close to an industry standard as possible. If amendments are made to the standard, all affected parties must be issued the amended specifications so that they know how to interact with the registry.

3.2.3.5 Service Composition

Until now, this section has discussed how one particular service is built, accessed, and discovered. But business processes are seldom made of just one service; modeling a group of services after an end-to-end business flow is the ultimate goal of the system. In SOA terms, this is known as *service composition*, that is, how services work together to achieve a business goal. BPEL (Business Process Execution Language) is an example of a language that can be used to coordinate a set of service invocations in order to produce a business result.

3.2.4 BENEFITS OF SOA

The SOA approach has several benefits including:

- **Reusability:** The federation of services frees software modules from being redundantly deployed in different silos in the same firm. By encapsulating business functionality in a service, SOA allows a software module to be used by any client that wants to use that functionality.

- **Integration:** Each service can be accessed using a standard interface that is outlined in the service contract. Even legacy components can be presented as services by putting a wrapper service interface around them. This allows easy integration of modules across disparate systems.

- **Agility:** Because libraries of well-defined services form the core of the SOA framework, new requirements that need those services can access and reuse them easily, thus shortening the time-to-market deployment of new applications.

- **Cost Savings:** The flexibility of reusing software components results in both a cost and time-saving benefit.

- **Business Process Alignment:** SOA is built around services, which are representations of business processes. It is one of the first times in the history of software architecture that business processes and software components are so closely aligned, making the technology a direct solution to a particular business goal.

3.3   SOA in Financial Services

Whenever a new technology or paradigm comes to the market, it is difficult to convince senior management that it is the best way to move forward. Architects can spend years trying to build consensus around a particular framework. This holds true in the securities industry as well. SOA has been greeted with both enthusiasm and resistance, and management has hesitated at what it sees as a costly overhauling of its enterprise architecture. However, SOA does not need to be rolled out in such a big bang way. In fact, it is easy to integrate new and old systems using SOA, because legacy software modules can be wrapped as services. In fact, the best way to spread the word about the benefits of SOA is to create this infrastructure in one project, and then to incrementally ripple it across the enterprise. This viral marketing of technology paradigms has been quite effective in the past. An increasing number of banks, such as Citigroup and Merrill Lynch, and industry utilities, such as the New York Board of Trade (NYBOT), are slowly shifting to an SOA-based IT infrastructure using this approach. The US bank Wachovia, however, did decide to use the "big bang" method for introducing SOA at the enterprise level, as will be described below.

In 2004, Susan Certoma was hired as CIO of Wachovia's $6 billion Corporate and Investment Banking (CIB) division, with the explicit mandate to equip the division with the kind of efficient IT infrastructure that would make Wachovia, the country's fourth largest commercial bank, a formidable competitor in capital markets as well. Certoma decided to overhaul the entire IT infrastructure of the division, starting with a new approach on how to develop software systems. She decided that the best way to achieve this goal was by creating a federation of services that could be shared among all of CIB's lines of businesses, and chose to use SOA as the blueprint for rolling out a robust, scalable, and powerful system for traders, quants, and risk managers.[3] It was a bold move, but one that would be applauded across the industry within

---

[3]"Certoma Floors It," *Waters*, June 1, 2006.

two years, when the bank would reap the benefits of services that could be leveraged across all nine lines of business, including research, advice, and trading.

Certoma immediately hired an elite team of SOA specialists and created a 50-person central architecture group that modeled business processes to existing and future services. The exercise, which involved extensive interaction with the business to understand its needs and goals, took five months and proved invaluable to everything that followed. Armed with their in-depth review of business requirements, the team was able to map out the high-level architecture. It included how to build services that could be used by multiple departments within CIB, such as trading and order management, and decisions on which hardware to use, such as grid computing for more power and scalability.

While the overall project plan ran out to three to five years, particular services were built in record time under the clear vision of SOA. Applications that traditionally took a year to build were now built in months given their ability to leverage services already built for other applications. The improvements in efficiency were immediate and significant. Fast forward to summer 2006 and Wachovia opened the doors to its new trading floor at 375 Park Avenue in Manhattan, home to more than 400 traders and 800 employees, and one very sophisticated service-oriented IT infrastructure. The trading floor has since become the trophy flagship for Certoma's successful implementation of SOA. In the 2006 American Financial Technology Awards, which every year recognizes achievement in IT in the securities industry, awarded Wachovia the top spot for Most Innovative Trading Floor.[4]

3.4 Role of the Enterprise Architect

The purpose of articulating the system architecture is to better understand and manage the project implementation and maintenance. It also allows the project team to predict roadblocks, make a timeline, see dependencies, and optimize the system. There are several layers to the role of an architect, from visualizing and documenting an architectural approach to guiding the development team on technologies for implementing the architecture. The responsibilities of the enterprise architect can be divided depending on the phase of the project.

3.4.1 DESIGNING THE ARCHITECTURE

In the beginning of any project, the key function of the technology team is to understand the business requirements of the clients. The *business analyst* is responsible

---

[4]American Technology Awards, 2006.

for understanding and communicating their business requirements to the technology team. Based on close discussions with the business analysts, the architect begins to map out the overall architecture for the various software components that will work together to satisfy business goals. The architect also examines which software applications already exist in the firm that can be *leveraged* to meet the requirements of the new project.

3.4.2   CREATING THE TEAM

The architect then chooses the most appropriate technologies, such as programming languages, hardware, operating systems, and number of human resources, required to implement his or her vision. At this point, the architect begins discussions with the *project manager* to map out the timeline for completing the business requirements of the project. Thus, in Stage 1 of the project, the business analyst, software architect, and project manager work closely together to distill high-level business requirements, model the architecture, choose the technologies, and estimate the time and resources required for implementing the proposed architecture. Once all three parties have documented their analysis, they present a case to the clients. If the clients approve the project plan, the architect has the go-ahead to staff the project team and begin work on the project. See Figure 3-7.

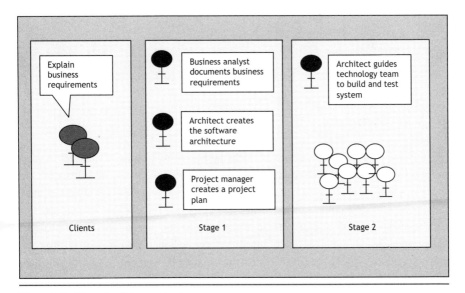

Figure 3-7   The role of the architect.

3.4.3 OVERSEEING DEVELOPMENT AND TESTING

The next stage from the software architect's point of view comprises choosing members of the technology team—developers, database administrators, and testers—and investing in the appropriate hardware and software applications. Whereas Stage 1 saw the software architect more in a strategic role, Stage 2 sees him or her more in a mentoring and oversight role. At every point, the architect addresses how to avoid technology risks and explains how his or her architecture can accommodate changes or additions to the business requirements. That is why choosing the right architecture is key to a successful project: requirements are always changing and growing, and a modular architecture can result in the lowest-cost expansion of the system.

RECOMMENDATIONS

SOA is the recommended architecture for implementing an STP system. A software architecture is the framework under which new components will be added, legacy systems integrated, and all parts of the system created in an interoperable manner to meet the business goals of STP.

1. Loosely-coupled services allow reuse of software modules.
2. Integration with legacy components possible through service wrappers.
3. Interoperability between applications made easier through standard interfaces.
4. Agility in expanding and scaling the system with addition of new services.
5. Services are closely aligned with business processes.
6. Proven success in financial services firms such as Wachovia.

3.5 Summary

SOA is the result of a collection of ideas and patterns that have evolved to meet more complex business requirements across industries, including the financial services industry. In essence, it is a set of loosely coupled services that represent business processes and communicate with each other via standard interfaces across a message bus. Moving to SOA can be costly initially, but in the long run, it provides better capability to integrate heterogeneous systems. It also lowers costs due to reusable component-based design, and provides higher ROI given its use of services, which can be accessed by multiple lines of business. SOA has been discussed independently of any particular implementation technology, and is presented as a blueprint of how to think of a software infrastructure at an abstract level. It is the recommended software architecture for an STP implementation because of its flexibility and scalability. The next three chapters discuss implementation specifics of SOA in light of STP requirements. Different messaging formats and industry standards for financial products are surveyed in Chapter 4, Industry Standards; message-oriented middleware is examined in Chapter 5, Connectivity; and data access, storage, and representation are discussed in Chapter 6, Data Management.

Chapter 4

Industry Standards

▌ 4.1 Introduction

The standardization of financial contracts has always been considered a necessary step in streamlining financial intermediation. Stocks, bonds, and futures each have generic contracts, making these instruments commodities with a predetermined set of parameters. Standardization not only makes a security easier to understand for investors, it is also necessary for automating the trade lifecycle of the security. When firms do not follow an agreed upon communication method and language, the result is that the communication is riddled with errors and interoperability becomes prohibitively difficult. Managing associated operational risks requires extensive and repeated testing, which is costly and time-consuming.

Industry standards are created after extensive discussion between experienced industry players, and are thus extremely helpful in reducing errors, managing risk, and increasing efficiency and productivity. If they are published free of license fees, they are also known as *open standards*. For an STP environment, three types of standards are relevant: (i) business standards, such as instrument contract specifications and business rules; (ii) technology standards, such as architecture paradigms and messaging models; and (iii) financial ontologies, which are domain-specific vocabularies created specifically for exchange of financial data between systems. While all three types are examined briefly in Section 4.2, the focus of the chapter is financial technology standards, as they are most relevant to creating an STP environment.

Modern architecture paradigms like Service-Oriented Architecture (SOA) advocate the use of industry standards for system communication. Section 4.3 introduces the industry's leading financial ontology standards—FIX, FpML, and SWIFT. It also compares Comma Separated Values (CSV) and Extensible Markup Language (XML), which are the two main message formats used by these industry standards. Firms have traditionally built their own communication vocabularies for exchanging financial data, and in order to use industry standards, they must build translators that can convert the industry format and vocabulary to their legacy ones. Section 4.4 provides insight into how firms can contribute to, transform, and extend industry standards to meet their own needs.

4.2   Industry Standards

An *industry standard* can be defined as a set of conventions that is accepted and followed by every participant in the industry. Often, it is agreed upon through meetings and iterative enhancements by the major players in the industry, usually via an organization that has been set up specifically for this purpose. Financial technology standards depend on business and technology industry standards to help them devise guidelines for system communication of financial data. For example, FpML (Financial Products Markup Language) publishes industry guidelines for processing of credit derivatives that builds upon protocols that ISDA has set for credit derivatives and that W3C (World Wide Web Consortium) has set for XML. This section introduces the major organizations that are involved in setting standards for the securities industry.

4.2.1   BUSINESS STANDARDS

In securities trading, standards need to be set for both content and operations, that is, everything from legal contracts to how to handle credit events (in which an issuer defaults on an obligation). Technology operations revolve around these business standards, and thus knowledge of these standards is imperative for technology managers in the securities industry. Examples of the kinds of standards that are important are below:

- **Master agreements** for asset classes. A master agreement serves as a template for all the possible terms and conditions that can be part of a contract, including definitions and business rules. Industry consortiums that represent the interests of market participants trading particular asset classes create master agreements. These can then be used as legal contracts between two parties, thus facilitating the trading process. The Bond Markets Association (BMA), for example, provides master agreements for fixed income products including corporate bonds, government bonds, and mortgage backed securities.

- **Reference data standards,** including unique security identifiers, business calendars, and reference codes for countries and currencies. The CUSIP (Committee on Uniform Securities Identification Procedures) system for identifying securities, for example, was created for establishing a standard for unique identifiers for securities for US stocks and bonds. Another example of reference data is the knowledge of holidays in different countries. In order to know good business days for trading around the globe, firms rely on business calendars provided by Swaps Monitor, which provides a database of holiday and trading hours data.

- **Credit event protocols** for handling events such as bankruptcy and default. For example, when the US auto parts manufacturer Dura Operating Corp filed for bankruptcy in October 2006, the ISDA announced the publication of a protocol to facilitate the settlement of credit derivatives trades involving the company.

- **Credit ratings standards** for expressing the creditworthiness of issuers. The leading credit ratings companies, Standard and Poor's, Moody's, and Fitch Ratings, employ proprietary rating algorithms to evaluate the potential for an issuer to default on a particular obligation. They have established different categories that have become universally acceptable in the industry. For instance, Moody's categorization for issues that have minimal credit risk is Aaa.

- **Financial reporting standards** are set by agencies such as the Financial Accounting Standards Board (FASB), which establishes standards for reporting financial data to shareholders, auditors, and the government.

The list above highlights how standards are set for every possible aspect of securities trading. Once a standard has been set, it must be followed by all market participants, usually by some predetermined date. Governments, central banks, and regulatory organizations are also closely involved in monitoring and setting standards in the industry. For example, the SEC mandated that by April 2001, all stock exchanges in the US must change their market quote conventions to decimals. Some organizations, known as Self Regulatory Organizations (SRO), set standards and regulate activities of the members in the securities industry. NASD is the primary private-sector regulator of the US securities industry, with over 5,000 brokerage firms and more than 660,000 stockbrokers and registered representatives under its jurisdiction.

4.2.2 TECHNOLOGY STANDARDS

Technology standards are the key to building good software solutions. They refer to architecture models, programming languages, messaging protocols, and data standards. An industry standard is considered viable if a large number of vendors begin to provide support for it. The longevity of a standard is usually measured by users as they test the standard's ability to accommodate new and complex business requirements.

4.2.2.1 Proprietary Versus Open Source

Standards are either proprietary, that is, they are owned by a company or individual, or they are open, which means that anyone is free to use, modify, and distribute that standard. The programming languages Java and C# were created by Sun Microsystems and Microsoft, respectively. Initially, they were both proprietary languages, which meant that the libraries for the standard could only be set by the companies. However, Microsoft presented the C# language to the International Organization for Standardization (ISO) for approval as an open standard, which means its specification will from now on be voted on and approved by the ISO. It was accepted as a standard in 2003. The ISO is a nonprofit organization that is made up of the standards institutes of 157 countries. It is the world's largest developer of standards, especially technical standards. That said, there is far more vendor support for Java because it is a more open technology, in that it can be run on multiple platforms. Microsoft, on the other hand, has been known to develop technologies that can run primarily on Windows. For instance, Visual Basic (now VB.NET) is the most popular business technology language in the world. It was developed by Microsoft and, by default, can only run in a Windows application (which is Microsoft software).

Open source refers to code that is publicly available. By definition, anyone is allowed to use, modify, and redistribute the source code without paying any royalty fees. Open source software is usually developed through collaboration by a community of software developers. Examples of open source software include the Apache and Tomcat web servers that have become very popular for trading applications. Firms find it very cost effective to use open source software, although sometimes it is problematic when such software does not have the kind of support that vendor products provide.

4.2.2.2 *World Wide Web Consortium (W3C)*

Ever since the introduction of the web, the W3C has become an important standard-setting organization for web technologies. W3C was created to develop protocols and guidelines that would help users take advantage of the web to its fullest potential. Since the standards created by this body are not owned by a company or person, they are said to be in the public domain. The standards for how messages can be exchanged between systems, and validated according to proprietary business rules, are most pertinent to this chapter. In this respect, the W3C oversees the standard for Extensible Markup Language (XML), a flexible platform-independent text format that is advocated by SOA architects as the lingua franca of system communication.

4.2.3 FINANCIAL ONTOLOGIES

Whenever financial managers build systems, they are careful to always use industry standards for two reasons: first, interoperability increases when everyone uses the same vocabulary and business rules; second, these standards have been vetted by the best experts in the field and are likely very conducive to efficiency and productivity. Financial ontologies define the concepts and the relationships between them pertinent to a particular domain. For example, an ontology for an equity derivative call option will include the concept of strike price, exercise date, underlying asset and underlying asset price, and the price of the call option itself. They are usually written in a standard data format language such as XML. FpML, a standard for exchanging data related to OTC derivatives, is written using XML. FpML is published by a subsidiary of ISDA, which represents the global OTC derivatives industry.

In general, communication standards for STP in the securities industry should cover representation of both *data* and *processes*. For instance, a standard is needed for representing the details of a credit default swap; a standard is also needed for the notification message which communicates a credit event that could affect the future cash flows of that swap.

In general, broker-dealers are always pushing more for the development of financial technology standards than buy-side institutional investors. One of the reasons is that the front office usually develops sophisticated trading applications that use industry languages for pre-trade and trade phases, and pushes the back office to develop its systems for automating post-trade and post-settlement processes.

Buy-side firms have traditionally been insulated from direct trading and associated front office systems in the market, and therefore are slower to adopt cutting-edge technologies. However, with the buy-side's growing interest for direct market access, it can be expected that its input in driving the growth and ubiquity of financial standards will increase significantly.

4.3 Financial Technology Standards

Financial ontologies have been created to cover all aspects of trade lifecycle events, from defining contracts and business rules, to reporting to the SEC, to receiving consolidated market data from sources such as Bloomberg. When standards are published, firms and industry utilities begin to build their IT systems around these specifications for use in electronic communication. This section discusses the major standards currently available in the industry for STP activities. But first, there is a discussion on the different message formats and their relevance to the choice of standard chosen.

4.3.1 MESSAGE FORMATS

Industry standards are used to communicate financial information. Once the vocabulary and rules have been agreed upon, the next thing to agree upon is the format in which this information will be exchanged. Only by documenting how machines can expect to receive the data can firms code their interfaces and modules to accept and process this information. The idea is similar to having two people decide that they want to talk about the weather; the question now remains whether they will have the discussion in English or Spanish. A shared understanding of the language and grammar in which content is exchanged is crucial for effective communication. In technology, this language and grammar can be referred to as the message format in which financial data is transmitted between and within firms.

In general, it is important for the chosen message format to be:

- **Descriptive:** The format should be able to capture the data and its relationships as richly as it can.

- **Flexible:** The format should be flexible enough to accommodate new types of information and process requirements.

- **Platform-neutral:** The message format should not be tied to any vendor product or platform; that is, disparate systems and programming languages should be able to receive and process data in the message.

- **Fast:** Data must be transported in a structured format that is easy to parse and process, especially given the high-speed requirements of electronic and algorithmic trading these days.

- **User friendly:** Human intervention is often required whenever there are exceptions in system communication. Operations teams struggle to locate errors when messages are written in opaque formats. Thus, it helps to have a message format that is easy to scan by the human eye.

There are two main kinds of message formats that are used in the securities industry: text formats that contain information that is separated by comma, tab, or tag delimiters; and the text format XML.

4.3.1.1 Message Formats Using Delimiters

The *de facto* data exchange language before XML was CSV. CSV is a platform-neutral message format that contains data separated by commas in a predetermined order. For example, if two firms agree that they will exchange legal entity data using CSV, they will specify that each row will refer to one legal entity and the data will come in the following order: *Legal Entity Identifier, Legal Entity Name, Country of Incorporation, Address of Headquarters*. This is known as the *meta-data* of the file, as it provides the attributes for which values are supplied in the file. It is usually carried in a separate template. An example CSV file for the specified meta-data could be: *MSFT, Microsoft Inc., USA, Seattle*.

Other examples of delimiters are tags and tabs. The most popular industry protocol FIX (Financial Information Exchange) uses tag delimiters to describe everything from a buy order to an allocation report.

CSV and such formats are very good for flat data records that do not have nested hierarchical relationships. For instance, it would be difficult in one file to describe several subsidiaries of Microsoft that are legal entities in their own right. XML, discussed in the next section, is much more flexible and richer in describing hierarchical data. CSV, on the other hand, has the advantage of being a small message in terms of byte size and therefore amenable to quick processing. It is important for technology managers to realize that different message formats are suited for different kinds of data needs and that there is no one solution for all problems.

4.3.1.2 Extensible Markup Language (XML)

XML is a platform-neutral text format that uses tags to describe data. It has become very popular in recent years, becoming the format of choice for exchanging data between disparate applications. XML's syntax and rules are published by the W3C, and a number of industry tools have come to market which can be used to construct XML documents.

XML is very simple to understand. To use XML to describe a legal entity, the values can be enclosed in tags around the data.

<LegalEntityIdentifier>**MSFT**</LegalEntityIdentifier>
<LegalEntityName>**Microsoft Inc.**</LegalEntityName>
<CountryOfIncorporation>**USA**</CountryOfIncorporation>
<Headquarters>**Seattle**</Headquarters>

Compare this to the CSV file:

MSFT, Microsoft Inc., USA, Seattle

The XML file has the advantage that the data tags describe the information, and thus it is easier for a software program to manipulate the data. However, the very fact that it has these self-describing tags makes it a far larger file size. As mentioned before, the order of the CSV file was described as follows: *Legal Entity Identifier, Legal Entity Name, Country of Incorporation, Address of Headquarters.* The order in which the data will appear in an XML document is outlined in an *XML schema.*

XML Schemas thus define the terms and rules that are permissible in an XML document; by following the rules on how to write an XML schema as defined by the W3C, anyone can write a schema that is relevant to a particular domain or process. This schema is used as a template to build XML documents, and the resultant documents are *validated* against it immediately upon receipt. Validation is useful as the receiving system can identify missing data or violated business rules automatically, reducing the risk of finding errors later in the trade lifecycle. XML schemas can be built easily using tools such as Altova XML Spy and Oxygen. The important thing is to understand how business concepts translate into XML schemas; knowing the exact syntax of how an XML schema is built is not necessary from a managerial point of view.

As an example, the associated XML schema may force the elements to appear in sequence or there may be no order specified at all; since the data is surrounded by descriptive tags, the sequence is not that important. In this way, XML is less rigid in terms of order than CSV files. XML also has the advantage of allowing nested elements lending itself to deeper hierarchical relationships that are harder to implement in CSV. However, as is obvious, XML has the issue of being a verbose language, which means that XML documents are bloated and take longer to process than CSV files. One solution is data compression, which is discussed in the next section.

FIX	FpML
1. Used widely in electronic trading of equities.	1. Becoming more prevalent in derivatives processing.
2. Primary message format is tag delimited format.	2. Message format is XML.
3. Performance is very fast.	3. Performance issues due to XML.
4. Primary execution venue is at exchanges.	4. Primary execution venue is the OTC market.
5. Used extensively by front-end applications as well as on the back-end.	5. Used primarily for back-end clearing and settlement processing.

Figure 4-1   Differences between FpML and FIX.

4.3.1.3   Message Compression

With the explosion in the volume of trading data, file size and the ability to process financial data quickly have come to the forefront. XML documents have the disadvantage of being bloated primarily because they contain the content descriptors within the document. This has resulted in larger file size and therefore slower processing and bottlenecks, which has discouraged securities firms from using it for high-volume high-speed transactions. Some believe message compression can reduce the overhead costs that accompany processing the extra tags in XML documents. One example of message compression is when the tags are made into binary tokens and the resulting document is zipped (compressed) as a message.[1]

4.3.2   FIX (FINANCIAL INFORMATION EXCHANGE)

The FIX protocol is a messaging specification created for the electronic exchange of trade-related information. Formed in 1992 as a protocol for equity trading between Fidelity Investments and Salomon Brothers, FIX has grown to become the most popular pre-trade and trade messaging language for equity trading in the world. The standard is published and maintained by FIX Protocol Ltd. (FPL), an industry

---

[1]Nina Mehta, "FIXing the Market Data Mess," *Financial Engineering News.*

consortium that boasts of having leading buy-side and sell-side firms as its members, along with exchanges, utility providers, and data providers. The mission statement of FIX Protocol is, "To improve the global trading process by defining, managing and promoting an open protocol for real-time, electronic communication between industry participants, while complementing industry standards." Members collaborate in working groups to come up with message formats for asset classes, markets, and phases of the trade lifecycle.

Since FIX predates most other trade communication protocols, its use is far more prevalent across securities firms than that of any other standard. According to the FIX Global Survey that was conducted by TowerGroup in 2005, 75% of buy-side firms and 80% of sell-side firms interviewed reported that they used FIX for electronic trading. In addition, 75% of the exchanges interviewed said they supported a FIX interface for trade communication, and further, over 25% of their trading total volume was handled via FIX messages.

4.3.2.1 Product and Process Coverage

Although FIX originally started with supporting mainly pre-trade messaging for equity products, it now includes many other asset classes and post-trade messaging in its specifications. The latest version of the specification FIX 5.0 has support for a variety of equities, fixed income instruments, foreign exchange trades, futures, and options. It also supports different pre-trade, trade, and post-trade messaging requirements.

Specifications for trading activities, including negotiated trade/bid or offer requests, order initiation, execution, and allocation, are provided by FIX for the instrument types listed below:

Collective Investment Vehicles (CIVs)

Mutual funds

- Unit trusts
- Managed investments

Equity

- Stocks

Fixed Income

- US Treasury bonds
- US corporate bonds
- Municipal securities
- Agency securities
- To-be-announced (TBA) mortgage backed securities

- Euro sovereign bonds
- Euro corporate bonds
- US and European commercial paper
- Repurchase agreements (repos)
- Related securities lending activities

Futures and Options

- Single-leg instruments including both standardized and nonstandard call and put options, future, and call and put options on a future
- Multileg instruments with futures, options, and other securities as legs

Foreign Exchange

- Spot
- Forwards
- FX swaps
- Vanilla FX OTC spot options

Depending on the phase of the trade, different components of FIX are added to a FIX message. The main trading activities covered by FIX are divided into pre-trade, trade, and post-trade phases. Examples of message types are given below. However, it should be kept in mind that FIX is used primarily for pre-trade indications of interest (IOI), for trade single and multiple orders (including cancel and amend orders), and for post-trade allocation orders. See Figure 4-2.

Pre-Trade

- EventCommunication, News, Email
- Indication, Advertisement, IOI
- MarketData, MarketDataRequest, MarketDataSnapshotFullRefresh
- QuotationNegotiation, QuoteRequest, QuoteResponse
- SecurityAndTradingSessionDefinitionOrStatus, SecurityDefinition, SecurityDefinitionUpdateReport

Trade

- CrossOrders, CrossOrderCancelRequest, NewOrderCross
- MultilegOrders, NewOrderMultileg
- ProgramTrading, BidRequest, ListStrikePrice, NewOrderList
- SingleGeneralOrderHandling, BidResponse, ExecutionAcknowledgement, OrderStatusRequest

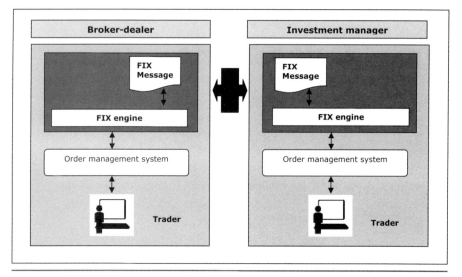

Figure 4-2 FIX is a popular message format for communicating trade order and detail information.

Post-Trade

- Allocation, AllocationInstruction, AllocationReport
- CollateralManagement, CollateralAssignment, CollateralInquiry
- Confirmation, ConfirmationRequest
- PositionMaintenance, AdjustedPositionReport, AssignmentReport
- RegistrationInstruction, RegistrationInstructionsResponse
- SettlementInstruction, SettlementInstructionRequest
- TradeCapture, TradeCaptureReport

4.3.2.2 Specification Formats

FIX is a vendor-neutral standard, which means that once the message has been created, it can be sent over any type of connection and security protocol between two firms. FIX was originally written only in tag and field format. However, unlike XML where the tags are self-describing, here the tag is an integer value that refers to a particular field.

For example, the tag 1003 represents a trade ID, which is defined as "The unique ID assigned to the trade entity once it is received or matched by the exchange or central counterparty." In the FIX document, it will appear as "1003 = SomeTradeIdentifier." Immediately upon encountering the tag 1003 in a message, the receiving firm (which has coded its IT system to process FIX messages) will know that the trade identifier for the trade this message is referring to is "SomeTradeIdentifier."

The FIX format as outlined carries information that is delimited by predefined codes. While this format has been successfully implemented and is considered lightweight, it is also viewed as more rigid and inflexible than XML. In response to the XML's growing popularity as a data format, FIX introduced an XML version of its specification called FIXML. In the above example, the FIXML tag name for trade ID is "TrdID" and would appear as

<TrdID>SomeTradeIdentifier</TrdID>

in a FIX message. However, the XML version has not seen widespread use by the industry.

4.3.2.3   FAST (FIX Adapted for Streaming)

The FAST (FIX adapted for streaming) protocol was developed specifically as an optimized version of FIX for transporting market data for electronic trading. Timely market data has become crucial in a fast-paced market environment. However, the proliferation of electronic trading has resulted in a spike in market data volume (up to millions of messages per second), and current message formats are not optimized for the acquisition and distribution of this data. FIX has developed FAST using data compression technology that encodes data optimally and therefore offers high-speed data in smaller packets, resulting in significant bandwidth savings. There is the question of decoding the data, but FAST proponents claim that the decoding can be done within milliseconds. In particular, FAST is interoperable with FIX messages, which is particularly attractive to firms that use FIX messages but that need to handle high-frequency high-volume data. Regulations such as Reg NMS and MiFID will likely result in even higher levels of pre-trade quotes and trade orders, leading some to believe that FAST will be adopted by a significant number of exchanges. Until now, some exchanges, such as the London Stock Exchange, have started pilot programs to test FAST.[2]

4.3.3   FpML (FINANCIAL PRODUCTS MARKUP LANGUAGE)

FpML is an XML-based industry standard for messaging and communication between systems for OTC derivatives. The aim of the FpML organization, which is managed by ISDA on behalf of a community of leading investment banks, is to

---

[2] Ivy Schmerken, "Exchanges Are Adopting the FPL's FAST Protocol to Speed Up Market Data Rates," *Wall Street & Technology*, August 21, 2006.

provide an ontology for the attributes of derivative products, as well as to process related messages for all the transactions involved in trading these instruments. Since FpML is written in XML, it is a platform-neutral ontology that can be used to exchange information over any kind of connection and can be processed by applications written in any software language.

The standard was first published in 1999 as a result of collaboration between JP Morgan and PricewaterhouseCoopers. It was created to facilitate automation for privately negotiated contracts, which are customized contracts and, therefore, difficult to standardize. Trading derivatives is usually phone based, with manual faxing of contracts and consequent input of trade information into computer screens by the middle office. This method of communication created backlogs of unconfirmed trades, and in general made the trade lifecycle more prone to errors and delays in settlement. The longer the time between trade confirmation and settlement, the greater the risk exposure of the parties involved in the trade. While equity trading was given a great boost through electronic trading with the help of protocols such as FIX, derivatives still lagged behind because of their complicated structures. With the introduction of XML Schemas, there was a way to construct a flexible, extensible ontology for a messaging infrastructure for derivatives. The FpML standards committee undertook this effort with great determination. Since its inception, FpML has published several versions with an ever expanding specification base for asset classes and trade processes. All the major derivatives players in the industry have been participating in its development and acceptance. Currently, the clearinghouse DTCC and SwapsWire, a centralized electronic platform for the trade capture and confirmation of OTC derivatives, are two market leaders that use FpML. See Figure 4-3.

4.3.3.1   Product and Process Coverage

The working draft of the latest version FpML 4.3 specification is now available on the FpML website. It includes expanded coverage of credit derivatives products and support for their post-trade processing. The following asset classes are represented in this working draft, the definitions of which have been taken from the ISDA Master Agreement specifications for these products.

Interest Rate Derivatives

- Single and cross-currency interest rate swap
- Forward rate agreement
- Interest rate cap
- Interest rate floor interest rate swap (European, Bermudan, and American styles; cash and physical settlement)

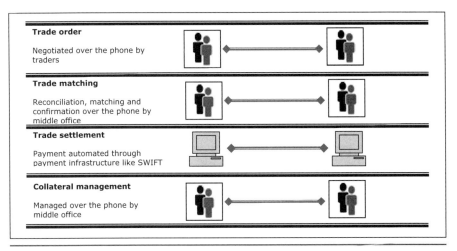

Figure 4-3   Derivatives trading was a highly manual process before FpML. Source: FpML.

- Extendible and cancelable interest rate swap provisions
- Mandatory and optional early termination provisions for interest rate swaps
- FX resetable cross-currency swap

Credit Derivatives

- Credit default swap
- Credit default swap index
- Tranche on credit default swap index
- Credit default swap basket
- Credit default swap on a mortgage
- Credit default swap on a loan
- Credit event notice

FX Products

- FX spot
- FX forward (including non-deliverable forwards, or NDFs)
- FX swap
- FX options (European and American; barriers, digitals, binaries, average rates; cash and physical settlement)
- Option strategies (multiple simple options)

Money Market Instruments

■ Term deposits

Equity Derivatives Options and Forwards

Broker equity option

■ Equity option transaction supplement

■ Equity swap transaction supplement

■ Support for long form equity forwards has been introduced

Return Swaps

■ Support for different legs of generic return swaps including equity swaps, total return swaps, and variance swaps

The FpML Business Process and Messaging Working Groups collaborate on creating specifications for the information exchanged during different phases of the trade lifecycle. For example, given that pricing and risk analytics are incredibly important for derivatives, FpML also has a separate committee to specifically create XML data structures for these data. Structures have been created for market data such as yield curves, volatility surfaces, and FX spot rates; market risk reporting such as convexity and time decay risk for interest rate swaps; and probability of default and credit spread for credit default swaps.

The business processes covered by FpML in its version 4.3 working draft are as follows:

■ Trade affirmation

■ Trade confirmation

■ Request for quote

■ Novations

■ Terminations

■ Increases

■ Amendments

■ Allocations

■ Cash flow matching

■ Contract notifications for messages between asset managers and custodians

4.3.4 SWIFT

SWIFT (Society for Worldwide Interbank Financial Telecommunication) is a provider of communications infrastructure that securities firms use for exchanging financial messages. SWIFT was created in 1973 by a consortium of over 200 banks from 15 countries in North America and Europe to automate communication of financial information in the industry. To achieve this goal, SWIFT built a communications network that ensures the secure and quick transmission of financial data between firms around the world. Today, over 8,100 financial institutions in 207 countries use the SWIFT infrastructure for their interbank communication needs in securities (equities, fixed income, and listed options), treasury and derivatives, and cash management and payments.

The SWIFT core application is the SWIFTNet FIN messaging middleware, which is a store-and-forward messaging service that can be used by participants as long as they follow the SWIFT message protocol. SWIFT members can connect to FIN in a variety of ways, including linking to it directly, using a SWIFT interface, or outsourcing its SWIFT connectivity requirements to a third party (see Chapter 5 for details). In 2005, FIN carried over 2.5 billion messages between firms in the financial industry.

The SWIFT message protocol is a proprietary format that consists of categories of messages called MT (message type) messages. For example, MT 306 is the message format that should be used by SWIFT members for transmitting a foreign currency option confirmation. In 1999, SWIFT decided that it would provide XML-based messages, called SWIFT MX messages, as an optional message format for its clients. It began working with the ISO to create an XML-based protocol for financial services under the name of the ISO 20022 standard. ISO 20022 is also known as the UNIFI (universal financial industry) standard, because it aims to converge all existing financial protocols into one universal standard.

In order to expand the variety of message types it supports, SWIFT also announced in June 2006 that it had entered an agreement with ISDA to support FpML messaging services over SWIFTNet. In 2002, SWIFT had also introduced SWIFTNet Fix, which allowed members to send FIX messages to counterparties over a SWIFT network. In 2007, SWIFT outsourced the back end processing of FIX messages to a third-party vendor, while it continues to provide this facility to its clients on the front end. By allowing flexibility in message formats, SWIFT has realized that its proprietary message format will eventually lead to a loss of clients. Over time, it is expected that SWIFT will continue to perform strongly as a provider of messaging infrastructure, but will also allow a variety of industry standard messages to be used on it. The goal of having a universal message format such as UNIFI for all the needs of the financial industry seems unlikely to be achieved in the short term, and so FIX and FpML must be accommodated by SWIFT if it is to retain its competitive edge in the industry. See Figure 4-4.

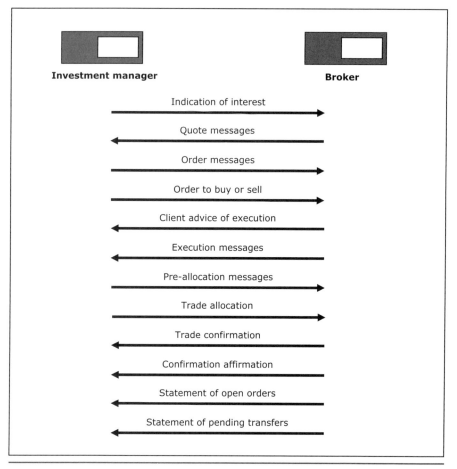

Figure 4-4 SWIFT pre-trade, trade, and post-trade messages. Source: SWIFT.

4.3.5 MDDL AND XBRL

Several XML-based standards have emerged to meet the requirements of other parts of the trade lifecycle. Two standards, in particular, have gathered some attention: MDDL (Market Data Definition Language) and XBRL (Extensible Business Reporting Language) for the transport of market reference data and financial reporting, respectively. Industry standards are judged by their ability to meet a business need. The nonstandardization of market data is becoming an increasingly big problem for market players who have to deal with translating it in a competitive environment. While MDDL provides a language and format for transporting reference data, pricing, and end-of-day close information, the fact that it is written in XML and therefore, its messages are large in size, has caused concern among users who need to process data effectively in real time. Its adoption has, therefore, been limited, and the need for a standard for exchanging market data still remains an important goal for the industry.

XBRL, on the other hand, has received a boost by the support of the SEC, the FDIC (Federal Deposit Insurance Corporation), Federal Reserve System, and other members of the Federal Financial Institutions Examination Council, which have begun to accept both quarterly and annual filings in XBRL mode. Over 8000 US banks now use XBRL to submit their quarterly balance sheet and income reports to FDIC and the SEC, benefiting from the advantage of having one standard that can be used to satisfy requirements of different regulatory authorities. One of the reasons XBRL is successful is that message size is not an issue in a reporting environment where reports are submitted only periodically and turnaround time is not immediate. The adoption of XBRL has greatly facilitated the processing of reports by staff members of regulatory authorities; systems can automatically check XBRL-tagged filings for incompleteness and inform submitting parties, replacing the old process of staff manually checking each report.

4.4 Using and Extending Industry Standards

The language and format in which an exchange, a clearinghouse, or a settlement bank advertises as an acceptable message format affects the broker-dealers and investment managers who must communicate with it. While market participants would ideally prefer there to be just one standard that everyone uses, different firms use different industry formats, and others use their own proprietary interfaces. This requires firms to sometimes support several protocols, including FIX, FpML, SWIFT, and exchange specific messaging protocols. Of all the standard financial ontologies, FIX is the most popular in the pre-trade and trade stages, while FpML is increasingly becoming the most popular for the OTC derivatives space.

Regardless of which protocol is used, it is almost always incomplete when it comes to meeting the internal data needs of firms. This is because firms have many proprietary fields that they need to communicate between systems in-house, and that are usually not included in protocols created for interfirm communication. Also, industry standards are relatively new in the industry and have been evolving over the last decade. During this time, firms have built their own messaging protocols and formats, and it is difficult for them to change these internally. Sometimes, they have used tag value pairs, which they have simply hard-coded into their systems. Even though such architecture is inflexible and inadvisable, it is one of the problems of dealing with legacy systems and must be accommodated.

In general, if a firm is building a new system, it is advisable that it utilize the most appropriate industry standard and *extend* it for internal use to include the fields that are proprietary to the firm. If the firm is extending an XML-based industry standard, then extra data fields can be added to an XML schema by using its *extension capability*. If a firm is using industry standards, but continues to use its legacy data format and ontology that it has developed in-house, then interfirm messages will have to be *transformed* through an adaptor when they enter the firm. This adaptor application maps industry messages into the appropriate in-house format and vocabulary. Many firms have built FIX engines or adaptors that translate FIX messages into their own protocols. If the firm is using an XML-based industry standard, XSLT (Extensible Stylesheet Language Transformation), which is a language for transforming XML documents into other XML documents, can be very useful.

The ability to *extend* XML schemas and *transform* XML documents allows firms to seamlessly use variations of the industry standard inside the firm, yet communicate with other firms by transforming it back into the market standard when needed. It is yet one more reason why XML is very popular among software developers.

Major broker-dealers such as Goldman Sachs and JP Morgan always participate in working groups, as do large buy-side firms such as AIG, in order to ensure that as many of their requirements as possible are included in the industry standard. The industry as a whole has begun to understand the value of electronic exchange of trade data, and members want to influence the development of any standard that will become the language of this communication. The utopia of having a universal data dictionary and messaging protocol is unlikely in the short term, but firms would like to have their internal protocols meanwhile be as close to the leading industry standards as possible. This saves them the cost of building adaptors and translation engines, which are costly to build; even more importantly, the process of translation takes time, which in a fast-paced electronic trading environment is increasingly unacceptable.

RECOMMENDATIONS

The use of industry standards is a necessary stepping stone to achieving system-to-system communication of financial data between market partners during the trade lifecycle. It is recommended that firms always use one of the industry's open standards for interfirm and intrafirm communication.

1. If speed is not a pressing requirement, XML-based standards are the best message format for an SOA environment.

2. FIX is the predominant pre-trade messaging format, particularly for equity trading.
3. FMPL is the industry standard of choice for derivatives processing.
4. When using SWIFT for post-trade payment messages, SWIFT messages can be used. If available, it is preferable to use SWIFT's FIX and FpML utilities.
5. Firms should align their internal standards to industry standards as much as possible, using extension and translation to switch between the two.

4.6 Summary

This chapter has introduced financial technology protocols and discussed the value of using industry standards for electronic communication of trade data. Different message formats including CSV and XML were reviewed, with pros and cons provided for using one over the other. Currently, three industry standards—FIX, FpML, and SWIFT—are used for system communication of financial data in the securities industry. FIX is used primarily for pre-trade and trade communication, and has significantly contributed to automating equities trading in the US. The OTC derivatives market has traditionally been difficult to streamline because of the bespoke and tailored nature of derivatives contracts. However, FpML has emerged as an XML-based standard that is flexible enough to accommodate variations in contracts. It has been successfully used by DTCC and Swapswire for automated trade matching and confirmation of equity and credit derivatives. SWIFT is a provider of messaging infrastructure for over 8000 clients across the world, and is introducing an XML version of its proprietary SWIFT MT messages in order to expand its operations base. Other standards such as XBRL and MDDL are also gaining traction as data format languages for reporting and market reference data. The move toward industry standards is crucial for achieving STP in the trade lifecycle, and more and more firms are adopting one of these ontologies for interfirm communication. However, concern remains over which format to use for high-speed high-volume trade and market data, and firms struggle to translate industry standards to their internal legacy data formats. The next chapter, Chapter 5, Connectivity, discusses how message-oriented middleware links systems and carries these messages back and forth between them.

Chapter 5

Connectivity

▌ 5.1 Introduction

One of the architectural constructs most important to creating an STP infrastructure is the structure that links systems externally and internally. Speed, reliability, and security in the trade lifecycle all depend on enterprise connectivity. The last chapter discussed industry standards that can be used to exchange trade-related information between systems. This chapter examines the mechanism by which this communication will take place. There are several ways to send information from one system to another, including FTP (file transfer protocol), uploading to a server via HTTP, and middleware (such as MQ Series). Middleware technology is expensive and is usually purchased by larger banks, while smaller institutions more often rely on FTP and uploading Excel spreadsheets to websites for their connectivity needs.

In an STP environment, linkages both within the firm and to various market participants outside the firm must be considered when designing a connectivity infrastructure. Section 5.2 of this chapter lists these system connectivity points in the context of the trade lifecycle, and explains how they are particularly important for newer trading strategies, such as program trading. The technical requirements for enterprise connectivity can be divided into two parts: transport infrastructure and message format, that is, how systems communicate with each other and the language they use for information exchange. Section 5.3 introduces basic concepts in computer networks, including the Internet protocol TCP/IP and applications, such as HTTP and FTP, that use TCP/IP to transport data.

Building middleware from scratch is a very difficult undertaking, and firms usually rely on industry network providers and vendor products to transport their messages. Section 5.4 discusses the various options that firms have when considering connectivity options. It uses connectivity to NASDAQ as a case study and reviews SWIFT, a leading provider of transaction processing, as an example of leveraging an existing network for interfirm connectivity. It also discusses message-oriented middleware (MOM) for intrafirm connectivity.

5.2   The Business Requirements

Trade lifecycle automation relies heavily on strong, reliable connectivity between systems, both internally within a firm and externally with other participants in the industry. Firms that exchange information electronically want to ensure that the transport mechanisms they use are fast, robust, and not vulnerable to security attacks.

There are numerous advantages to having a robust connection network. Firms can trade electronically with their trading partners, adding and removing partners transparently, without causing disruption in services. They can access markets directly and route orders to the most appropriate marketmaker, broker-dealer, or ECN automatically, which allows them to find liquidity more easily and reduces transaction costs per trade. When trade data is communicated electronically, it is less susceptible to the operational risks, errors, and processing delays that come with manual processing. Exceptions are immediately identified because the transaction can be monitored throughout the trade lifecycle. Direct connectivity to clearinghouses, such as DTCC, reduces time to settlement, lowering the risk exposure of parties. And finally, a firm whose internal systems are linked can quickly calculate enterprisewide risk metrics by combining position data from all trading desks with real-time data from market vendors.

Within a firm, the front office must connect to the middle and back offices for trade enrichment, risk management, and profit and loss reporting. Across the industry, firms must link to exchanges, clearinghouses, and custodians for trade matching, confirmation, and settlement. Apart from the regular trade lifecycle requirements, new business models, such as algorithmic trading, and regulations, such as Reg NMS, have the industry striving for electronic trading, and consequently for better connectivity. This section looks at some of the main business junctures where system-to-system connection is crucial.

5.2.1   THE TRADE LIFECYCLE

The trade lifecycle has many points in the pre-trade, trade, and post-trade stages where communication and connection between systems is required. These points are enumerated below.

5.2.1.1   Pre-Trade Analytics

Pre-trade analytics requires connectivity between the front-office risk analytics applications, back-office databases, and external data vendors for historical and current market data. This data is then combined with the multiple scenarios chosen by the traders for Monte Carlo simulations to estimate the risk of buying and selling particular securities.

5.2.1.2   Real-Time Data Feeds

Every securities firm requires connections with data vendors, such as Bloomberg and Reuters for real-time market data. This data is used to make trading decisions, calculate prices, and estimate portfolio risk.

5.2.1.3   Order Routing and Execution

After the pre-analytics phase, the front office creates an order that is then routed for execution to a liquidity pool. Links to multiple brokers, exchanges, ECNs and other liquidity pools are needed to find the best execution venue for the trade.

5.2.1.4   Trade Matching, Confirmation, and Affirmation

A central clearinghouse, such as DTCC, provides matching engines that are used to match trade information sent by parties. This requires connectivity between the firm, the exchange where the trade took place, and the clearinghouse. Once the trade is matched by the clearinghouse, it is deemed confirmed and the agreed upon document becomes equivalent to a legal document.

5.2.1.5 Trade Amendments, Terminations, and Assignments

The affirmed legal copy of a trade is kept in a central repository in the clearinghouse. Whenever a trade is amended, terminated, or assigned to a third party, this information needs to be communicated to all the parties involved, and again records need to be matched and reconciled on both sides.

5.2.1.6 Trade Clearance and Settlement

Calculating the amount due on a trade and ensuring that the money and securities exchange hands occur during the clearance and settlement phases, respectively. Messages regarding payments must be exchanged between the clearinghouse, the parties, and the settlement banks of the parties.

5.2.1.7 Reconciliation and Allocation

Reconciliation is very important and occurs at multiple places in the trade lifecycle, between both internal systems and external systems. It requires connectivity across the industry with all participants who are involved in the transaction at any level. For example, asset managers must reconcile their records with those of the custodian to make sure that trades are allocated to the correct client accounts. Reconciliation is discussed in more detail in Chapter 7, Reconciliation and Exception Handling.

5.2.1.8 Risk Management and Accounting

After the trade has been settled, it is monitored and "marked to market" on the books of buyers. Firmwide market and credit risk calculation needs information from all the different trading divisions in the firm, necessitating connectivity between front-office trading applications and back-office position management databases for all the major asset classes. Real-time connections to market data vendors can help engines create mark-to-market figures, which are then also used in the quarterly and annual reports that are generated by the accounting systems.

5.2.2 DRIVERS OF ELECTRONIC TRADING

In Chapter 1, trends in the securities industry were discussed that highlighted the drivers pushing the industry toward electronic trading. Chief among them were the buy-side's increasing demands for best execution; the emergence of direct market access technology coupled with exchanges, such as ECNs that allow electronic trading; and regulations that call for efficient marketplaces and transparent firmwide risk management. In this section, that discussion is briefly reviewed in the context of connectivity requirements.

5.2.2.1   Hedge Funds

Traditionally, institutional investors have depended on broker-dealers to give them quotes for prices and to execute trades for them in the market. This was frustrating for buy-side investors because it essentially made them completely dependent on the sell-side's expertise and their inroads into marketplaces, such as the NYSE, where sell-side banks had placed their specialists. The proliferation of hedge funds began to change that equation. Run by former traders from sell-side firms, hedge funds did not want to rely on broker-dealers for their execution. They wanted to make decisions on prices and markets where they traded themselves. However, given that they were small, they wanted to leverage the expensive trading infrastructures, including connectivity to liquidity pools, of broker-dealers. This leasing of infrastructure to smaller buy-side institutions is known as *prime-brokerage*. Given that hedge funds rely on sophisticated statistical algorithms to wean profits from small arbitrage opportunities, they began to assert that their prime-brokerage providers give them superior electronic connectivity to marketplaces. To meet this demand, the market saw the emergence of direct market access (DMA) technology firms, which began offering these services and taking order flow away from the sell-side. To stop DMA firms from undercutting their revenues, broker-dealers began to acquire leading DMA vendors and to present them as part of their service offering to institutional investors. For example, in the last two years, Bank of America has acquired Direct Access Financial Corp., while Citigroup has acquired Lava Trading, to strengthen their ability to offer electronic trading to clients.

5.2.2.2   Algorithmic Trading and Transaction Costs

Mutual funds, trust funds, and those money managers who had believed that portfolio management was their realm and trade execution was the realm of broker-dealers began to see things differently, too. Portfolio managers often represent the assets of hundreds of individual investors, so when they change the asset distribution of their portfolio, it usually involves buying and selling hundreds of thousands of shares. For instance, if a portfolio manager decides that Google will give high returns in the long run to his or her clients, he or she may switch 50% of the money that the portfolio invested in Microsoft to Google. This might translate into selling 500,000 shares of Microsoft and buying 300,000 shares of Google. The size of these trades is so huge that flooding the market with Microsoft shares or raising the demand of Google shares in one go would drastically impact their price, bringing down the price of Microsoft and increasing the price of Google. To avoid such *market impact*, institutional investors would give the whole order to broker-dealers who would then divide the order into smaller *blocks* and spread the buy and sell orders in different markets. There was no way for institutional investors to measure whether broker-dealers achieved this execution at the best price or not. But this status quo changed when electronic publishing of prices made it possible for everyone to view the prices displayed in marketplaces. A metric called *transaction cost analysis (TCA)* came to the forefront of discussions on best execution, which included assessment of the algorithms used to choose execution venue and achieve best price. Institutional investors demanded that if broker-dealers wanted their business, they would have to provide them with the lowest transaction costs for trades. Broker-dealers once again found themselves frantically building faster connectivity to marketplaces, and offering a set of algorithms for best execution of block trades.

5.2.2.3 Electronic Marketplaces

The sophisticated infrastructure of institutional investors and broker-dealers would be of little value if marketplaces could only be reached through specialists, market-makers, and floor brokers who physically sat in exchanges. In fact, the ability to trade electronically has been an offering that marketplaces have been providing for some time. Every major stock exchange in the world now offers the ability to trade electronically in it, a trend that was started with NASDAQ, the first electronic stock exchange in the world. With competition from alternative trading systems, such as ECNs, this conversion from floor brokers to computerized trading was accelerated. The last year has seen consolidation of exchanges across the world, with acquisition of ECNs along the way, as exchanges grow to offer better and better electronic trading interfaces to their clients.

5.2.2.4 Compliance

Market competition has not been the only driver of the computerization of marketplaces. In recognition of the contribution of capital markets to the vitality of the macro-economy, governments in North America, Europe, and Asia-Pacific have all mandated new regulations to make markets more transparent and streamlined. Basel II and Reg NMS (Regulation National Market System) are just two examples of an ever-growing array of regulations to govern market activity and protect investor interests. The firmwide risk management clauses of Basel II have required firms to improve connectivity between all their departments, and with data provider vendors to calculate up-to-date risk assessments. And Reg NMS, formulated to modernize the markets for equities in the US, is forcing markets to display their best prices and brokers to trade only at the best price available across markets. Compliance with Reg NMS necessitates electronic connectivity and communication between markets and broker-dealers.

Electronic trading thus has been a long way in the making, driven by a number of forces in the market. But its ubiquitous presence in the industry is going to prove a seismic shift in the trade lifecycle, forcing all players to up their game to retain their competitiveness.

5.3   Computer Network Basics

Since this book is a manager's guide to financial technology, it will not delve deeply into technical details of computer networks. However, it is important for the reader to have some knowledge to be able to ask the right questions when speaking to technology teams. This section introduces basic concepts in computer networks, including types of networks, network design, and network protocols.

5.3.0.1   Network Connectivity

A network is when two or more computers are linked together to exchange information and share resources. Networks can physically be linked in two ways: wired and wireless. The norm up to now has been that networks have been connected with cables, whether Ethernet, copper, or fiber-optic, and this still remains the predominant way of connecting computers in the securities industry. Recently, however, wireless networks have also made significant inroads, at least in personal communication. Wireless networks use radio waves or microwaves to transmit information between computers. There are several different types of wireless networks, with Wi-Fi and GSM being the most well-known since they are used to connect computers to the Internet (Wi-Fi) and mobile phones to each other (GSM).

5.3.0.2   Types of Networks

There are many axes along which a network can be defined. One way to categorize networks is by the area that the network covers. Local area networks (LANs) span a small geographical area, such as a home or an office building. Wide area networks (WANs), on the other hand, can cover much larger areas, such as cities, states, and even countries. The Internet is the largest public WAN in the world. If a network is not public, it can either be an intranet or an extranet. In an intranet, computers are limited to a single organization. In an extranet, several organizations have limited connectivity to each other that allows private and secure exchange of data. One example of an extranet is SWIFTNet, a private network provided by SWIFT for exchanging trade and payment information for securities. With a client base of over 8000 leading financial institutions in 205 countries across the world, SWIFTNet is one of the major providers of interfirm communication in the securities industry. SWIFTNet is discussed further in Section 5.4.

5.3.0.3   Network Design

Networks are constructed using certain design paradigms. The most common network designs are client-server and peer-to-peer. In client-server networks, a central computer (known as the server) serves the needs of many different clients. For instance, office email is always stored in the office server, even though it is accessible from

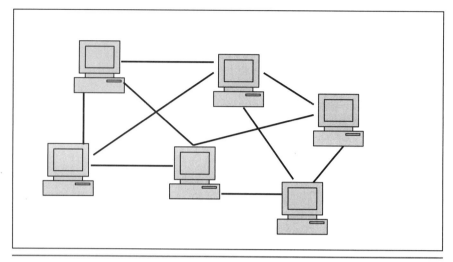

Figure 5-1 Peer-to-peer network topology.

a web-based client anywhere in the world. In a peer-to-peer (P2P) network, every computer can function as both a server and a client. This kind of design came into mainstream discussions when applications, such as Napster and Kaaza, enabled everyone's computers to link to each other and share multimedia files, both as providers and consumers of these files. See Figure 5-1.

5.3.0.4 Network Topology

Another way to look at computer networks is by tracing how data flows occur within the network. This is also known as looking at the topology of the network. There are several kinds of topologies, but one that is particularly relevant to our discussion is the bus network topology, in which all computers share resources over a conduit called a message bus. Other topologies include the star network, in which data flows through a centralized device out to all the computers on the network. See Figure 5-2.

5.3.0.5 Network Protocols

A protocol defines the rules by which computers communicate with each over a network. It defines the most basic way in which information packets are exchanged between computers. The most common protocol for computer networks on the Internet is TCP/IP, which stands for Transmission Control Protocol/Internet Protocol. It was developed by the Department of Defense (DoD) in the 1970s to robustly and securely connect a large network of computers. TCP/IP officially replaced the older Network Control Protocol used by computers connected to the DoD on January 1, 1983, a move that improved network communication tremendously and created a

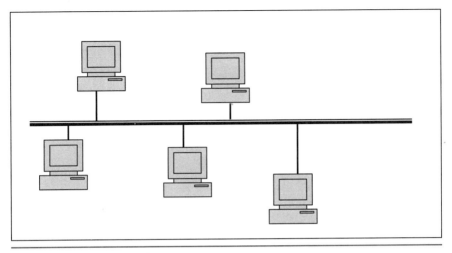

Figure 5-2 Bus network topology.

protocol standard that was strong enough to eventually accommodate a much bigger network—the Internet. In the words of *Wired* magazine, "Call it one small switch for man, but one giant switch for mankind.com."[1]

At its most simple, IP is responsible for forwarding bytes of data from node to node, with each node identified by a unique IP address, until information from the sender reaches the receiver. TCP is responsible for creating IP packets out of the data that has to be sent, and reassembling it into the original data after it has been received. This way TCP can also verify that none of the data was lost during the transmission. TCP/IP connections work through sockets, which are ports specifically created for sending and accepting messages for data interchange. Another way to transmit data is via a higher-level application that uses TCP/IP as its underlying transport layer.

5.3.0.6 TCP/IP Applications

While TCP/IP is an underlying transport mechanism not familiar to most users, people are acquainted with two popular applications that run on TCP/IP—HTTP and FTP. Hypertext transfer protocol (HTTP) is used to transfer information over the Internet. One example is when information in an Excel spreadsheet is uploaded to a custodian's site, or when a form is filled out on the web with trade data. File transfer protocol (FTP) is a common way to connect two computers over the Internet so that one computer can transfer files to another computer. It can be used, for example, to get a nightly batch of market data from Bloomberg. A third application relevant to

---

[1] Justin Jaffe, *Happy Birthday, Dear Internet,* Wired magazine, December 31, 2002.

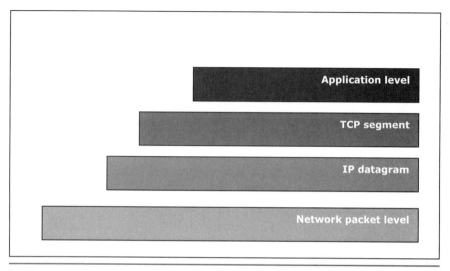

Figure 5-3   Layers of communication protocols.

this chapter is a message bus, also known as message-oriented middleware (MOM). MOMs are discussed in more detail in Section 5.3.1. See Figure 5-3.

5.3.0.7 Message Format

The messages that are carried by applications, such as FTP, can come in various formats—CSV, tab delimited, and XML to name a few. It is crucial to consider which message format will be used whenever interfirm communication is proposed. Traditionally, data separated by delimiters were used by firms as the message format of choice. But more recently, XML has become the lingua franca of system communication given its platform-neutrality, self-describing tags, and flexibility. FIX, which is the most popular financial exchange protocol, was originally in code-delimited format, but has also begun to publish the specification in XML as well. XML's drawback is that XML tags tend to bloat the document, making it time consuming to transport and process. However, with computing costs becoming cheaper, this is deemed by some to be not as big an issue as it was a few years ago. Note that messages, whether in CSV or XML, can be carried over TCP/IP and any of the three TCP/IP applications, HTTP, FTP, or MOM.

For the purposes of this book, the two most important aspects of connectivity are (i) transport layer and application, and (ii) message format. When speaking of connectivity, it would be good to highlight both transport and message format. For example, one can say that a CSV file was downloaded via FTP from Bloomberg every night, or an XML message regarding settlement state was transmitted via a message bus, such as MQ Series.

5.3.1 MESSAGE-ORIENTED MIDDLEWARE (MOM)

Message-oriented middleware (MOM) is an application that supports asynchronous messaging in a distributed system environment. It is often used in conjunction with a SOA, as a medium for exchanging messages between software services. Asynchronous messaging means that the sender and the receiver of the message do not need to be linked to the middleware at the same time. The middleware will store the message in a queue and deliver it to the receiver when the receiver is connected and ready to receive the message. There are several advantages to using MOMs:

- *Asynchronous messaging*—Both sender and receiver can continue with their normal processing; the receiver does not have to immediately accept the message, and the sender does not have to wait for a confirmation to continue to function.

- *Guaranteed delivery*—Since the middleware has the ability to store messages, it provides a guarantee that the receiver will always receive the message even if there is a network failure, in which case the middleware will send the message when the network is operational again.

- *Interoperability*—The middleware adds a layer of abstraction between the sender and receiver systems, insulating them from knowing any details of each other's platforms and operating systems. The middleware, in turn, can have functionality built into it that maps the sender's message to the format that the receiver is capable of processing.

- *Reduction in complexity*—Since all parties communicate with just one medium for communicating with any number of partners on the network, this greatly reduces the number of independent connectivity points that exist in a distributed network.

- *Broadcasting*—The middleware can deliver the message to more than one receiver (this is known as a broadcast message).

Despite the many advantages of MOMs, technology managers should consider a few things carefully before buying middleware products. Disadvantages include:

- *Cost*—The biggest hurdle to using MOM is that it is expensive to buy and requires both receiver and sender to have the application installed on their servers. For smaller firms, this is an expense they cannot afford to undertake; they prefer connecting directly with TCP/IP or using an application, such as FTP or HTTP, to exchange data. Larger firms, however, can afford to take advantage of MOM products and do so with the advantage of the superior reliability and security that comes with these products.

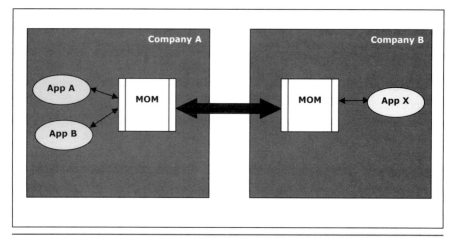

Figure 5-4 Message-oriented middleware connectivity to communicate messages between applications both within and between firms.

■ *Speed*—Firms should also consider speed of message transfer when considering whether to use TCP/IP and program to sockets, or to use MOM for message transfer. One important difference between the two is that TCP/IP, though efficient and reliable, is tightly coupled. This means that both the receiver and sender must be up and running for the message to be relayed correctly. MOM, on the other hand, can store the messages in a queue if the receiver is unavailable. This is very useful for asynchronous messaging, but the additional application layer on top of TCP/IP results in less speed, which makes it not as suitable for request/response synchronous messaging.

■ *Partner connectivity*—Since MOM needs to be installed on both the sender's and the receiver's machines, it is important for external connectivity to ask partners whether they use MOM or not. Often, firms just use MOM internally to take advantage of its benefits, and use TCP/IP to connect to firms in the industry, as it is rare to find partners that have the same vendor MOM product. See Figure 5-4.

5.4 Connectivity in Financial Services

As discussed in Section 5.2, connectivity between systems is needed at every point in the trade lifecycle. Connections to industry participants are needed for both internal and external workflows. For instance, to calculate risk, a firm must get real-time market data from external data vendors and updated position data from internal firmwide trading systems. Firms have two ways of connecting to each other externally:

1. Directly connecting to a market partner, either through connections they build themselves or by using vendor products, such as IBM WebSphere MQ.
2. Using the infrastructure of network providers, such as SWIFTNet and OMGEO Oasys.

This section gives an overview of connection options to marketplaces in light of connecting to NASDAQ as a case study. It then evaluates leading industry networks that are leveraged for their connectivity and messaging infrastructures. Finally, it evaluates MOM for in-house or external connectivity.

5.4.1   CONNECTING TO MARKETPLACES—NASDAQ CASE STUDY

NASDAQ is a US electronic stock exchange, which was the world's first electronic stock exchange when it was founded in 1971. In the beginning, it only published prices over a computerized bulletin board, but since then has evolved to provide full service electronic trading facilities that can bring buyers and sellers together. In 2003, facing increasing competition from ECNs, NASDAQ Stock Market Inc. bought Brut ECN from SunGard in a $190 million cash deal, making it one of the world's largest ECNs as well. NASDAQ provides market quotes for investors, receives orders from them, and sends post-trade information to clearinghouses and to trading parties. NASDAQ publishes information on how to connect to it, along with connectivity charges. As always, two parameters define connectivity: transport mechanism and message format. Firms can connect to NASDAQ in three ways: (i) through an extranet; (ii) through a direct circuit connection; and (iii) through a service bureau that has a front-end workstation for using it.[2]

5.4.1.1   Direct Connectivity

Directly connecting to NASDAQ is much harder, since not only does all the connectivity software need to be written, but lines have to be leased from providers, such as Con Edison. The added advantage of high speed is that being the only firm on the connection may be considered very useful, especially for algorithmic trading where advantages are measured in milliseconds. Some firms are even putting their algorithmic trading applications in the datacenters of the exchanges themselves to

---

[2]NASDAQ Connectivity Providers, NASDAQ, November 7, 2006.

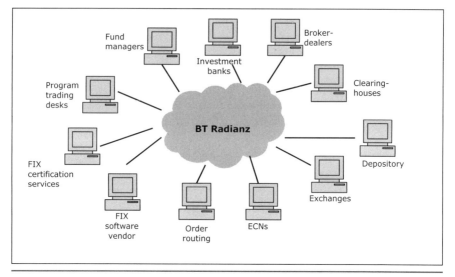

Figure 5-5 BT Radianz extranet. Source: Radianz.

benefit from massive reductions in latency. For Direct Circuit connectivity to the NASDAQ facility in Carteret, New Jersey, NASDAQ recommends contacting the following providers:

- Con Edison Communications
- Level 3 Communications
- Verizon Business
- Yipes

5.4.1.2 Extranets

An extranet is a third-party private network connecting organizations. Outsourcing their connectivity infrastructure through an extranet provider like BT Radianz simplifies development efforts for firms. The service agreement with such providers ensures fast, reliable, and secure access to multiple market participants, along with customer support 24 hours a day, 7 days a week (see Figure 5-5). The fact that extranets also have limited membership and have extensive mechanisms in place for avoiding bottlenecks makes them fairly fast. NASDAQ lists the following six extranet providers that can be contacted to provide connectivity to NASDAQ:

- BT Radianz
- SAVVIS
- Sector Inc.

- TNS
- Verizon Business VFN
- Yipes

5.4.1.3   Service Bureaus

There is also another option for those firms that would rather not deal with the back end connectivity infrastructure: they can license NASDAQ Workstation, which can be accessed over the Internet. Since it is web-based, it can be accessed from virtually anywhere in the world. Using front-end products to access liquidity pools is fairly common, especially for smaller firms that cannot afford to build the infrastructure themselves. For instance, the New York Stock Exchange can be accessed by a large number of service bureaus, such as Bloomberg, Lava Trading, and NASDAQ Tools.[3]

5.4.1.4   Message Protocols

Once the connectivity layer has been decided, the next step is to decide the language in which communication will take place. NASDAQ provides a number of communication protocols for exchanging quotes, orders, and post-trade messages. One of the most popular industry standards is FIX, and as can be seen from Figure 5-6, it is used for order and post-trade communication with NASDAQ. NASDAQ also allows firms access through its own proprietary protocol QIX. According to NASDAQ, QIX can carry richer order types and is two to three milliseconds faster than FIX. Details of how to code message documents, whether in QIX, FIX, or any other protocol specified, are provided by NASDAQ to interested firms.

5.4.2   NETWORKS FOR INDUSTRY CONNECTIVITY

Two industry networks that are used extensively by market participants are SWIFT-Net and OMGEO Oasys. In exchange for a service fee, both of these firms provide clients a private financial messaging network with connectivity to major broker-dealers, custodians, industry utilities, liquidity pools, and service providers. Networks are also interconnected as OMGEO Oasys connects to SWIFTNet.

5.4.2.1   OMGEO Oasys

OMGEO Oasys, one of the leading providers of post-trade pre-settlement trade management, processes over 800,000 trades a day. Owned jointly by DTCC and Thomson Financial, it has over 6000 users worldwide, and provides STP of equity,

---

[3]NYSE website, *Connecting to Our Markets.*

Table 5-1 Institution-type decision tree for SWIFT users. Source: SWIFT.

Institution Type A	Institution Type B	Institution Type C
1. Are you a global institution? 2. Do you have multiple business lines? 3. Do you want to connect to a multitude of counterparties? 4. Do you have high volumes of SWIFT traffic (more than 10,000 SWIFT messages per day)? 5. Do you consider SWIFT critical to the nature of your business? 6. Are you looking for a connection with high availability and service levels?	• Are you a regional institution? • Do you have a couple of business lines using SWIFT? • Do you have medium volumes of SWIFT traffic (around 1,000 SWIFT messages per day)? • Are you looking for a cost-effective connection that is simple to operate?	• Are you mainly a domestic player? • Do you have limited cross-border transactions? • Do you have just one business line using SWIFT? • Do you have low volumes of SWIFT traffic (less than 50 SWIFT messages per day)? • Are you looking for a low-cost and "must work" connection?
If your answer is yes to most of the above, you should consider: • a high-end direct connection to SWIFTNet; or • having your connection managed by a Service Bureau, if it is your company's policy to outsource IT operations to a third-party service provider	If your answer is yes to most of the above, you should consider: • a direct connection • a connection via another SWIFT User; • a Service Bureau; or • a connection via a Member/Concentrator, if you want to outsource the SWIFT administration and invoicing in addition to the	If your answer is yes to most of the above, you should consider: • a low-end direct connection • a connection via another SWIFT User; • a Service Bureau; or • a connection via a Member/Concentrator, if you want to outsource the SWIFT administration and invoicing in addition to the

Product	Quoting	Orders	Post-trade	Firm-to-firm routing
Connectivity				
QIX	√	√		
OUCH		√		
RASHport		√		
FIX		√	√	√
CTCI		√	√	√

Figure 5-6 Message formats accepted by NASDAQ. Source: NASDAQ.

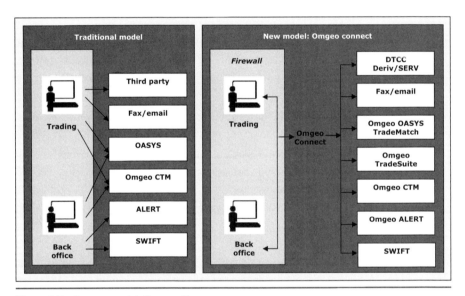

Figure 5-7 Omgeo model. Source: Omgeo.

fixed income, and FX trades for investment managers, broker-dealers, and custodian banks. It is used by institutional investors to inform brokers how to allocate trades to different accounts, and in order to communicate trade details and confirmations to their clients. Unlike SWIFT, however, it does not provide any payment services, and therefore links to SWIFT as a preferred provider of payments processing. See Figure 5-7.

5.4.2.2 SWIFT

SWIFT (The Society for Worldwide Interbank Financial Telecommunication) gives subscribers access to SWIFTNet Fin, a TCP/IP-based network that provides a worldwide financial messaging. Established in 1975, SWIFT has been providing communication services to companies since its inception and now boasts a membership of over 8000 leading financial institutions in 205 countries around the world.

Firms that use SWIFT rely on its standardized communication and processing facilities for all phases of the lifecycle of equity and fixed income trading. Since SWIFT has a private network of over thousands of clients, it provides ready-made connections to a number of trading partners and industry utilities. By outsourcing their connectivity requirements to SWIFT, firms reduce the complexity, risk, and cost of setting up their own connections. In January 2007, SWIFTNet Fin processed over 12 million messages per day on average.[4]

SWIFT provides the following services for equities and fixed income:

- *Pre-trade/trade*—Includes trade order and execution messages, and all communication between an institutional client and broker-dealer that occurs prior to that. This includes indications of interest in buying or selling a security, orders, and status and confirmation messages.

- *Post-trade/pre-settlement*—Includes ETC (electronic trade confirmation) messages, along with allocations and confirm/affirm messages.

- *Clearing and settlement*—Includes all clearing and settlement activities, such as settlement instructions and confirmations between institutional clients, broker-dealers, custodians, and clearinghouses.

- *Custody services*—Includes data distribution, corporate actions, securities reporting, and collateral management. See Figure 5-8.

Firms can connect directly or indirectly to SWIFTNet depending on their size and requirements. A large firm can choose to have a direct connection because it requires high throughput (measured by transactions per second). On the other hand, it may decide to outsource the connectivity infrastructure to a service bureau such as Automatic Data Processing (ADP), a Member/Concentrator, such as Citibank, or share it with another SWIFT user who has direct connectivity. SWIFT presents the guidelines shown in Table 5-1 to firms that are deciding on which kind of connectivity to use.[5]

5.4.3 TRADING AND ORDER MANAGEMENT SYSTEMS

Buy-side firms, such as pension, insurance, and mutual funds, often use vendor products, such as Charles River and Murex, to connect to broker-dealers, market-

---

[4]SWIFT in Figures—SWIFTNet FIN Traffic January 2007 YTD.
[5]SWIFT website: *Direct or Indirect Connectivity?*

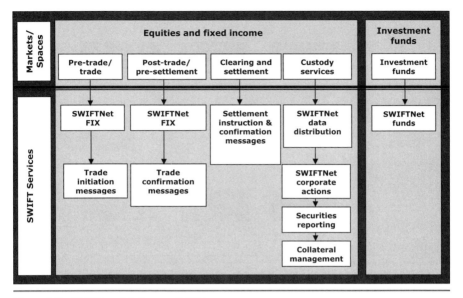

Figure 5-8   SWIFT model. Source: SWIFT.

places, and industry networks, such as Omgeo. Unlike broker-dealers, buy-side firms do not usually build their trading or order-management systems. Instead, they use off-the-shelf trading and order management applications for their pre-trade analysis and compliance checks, and for sending FIX trade orders to multiple broker-dealers. Platforms usually support multiple asset classes, such as equities, foreign exchange, credit derivatives, and commodities. These products can also automatically send allocation instructions to settlement venues. The advantage of using ready-made tools is that companies can save on building expensive network infrastructures. See Figure 5-9.

5.4.4   MIDDLEWARE OPTIONS FOR CONNECTIVITY

There are currently many different vendors providing middleware technology solutions for firms, with the leading vendor in the marketplace being IBM WebSphere MQ, known formerly as MQ Series. Other leading vendors include TIBCO Rendezvous, Sonic Software, and Microsoft BizTalk. In general, using MOM is the best way to connect systems within a firm.

One issue with choosing a particular vendor is that the firm is then tied to that vendor's implementation of MOM. This is because there is no standard implementation for MOM. Each vendor has its own implementation, which is incompatible with

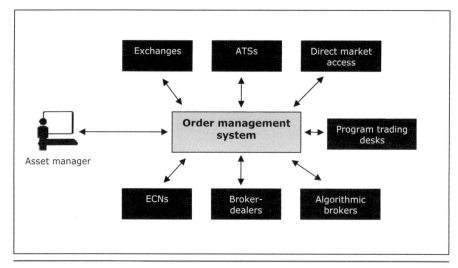

Figure 5-9 Buy-side trades using an order-management system.

other vendor products. In other words, it is not possible to send a message from TIBCO to MQ. In order to address this lack of standards, Sun Microsystems introduced a set of standards called Java Messaging Service in 1999. *Java Messaging Service (JMS)* provides a reference implementation for MOM, which has been implemented by vendors, such as BEA Systems, IBM, and Oracle. JMS is thus an additional layer on top of the queue and allows messages using different vendor middleware applications to communicate with each other. Microsoft does not support JMS.

In order to build a protocol that would allow messages to be exchanged even between .Net clients and JMS-supported applications, JPMorgan Chase formed a consortium that includes open source vendors, such as Red Hat, to develop an open source middleware application. This messaging middleware would be an alternative to expensive proprietary vendor products, such as IBM's MQ, and would be completely technology agnostic. Currently, over 90% of the market uses IBM MQ and TIBCO RV. The impetus came from the realization that although more firms were signing on to industry standards, such as FpML, they still lacked a standard way of communicating messages with each other. The consortium published the Advanced Message Queuing Protocol (AMQP) in June 2006, which is an open standard for queue-based messaging. AMQP comprises an application layer for messaging, just as HTTP and FTP is an application layer. This is different from JMS, which was an API on top of an application layer and was unable to achieve the kind of interoperability it hoped.[6]

---

[6]Floyd Marinescu, *Advanced Message Queue Protocol to Commoditize Messaging*, InfoQ, June 20, 2006.

RECOMMENDATIONS

Firms must connect and exchange information with each other at multiple stages of the trade lifecycle. Making the right choice of network connectivity involves assessing the requirements for the connection (especially speed) and the budget for the connection.

1. MOM is recommended for connecting systems internally.
2. For external connectivity, firms may choose from the following.

   a. Direct connection—for high-speed algorithmic trading (if budgets permit).

   b. Extranets—private networks with limited membership for fast access to market participants.

   c. Industry messaging infrastructures, such as SWIFT and OMGEO Oasys.

   d. Vendor order management systems.

5.5   Summary

This chapter discusses the connectivity infrastructure that is crucial to implementing STP. It reviews the business requirements that make system-to-system linkages important both from a trade lifecycle perspective and from the perspective of new trading models, such as algorithmic and electronic trading. The reader is introduced to the basics of computer networks and its two most important features—transport layer and message format. Message-oriented middleware (MOM) is recommended as the best transport layer for system-to-system communication within a firm, whereas either direct connectivity, an extranet, or a third-party messaging infrastructure can be used when connecting to systems outside the firm.

Chapter 6

Data Management

6.1 Introduction

The rapidly changing landscape of securities trading has put issues surrounding data management into the spotlight. Electronic trading has brought with it high-speed high-volume data for everything from market quotes to payment confirmations. More regulations exist than ever before, putting pressure on market participants to store large volumes of data for audit and reporting. In addition, commoditization is shrinking margins and driving the development of complex financial securities, whose details must be exchanged and stored, and which must be priced using extensive reference and market data. These are just some of the factors that are transforming the market, and making data management more challenging for all participants.

Data is crucial at every stage of the trade lifecycle—transaction flows, analytics and risk management, and accounting and reporting—and touches every part of the front, middle, and back offices of a firm. Thus, it has the potential to either accelerate or paralyze the quest to build a straight through processing (STP) infrastructure. In the past, data issues have often created bottlenecks in workflows, with inaccurate, untimely, and inaccessible data. According to a Reference Data survey published by Tower Group in 2005,[1] "institutions reported that 9% of all trades failed automated processing routines. Inaccurate reference data was the cause of 36% of these failed trades (or it caused fails in 3.3% of all trades), and poor data management processes led to an additional 43% of failed trades."

Under the pressures of competitiveness and shrinking margins, securities firms know that they cannot afford the costs that come from data errors, and are rethinking the focus they have traditionally placed on data as an asset. They are beginning to value data as a key enabler of business processes, and revenue and profit generation for the firm. For the first time, the ranks of CEOs, CFOs, and CIOs have been joined by a new officer, the Chief Data Officer (CDO). Citigroup and JP Morgan are just two leading financial services firms that have instituted this role, with the mandate to provide accurate consolidated data that is accessible real-time 24/7 from anywhere in the world.[2]

This chapter discusses the many facets of data management in the securities industry. Section 6.2 examines the present state of affairs in the industry. Market participants are currently plagued by the inefficiencies caused by data streaming in from disparate sources and stored in isolated silos across the firm. Coupled with the fact that these databases often vary in schema design and store data in a different format, the integration of such a group of databases is costly and time-consuming. Yet a consolidated integrated global view of data is exactly what is required in an STP environment.

The costs of having poor data can run into millions of dollars, caused by a range of problems from unsettled trades because of incomplete information to high-risk exposure due to inability to calculate firmwide risk management. In order to address the state of scattered data throughout the enterprise, firms need to have a strategy, supported by a competent staff well-versed in the fundamentals of data management. Section 6.3 introduces basic concepts in data management systems, followed by recommendations for an enterprise strategy for data management. The last section of the chapter enumerates the types of data that are needed for the implementation of such a strategy.

---

[1]TowerGroup, TowerGroup Research Note V46:08M "Measuring the Securities Industry's Progress on Reference Data, 2002–05," published February 2006.
[2]Greg MacSweeney, *Citigroup Names Bottega CDO*, Wall Street & Technology, March 16, 2006.

6.2   The Current State of Affairs

The data needs of securities firms are numerous and immediate, with market competition and regulation driving firms to aggressively improve their legacy data management systems. As discussed in Chapter 1, the securities industry is undergoing radical transformation that will have a significant effect on the way data is acquired and processed today. The decimalization of stock prices and electronic and algorithmic trading have all led to the ability of computers to trade in small lots, driving market quotation data to unprecedented volumes as more trades occur per second than ever before. At its highest volume, a broker-dealer could receive hundreds of orders a second from buy-side institutions, such as hedge funds, which use computer algorithms to eke out profit opportunities in the market. This puts enormous pressure on the broker-dealer's data management systems, which must process and store these orders at incredible speed. Simultaneously, such regulations as MiFID and Reg NMS have increased the requirements for transparency and best execution, both of which also lead directly to a huge surge in market quotation data. Other regulations, such as Basel II mandate better risk management overall, which requires more integrated internal data feeds to enterprise risk management systems.

Firms are thus facing a whole new set of requirements based on market changes to acquire and process larger volumes of data at a faster pace. But the fact is that today, they are still struggling to create a coherent strategy for their data management requirements, and are ill-equipped to meet the recent challenges in the market. For decades, firms have haphazardly met with new demands to accommodate larger volumes and types of data, more applications that need to access it, and greater speed of data access. More often than not, databases have been added in an ad hoc manner from an enterprise viewpoint, serving the needs of specific departments, even when this data exists in some other location. Sometimes, there can be over 50 databases in a large firm storing the same data in different formats, with varying levels of accuracy. In securities firms, many departments just used Excel files to organize and store data locally on their PCs. Other departments created their own databases, acquiring their data from various multiple data vendors, such as Bloomberg and Reuters. Since there is no widely used industry standard for representing reference data, data vendors usually supply their data in disparate formats, using different naming conventions. Firms then spend time and money building software components that mapped the vendor data to the firm's data representations.

The problem runs deeper than just having redundant data and the costs associated with such redundancy. Data vendors sometimes give different or incomplete information for the same record. This essentially means that the same security can have two distinct values for the same attribute in different databases in one firm. In addition, if one of the vendors provided an incomplete record, it was most likely manually completed via research by the middle office, opening the possibility of

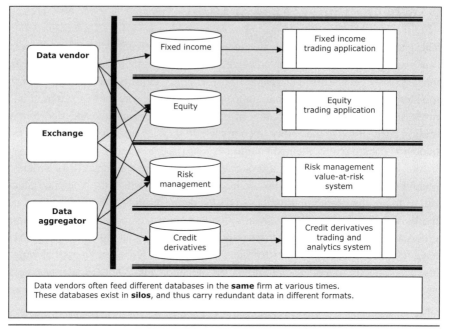

Data vendors often feed different databases in the **same** firm at various times. These databases exist in **silos**, and thus carry redundant data in different formats.

Figure 6-1   Financial firms find that their data is stuck in silos.

human error. Over time, the majority of firms in the securities industry have reached a decentralized and fragmented reference data acquisition and storage process that contains poor quality reference data that is inconsistent among its data stores. See Figure 6-1.

The decentralization of reference data management is especially problematic when trying to assess the overall financial profile of a company. With inconsistent data on the same securities, traders are functioning under a different set of assumptions from risk managers. This is precisely the kind of operational risk that leads to inaccurate financial reporting.

Revamping legacy systems that were developed in a hurry to meet market demands, and aggregating, integrating, and consolidating data in the firm, have now become the primary focus of technology managers. The rest of this chapter examines strategies that both address the old reference data problems faced by firms and create a data management system powerful enough to meet the new demands of the market.

6.3   Data Management Basics

Data management is a set of procedures and infrastructure that allow a firm to store, transport, and manipulate data. Databases form the core of any data management system. They are software programs that store information in an organized and structured manner. Lightweight databases, such as Microsoft Access, can be installed locally on a PC desktop, but firms usually deploy databases, such as Oracle or Sybase that can handle large volumes of data and queries, and are installed on servers. The most common type of a database is a relational database, in which data is organized in tables and relationships exist between data in different tables.

6.3.1 RELATIONAL DATABASES

Relational databases organize information by categorizing it into entities that have attributes, and then linking these entities through relationships. An *entity* is a real-world item or concept that exists on its own. For example, BOND, EQUITY, and PARTY are all entities. Each entity has *attributes*, or particular properties that describe the entity. For example, a BOND has such attributes as Issuer, Principal, Maturity, and Coupon Rate. The *value* of the attribute Principal may be $100. See Table 6-1.

A *relationship* type is a set of associations among entity types. *Constraints* are cardinality and format rules pertinent to a particular relationship. For example, there is a one-to-many relationship between the entity Issuer and the entity Bond: *one* Issuer can issue *many* Bonds. Database design architects model the entities, attributes, relationships, and constraints in what is known as an *entity-relationship (ER) diagram* (Figure 6-2).

Tables in databases are very much like Excel spreadsheets. In good database design, a table represents an entity. A table representing the entity BOND is one example. The columns in the table represent the attributes of the entity. Thus the BOND table contains the columns Issuer, Principal, Maturity, Coupon Rate, Callable, and Rating. Each table has a *primary key* that is a unique identifier for the combination of attributes for a particular bond. See Table 6-2.

Table 6-1 Typical bond attributes and values

ENTITY	Bond					
ATTRIBUTES	Issuer	Principal	Maturity	Coupon rate	Callable	Rating
VALUES	IBM	$100	30 yrs	10%	No	Aab

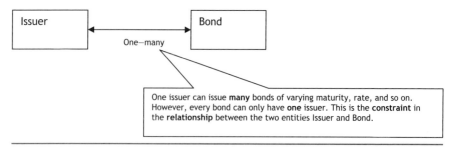

Figure 6-2   One-to-Many Bond Relationship Constraint.

Table 6-2   Three corporate bonds listed by Bond_ID

Bond_ID	CUSIP	Issuer	Principal	Maturity	Coupon rate	Callable	Issue rating
1	43333100	IBM	$100	30 yrs	10%	No	Aab
2	37833201	APPLE	$50	10 yrs	5%	Yes	Aaa
3	67833100	IBM	$1,000	12 yrs	7%	No	Aab

Primary Key: Bond_ID
Unique identifier for this combination of attributes for this entity. Automatically generated sequentially by the database as new rows are added to the table.

6.3.2   NORMALIZATION

Data is divided logically into different tables and linked together if it can be divided into different entities. For instance, if IBM has issued two bonds, one with maturity 30 years and one with maturity 12 years, the risk managers would like to monitor the performance of IBM and need more details on it, such as Issuer Rating and Country of Incorporation (in case the country where the headquarters are has an unforeseen political or natural hazard). These two attributes can be added to the BOND table as shown in Table 6-3.

However, ISSUER is really another ENTITY. It should be in the PARTY table with the attributes Role (whether it is an issuer, a guarantor, or a counterparty), the Name, Country of Incorporation, and Credit Rating. See Table 6-4.

Table 6-3 Three corporate bonds compared, coming from different countries of incorporation

Bond_ID	CUSIP	Issuer	Principal	Maturity	Coupon rate	Callable	Issue rating	Issuer rating	Country of incorporation
1	43333100	IBM	$100	30 yrs	10%	No	Aab	Aaa	USA
2	37833201	APPLE	$50	30 yrs	5%	Yes	Aaa	Aaa	FR
3	67833100	IBM	$1,000	12 yrs	7%	No	Aab	Aaa	USA

Table 6-4 Two corporate bonds compared, stored by Party_ID

Party_ID	Role	Name	Country of incorporation	Credit rating
1	Issuer	IBM	USA	Aaa
2	Issuer	APPLE	FR	Aaa

Table 6-5 Party_ID helps find which bond is the one of interest

Bond_ID	CUSIP	Party_ID	Principal	Maturity	Coupon rate	Callable	Issue rating
1	43333100	1	$100	30 yrs	10%	No	Aab
2	37833201	2	$50	10 yrs	5%	Yes	Aaa
3	67833100	1	$1,000	12 yrs	7%	No	Aab

Foreign Key: Party_ID

The foreign key in one table is the primary key in another table and helps to connect two tables together. So for Bond_ID 1, we know the Party is IBM because we look up Party_ID = 1 in the Party table.

This is a much cleaner way of representing the two entities. Now, instead of IBM and APPLE in the BOND table, we can put the identifiers Party_ID 1 and Party_ID 2 in the BOND table and link it to the PARTY table. The Bond_ID is the primary key, and the Party_ID is the *foreign key* of the BOND table. The process of separating tables into logical entities is known as *normalization*. See Table 6-5.

Normalization is the process of separating data into different tables to ensure that the data is not redundantly stored in several tables and to create consistent relationships between these tables. The more data is separated at a granular level, the more normalized is the data schema or modeling approach. For example, it would be redundant to store the issuer information in both the BOND and the PARTY table. Each time some information regarding a party changed, it would have to be updated in both tables. This kind of redundancy leaves too much room for error and inconsistency between tables. It is far better to normalize the information and to link the tables that store this information separately.

6.3.3 DATA MODELS

When designing how a database will hold information, a database architect usually refers to three levels of data modeling: conceptual, logical, and physical. The *conceptual data model* is the most abstract view of the database and is most closely aligned with how the business views the data. It only includes the important entities and the relationships among them, and can be visually presented by the database architect in an entity-relationship diagram. The *logical data model* adds more information to how the database will hold business data, by including attributes for entities, the primary and foreign keys for each entity, and the level of normalization that will determine the number of tables in the database. The logical model is used by database administrators to create the physical representation of the tables, columns, and relationships between tables in a database software program, such as Sybase. This is known as the *physical data model*, and data can now be entered, stored, and retrieved from this database.

Technologists often refer to mapping and normalizing data before entering it into a database. For example, if a bank wants to store market data from Bloomberg, it must first *map* the Bloomberg field names to the column names in its database. Bloomberg may call a field that describes the issuer of a bond by the name "issuer," whereas the firm's database may call the same field by the name "security issuer." In order to ensure that data is put into the correct tables and columns in its database, the firm must map all the Bloomberg field names to its internal data model. The entire set of data from Bloomberg may come in a flat CSV file that then has to be parsed and put into all the different tables in the database. In other words, the Bloomberg data has to be normalized to match the normalized data model of the firm's database. It is important to understand that the heterogeneity in data formats, field names, and normalization require careful translation when data is loaded from a data source. This translation process is often quite time-consuming and costly to build, which is why the industry is always clamoring for a universal data dictionary or standard for different kinds of market and reference data.

6.3.4 STRUCTURED QUERY LANGUAGE (SQL)

Data is physically inserted, deleted, updated, and queried from databases using a database language. The most common language for data manipulation in databases is *Structured Query Language (SQL)*. Basic SQL queries are quite simple; however, to construct fast updates and queries, database developers use a variety of sophisticated techniques. The format of a simple query to select data from a database is:

Table 6-6 Bonds in a table under Bond_ID

Bond_ID	CUSIP	Issuer	Principal	Maturity	Coupon rate	Callable	Issue rating
1	43333100	1	$100	30 yrs	10%	No	Aab
2	37833201	2	$50	30 yrs	5%	Yes	Aaa

Table 6-7 CUSIP numbers in a CUSIP lookup table

CUSIP
43333100
37833201

SELECT column_name **FROM** table_name **WHERE** some condition

If the goal is to select all the bonds in the BOND table with a maturity of 30 years, the following SQL statement will return the desired result set (note that when the entire dataset is needed, specify column_name as *).

SELECT * **FROM** Bond **WHERE** Maturity = 30

The result set returned from the query would be as shown in Table 6-6.

If the goal were to get all the CUSIPs (an industry security identifier for bonds) for bonds with maturity equal to 30 years, the following SQL statement would be used.

SELECT CUSIP **FROM** Bond **WHERE** Maturity = 30

The result in Table 6-7 would be returned from this query.

6.3.5 OLTP VERSUS DSS

Databases are often categorized as OLTP (Online Transaction Processing) or DSS (Decision Support System). Online Transaction Processing (OLTP) is used by applications that need quick transactions to be conducted, usually involving fetching, inserting, and updating data from a few rows in a table. The response time required for these SQL functions is very fast, and it is beneficial to have a highly normalized data model for an OLTP database. Databases connected to trading systems should by styled as OLTP databases so that they can effectively work in a high-speed market environment, quickly processing requests for data and updating transaction data as it happens.

Decision Support Systems (DSS) are usually read-only data warehouses that are used to generate reports. DSS queries usually require querying and aggregating large volumes of current and historical data, typically involving thousands of rows. Accounting systems that produce nightly profit and loss reports are often linked to DSS databases. These databases are usually de-normalized since it is better to have as much data as possible in one table; this saves time as SQL queries do not have to traverse several tables to acquire data.

If possible, it is advisable that OLTP and DSS databases be kept separate, and synced periodically to ensure data is consistent between the two. However, this is not always the case, and databases in firms usually have a mix of OLTP and DSS-level normalization for different types of data depending on which application will use it. Database administrators may employ various techniques when querying DSS-type results so as not to slow the performance of the database for OLTP-type transactions.

6.4   Data Management Strategy

Realizing that data management requires an enterprise-level strategy has spurred firms to create independent departments to specifically oversee the efficient management of data. In 2006, Citigroup led the way by naming John Bottega as its Chief Data Officer (CDO), the first executive position in the securities industry for planning the investments in and architectures chosen for Citigroup's enterprisewide data needs. Some firms chose the alternative data management executive title of Data Czar. Regardless of the title, data managers have steadily moved from the back-office to the top of the corporate ladder, underscoring the fact that data is now beginning to be regarded as a valuable asset in the firm.

Securities firms need a *centrally managed data solution* that meets the data requirements of all the lines of business in the firm. Note that centralized data management does not mean that all the data must necessarily be stored in one physical location. What it means is that decisions on how to acquire, store, and distribute the data a firm needs are managed by one central department that defines a strategy and takes a three-pronged approach to streamline people, technology, and content around the firm's data requirements. The remainder of this section discusses some of the important features of enterprise data management systems that need to be implemented by the CDO's office.

6.4.1 DATA MANAGEMENT SYSTEM ARCHITECTURE

In general, the best strategy is to have a set of read-only data warehouses that store the golden copy of reference data and distribute it to various local databases through a high-speed message bus. These local databases are then accessible throughout the firm using data access services using the SOA framework.

The first goal of a data strategy is to create a *golden copy* of reference data, which means that data will always be the same in all data stores and applications in the firm; and to eliminate multiple feeds by leveraging data acquired from an external source by one department by propagating it locally across all the databases in the firm. The golden copy is the official master version of a record. When data management is integrated, only this version of the data exists in every database and application in the firm. Having one master record that is created once centrally and distributed globally is one way of achieving this level of consistency across the enterprise. The golden copy of reference data, such as historical pricing, end-of-day pricing, and security reference data, is sourced either directly from marketplaces or through data aggregators. Regardless of the source, it is kept in one or several *data warehouses* and then distributed to other databases via a message bus. Data warehouses are usually read-only warehouses that are the central repository for reference data in a firm. See Figure 6-3.

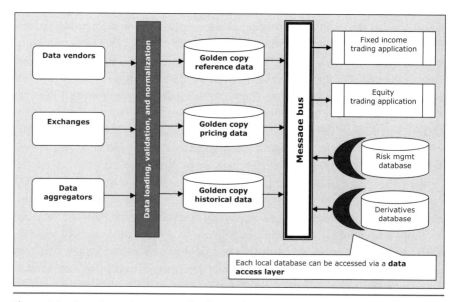

Figure 6-3 Central warehouses can distribute reference data to both applications and local databases via a message bus.

Building data warehouses has received a great deal of attention in the securities industry. The traditional technology approach to load data from multiple feeds into a warehouse has been to use *ETL (extract, transform, load)* tools. ETL tools were very popular because they would read data from a source, transform it into the database schema (taking into account naming conventions, data formats, normalization, tables, and so forth) and load it into the data warehouses.

Data can be propagated locally in databases through the firm by using the SOA approach of message buses and services. A data access layer or service provides an interface through which to load data in a local database. Every database needs to have a data service API that allows applications to use it via a middleware application. All the heterogeneous data stores are thus linked by one system connecting all of them. The interfaces abstract away from the type of database its model and even the underlying SQL by using a programming interface using XML to access it. It is important for data from the central warehouses to be sent in industry standard XML-based format for the SOA framework to be effective.

6.4.2 MARKET DATA INFRASTRUCTURE

Electronic trading and algorithmic trading are all resulting in the requirement to access market data at lightning speed. In the quest to achieve millisecond improvement over a competitor's access to the market, large broker-dealers are starting to develop direct connections to exchanges, such as NASDAQ, NYSE, and AMEX. Building market data infrastructure that acquires, stores, and distributes low-latency (high-speed) data access has become a top priority for securities firms.

Acquiring high-speed market data directly involves building a whole new set of procedures for firms that were traditionally used to getting this data from vendors, such as Bloomberg and Reuters. These vendors would aggregate and normalize the data from multiple exchanges and ECNs around the world and send it in a consistent data feed to firms. Since each source provides data in disparate formats and naming conventions, the value-added of using these vendors was very high. The downside of using this intermediary data consolidation layer was that there was a time lag between the time the data was available at the market source and the time it reached the firm. Even though these delays might have been measured in seconds, they are still unacceptable in an environment where black box trading systems compete to send orders out in milliseconds. With the need for faster access to market data and the consequent decision to build direct connectivity, the functions done traditionally by data vendors now need to be done by the firm itself.

Instead of building interfaces that would normalize direct feeds internally, several firms are deciding to use feed handlers, which are vendor products that normalize market data feeds at very high speed. Merrill Lynch and Bear Stearns, for example, are both using Wombat Financial Software,[3] which provides feed handlers for multiple exchanges and ECNs around the world for multiple asset classes including equities, futures, and options. According to Wombat, it has a median latency of one millisecond, which is the lowest in the market.

This data is then stored in time-series databases and supplied to their algorithmic trading systems that they use internally and provide to institutional clients over fast messaging middleware.

6.4.3 MANAGED OUTSOURCING

Recently, the market has seen the emergence of a number of *turn key management solutions*, which essentially allow a firm to outsource all its data needs to an outside service provider. These providers take care of all reference data requirements including data acquisition, normalization, validation, exception-handling, and distribution. In addition, these providers help a firm manage its compliance-related activities, such as Anti-Money Laundering (AML) and Know Your Customer (KYC) regulations. Examples of popular providers of such services are Cicada and TAP Solutions. The outsource solution, however, does have two drawbacks: first, it makes the firm entirely dependent for time critical data on the robustness and reliability of another firm; second, the process of data aggregation and consolidation adds a layer of abstraction to data acquisition, which takes up time, sometimes too precious a commodity in a fast-paced electronic trading environment.

6.4.4 ENSURING LOW LATENCY AND HIGH AVAILABILITY

Once data has entered the firm, it has to be distributed to multiple applications within the firm. *High availability* and *low latency* means that data is always available and the speed of access is fast. Technology teams have to build systems that redistribute this data using high bandwidth connections within the firm, and be able to store it in an optimized manner that allows fast retrievals and updates. In addition, business users must be guaranteed that the databases will always be up and running. Virtualization and grid computing have become the mantras for this kind of fast-changing data environment. Virtualization relies on the paradigm of distributed data caching, with fast access possible as data is stored in-memory across a grid of resources, as

---

[3]Tim Clark, *Surging Electronic Trading Volumes and Reg NMS Require Financial Firms to Enhance Underlying Technology Infrastructures*, Wall Street & Technology, January 24, 2007.

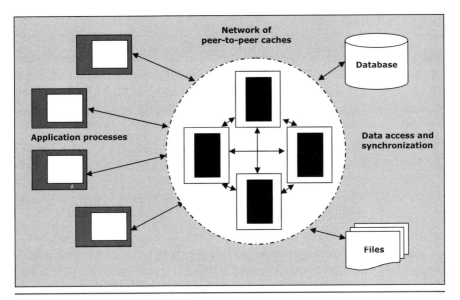

Figure 6-4   Virtualization of data sources. Source: Gemstone.

opposed to formerly stored on disk-based data management systems. Data is synched and shared among nodes of CPU, allowing for much higher data access rates than ever seen before. Applications can then access this data on-demand using an SOA messaging architecture that provides standard interfaces to data resources wherever they exist in the distributed environment (see Figure 6-4). Leading vendors in this space include DataSynapse and GemStone. Chapter 10 discusses the concept of virtualization in more detail.

6.4.5   USING INDUSTRY STANDARDS

The core of STP lies in having a standard manner of describing the same information so that it can be exchanged between disparate systems. Either all systems use the same vocabulary, or data has to be transformed from one vocabulary to another when it is exchanged between systems. Technologists agree that XML, given that it is flexible and it can be easily manipulated programmatically, has become the best data format for exchanging information. Using industry standards, written in XML or another format, that define how to represent financial information increases interoperability between applications, reducing the need to build software modules that transform data from one format and vocabulary to another.

6.4.6 VALIDATING DATA

Validation rules look for data anomalies and determine the accuracy of completeness of a record. A rules engine is automatically loaded and used on any data coming to the repository before it is stored. As data violates rules, error flags are generated and the data is manually investigated. There are four main kinds of rules that are recommended for data validation.

■ **Completeness Rules:** Rules of this type ensure that all required fields are returned. For example, if a call schedule is populated, then the call flag must be populated as well. The purpose of the completeness rules is to ensure that all required data fields are populated.

■ **Domain Rules:** These rules provide a range of values of parameters to flag outliers for review. For example, there can be a rule that the payment price in any call, put, or convertible schedule should be greater than 90 and less than 120. Two subsets of domain rules are Valid Identifier Rules and Referential Integrity Rules.

  • **Valid Identifier Rules:** These rules guarantee that data in an identifier field is in fact a valid identifier. For example, the ISIN number should be 12 characters.

  • **Referential Integrity Rules:** These rules guarantee that data in a dependent table has matching records in the table(s) on which it depends. For example, coupon currency should be found in the Currency reference table.

■ **Data Type Rules:** Type rules ensure that the data type for each field is in accordance with the type specified in the XML schema. For example, the maturity Date of an instrument must of type Gregorian Date.

■ **Comparison Rules:** These rules exist to help ensure that the record cleansed and returned by the data vendor is the record requested. This involves checking multiple sources to see if the different types of security IDs (SEDOL, CUSIP) on a security point to the same security (in terms of key values, such as issuer name, maturity date, coupon, and currency).

Rules are a very important piece of a data management system since the goal is to have a clean, trusted copy of the internal and reference data. Not only must the business analysts of the group building the system determine the rules but they must also consider when, where, and in which sequence each rule should be applied to the data. If the data has passed the validation rules, it can be stored in the repository and transported to all the departments in the firm reliably. If the validations fail, they will go through an *exception processing* procedure that will involve investigating and cleansing the data.

6.4.7 SECURITY AND OTHER CONSIDERATIONS

In addition to the business requirements for an enterprise data management system outlined above, these other features should also be kept in mind:

- **Security:** Database security involves putting stringent access controls on who can view and manipulate records. This is particularly important when it links to client information, in which data privacy is paramount.

- **Business Continuity:** Data is one of the most important assets of a financial firm. Firms go to great lengths to ensure that this data is not corrupted or lost due to unforeseen disasters, such as earthquakes and terrorist attacks. Protecting data from the hazards of unexpected events is part of the overall business continuity strategy of a firm, and primarily focuses on a state-of-the-art storage and replication infrastructure.

- **Exception Handling:** Whenever data is being queried, stored, or distributed, there are certain exceptions that can occur. For example, if a trader searches for a particular security and that security is not in the database, a "data not found" exception can be put in a user-friendly message. Graceful exception handling is a tenet of good code design and is as important in data management as in any other part of the software system enterprise.

- **Database Optimization:** The data must be stored in such a way that it is easy to retrieve and manipulate. There is no point in having all the necessary data, cleaned and enriched, sitting in the firm's databases, if it takes hours to conduct one calculation on the data. Solutions for database optimization include using specific SQL queries and storing data using indexes.

- **Data Governance:** Regulations, such as Sarbanes-Oxley, encourage firms to exercise good corporate governance for data management. This translates directly into keeping audit trails of any and all changes to data in a warehouse. Only authorized employees, such as database administrators or authorized applications, should be allowed to change data, and each of these changes should be logged.

6.4.7 DECIDING BETWEEN BUILD AND BUY

In general, no firm wants to outsource its entire data management system to one vendor. First of all, securities firms have proprietary data that is updated by algorithms that they do not want to make public. And more importantly, buying a black box vendor solution puts the firm at the mercy of the vendor, which makes adding new features a long process of negotiation with the vendor, not to mention a costly undertaking. What firms are doing instead is outsourcing different parts of the system to various vendors. For instance, the data grid is bought from one vendor, while data aggregators are used for some data needs. In other cases, the firm will build and maintain internal databases and direct connections to data sources. This kind of hybrid solution puts the build versus buy debate in a new light. The question has now become one of how much to build and how much to buy.

6.5 Types of Data

Effective data management is important for STP for four main reasons: (i) completing a transaction; (ii) risk management; (iii) accounting and reporting; and (iv) meeting regulatory requirements. Given how data is crucial for all major business processes, it requires senior management to fundamentally change its view of data, seeing it as a core business asset that needs to be developed and utilized more efficiently.

Broadly, data can be defined as static or dynamic. *Static data* are data that do not change very often, whereas *dynamic data* are data that continually change over time. For example, attributes of a bond, such as its maturity and issuer, are most likely going to remain constant over the life of the security, and are referred to as static data; however, its price continually changes, and thus price data is referred to as dynamic data. In addition, some data is public to all participants, such as currency codes and interest rates, whereas other data is kept private to a firm, such as client account information. With these high-level categorizations in mind, the following list shows the main types of data needed for securities operations.

- **Historical Time Series Data:** Historical market data is needed in both analytics and risk management for strategy back-testing, instrument pricing, and Monte-Carlo simulations. For example, a quant may require interest rates for the past ten years in order to simulate how they may behave and affect the fixed income portfolio of the trading desk in the future. For credit risk management, the fluctuating credit rating of an issuer in the past is helpful in determining whether it will default on its current obligations. Getting historical time-series data is a one-time download of the relevant dataset from a market source for a fee. Prominent data vendors for financial data include Bloomberg, Reuters, Telekurs, and FTID.
- **Static Reference Data:** Static reference data refers to the kind of data fields that do not vary over time. This includes the defining parameters of a security and

the legal entity structure of different counterparties. Static data is retrieved in a one-time download every time a new security, counterparty, or market partner is used, with updates triggered by events. For example, in the event of an acquisition, the name of the legal entity that has issued a security will have to be changed.

■ **Dynamic and High-Frequency Market Data:** Dynamic data varies on a regular basis and is most often used to refer to the changing prices of a security. Quotes received from a multitude of sources for a variety of asset classes have to be normalized and stored in the firm's database. These prices are then used for analytics, daily mark-to-market, and risk management. This includes high-frequency data, such as tick data, which is a constant stream of tick-by-tick price quotes from marketplaces, such as from NASDAQ, NYSE, and AMEX. There was a time when end-of-day price data was sufficient for most kinds of proprietary algorithmic trading (i.e., statistical arbitrage), but with electronic trading, margins have shrunk and competitiveness in finding small opportunities in the market has skyrocketed. Hedge funds in particular now need intraday high-frequency tick data for trading. Intraday market data is also needed by broker-dealers who must provide best execution to their clients, and therefore need to have a view of real-time current prices in all major marketplaces.

■ **Legal Entity and Corporate Actions Data:** Keeping track of corporate actions and legal entity data, such as mergers and stock splits, is very important because they can significantly affect the price and future returns on a security. They have been a sore spot for the industry since there is no consolidated data feed for this information, and the middle-office would notify business users after looking at press releases and company websites. Firms now increasingly outsource their needs to corporate actions aggregators, who provide updated information in feeds to the firm.

■ **Transaction and Position Data:** A firm keeps track internally of transaction details, including internal trade identifiers, position data, and profit and loss histories.

■ **Account Data:** There are two types of account data that each firm holds: the account information of clients that use the firm, and the account information when the firm itself is a client of another firm. Details of clients, including names, assets under management, client-directed rules, and transaction history, are kept in account-related databases. In addition, the firm may have several accounts of its own with data vendors, marketplaces, and clearinghouses and must store this information internally.

RECOMMENDATIONS

Effective data management requires that firms have a centrally managed data management solution that ensures that the data throughout the enterprise is accurate and consistent, and that data access is fast and always available.

1. Data stuck in silos must be replaced with an SAO consisting of data warehouses and data services that represent databases.
2. Data warehouses can be used to store static read-only reference data, which is then propagated throughout the firm using a high-speed message bus.
3. For fast access within the firm, data virtualization can be utilized.
4. Some types of data acquisition and aggregation, such as corporate actions, can be outsourced to data aggregators.

6.6 Summary

Reference data are the key to implementing the STP architecture. Usually, reference data storage is a redundant, inconsistent, expensive, and sometimes manually intensive process. It leads to delays and failure of transactions, misreporting, and inaccurate risk analytics. Senior management now agrees that data should be effectively administered by a centralized group and at an enterprise level. This chapter has reviewed the strategies and steps a securities firm can take to implement an effective data management system. It focuses on the procedures and concepts relevant to reference data management, with the underlying messaging and exception processing architecture based on an SOA framework.

Chapter 7

Reconciliation and Exception Handling

7.1 Introduction

Straight through processing (STP) is envisaged as an industrywide infrastructure in which automation of the trade lifecycle reduces operational risk. If and when processing exceptions occur in an STP environment, they are identified quickly and rectified effectively. Discussions of STP usually revolve around scenarios that highlight its efficacy in facilitating financial transactions; however, the critical processes of dealing with mismatched information between market participants, and workflow exceptions in general, are seldom discussed in detail. This chapter addresses the reconciliation requirements of the securities industry and overall strategies for expedited exception handling.

Continual reconciliation between systems, both internal and external, is the primary measure of ensuring that discrepancies are identified and resolved as early in the trade lifecycle as possible. For example, the SEC requires that the Net Asset Value (NAV) of a mutual fund be calculated at least once daily for investor information. This requires transaction details from mutual funds to be sent to a fund accountant, such as JP Morgan, so that the accountant can calculate the daily NAV. The fund and its accountant reconcile their transaction data either in a batch process periodically or on a real-time basis to check that the correct information has been received at the accountant. Another example that underscores the need for reconciliation is the demands of regulations such as Basel II, which calls for accurate global risk management. Firms must reconcile records between their front-end trade applications and middle-office position management systems across all departments to be able to publish a consolidated number for the market risk exposure of the firm. Section 7.2 steps through the trade lifecycle to examine the key points where reconciliation is needed both internally within the firm and externally between firms in the industry. Firms now rely on reconciliation engines to flag reconciliation errors through a variety of business rule checks. Section 7.3 reviews the most important features a reconciliation engine should have, whether it is built in-house or bought off-the-shelf.

Exceptions are not only related to reconciliation errors. They can be triggered by a number of events, including incomplete information, invalid message formats, and delays in payment. As a rule, an exception is said to occur each time the workflow is disrupted due to an unforeseen or unexpected event. Exception handling comprises the automated identification of errors and their resolution either by automated system responses or by manual investigation by Operations personnel. For example, an exception may occur if all the details of the trade are not included in a trade message from a broker-dealer to DTCC, preventing the trade from being matched and settled. This would be an example of an exception raised due to incomplete information. To be able to meet the T+1 settlement deadline, all market participants must have an exception handling strategy that includes automated exception flagging and resolution procedures by the system or by Operations personnel. In the example, the DTCC system will automatically send a message back to the broker-dealer that explains the reason as incomplete trade details. The broker-dealer's system then automatically forwards this message to Operations, where a staff member investigates why the details were missing. Section 7.4 provides a framework and reviews best practices for exception handling.

7.2   Reconciliation and Trade Lifecycle

Reconciliation is the comparison of two sets of information to see whether they match or not. This can include any data related to transactions, including trade and payment details, position and cash accounts, and corporate actions events. Reconciliation has traditionally been a back-office function, conducted end-of-day in batch cycles. However, risks associated with trades that fail to settle due to mismatched trade details are forcing firms to reconsider the way they have viewed reconciliation in the past. Not only do mismatched transaction records increase the pre-settlement exposure of parties involved, they also result in a long, costly, and involved procedure of correction. It is much better for reconciliation between trade details to occur as early as possible in the trade lifecycle, far before settlement time, so that the mismatches can be resolved quickly. Reconciliation should occur not only during trade matching, but between different market players at various other points in the trade lifecycle as well. This section highlights the different points in the trade lifecycle for which reconciliation is crucial.

7.2.1   TRADE MATCHING

In the pre-settlement stage, the two parties involved in the transaction must agree on all the trade details with each other. Details include key data attributes like security identifier, price, quantity, and counterparty. For example, if Party A and Party B have different prices for the same trade, the trade will not be confirmed and therefore will not be settled. Trade matching can be achieved in three ways: (i) by the marketplace in which the trade takes place; (ii) by a third party such as a clearinghouse; and (iii) privately between the two parties.

Generally, if the trade occurs at an exchange, the computer systems of the exchange match the trade details and send the "locked-in" (already matched) trade to the clearinghouse for settlement. For example, trades at NYSE and AMEX are matched before they are sent to the NSCC (National Securities Clearing Corporation) for clearing. In electronic trading, transaction details are usually agreed upon by the buyer and the seller prior to submitting the trade to a marketplace, such as NASDAQ, and thus are automatically matched and locked-in at the time of the trade.

In case of OTC derivatives, a service provider, such as Swapswire, can be used for real-time trade matching, resulting in legal confirmations within minutes of execution. This is also the case for fixed income securities, where trade detail reconciliation is provided by Fixed Income Clearing Corporation's (FICC) Real-Time Trade Matching (RTTM) service.

Firms can also match their trade details directly with each other. However, this is increasingly rare as market players prefer to use one place to match their trades instead of individual trade detail matching with each trading partner.

7.2.2 POSITION RECONCILIATION

Reconciliation takes place not only between firms, but also within systems at a single firm. The front-office is constantly buying and selling securities, and this information has to be reconciled with the information kept in the back-office systems for generating profit and loss accounting. Position reconciliation is also needed for collateral management, which bases calculations on mark-to-market of current positions. Finally, the position management system is also used by the global risk management desk to calculate enterprisewide market and credit risk.

7.2.3 PERIODIC PAYMENT RECONCILIATION

In the case of derivatives contracts, periodic exchange of cash flows occurs during the lifetime of the contract. The DTCC's Deriv/SERV provides a payment matching and settlement service that calculates and confirms payments with parties before the quarterly payment date. This reconciliation is helpful in making sure that payments are agreed upon before any transfer of funds takes place.

7.2.4 NOSTRO RECONCILIATION

A Nostro account is an account that a bank keeps with another bank in a foreign country. This account is kept in the currency of the foreign country. This is very convenient for banks that want to carry out transactions in foreign countries, because now they do not have to convert cash from their native currency to the foreign currency. Thus, if a bank maintains an account in a foreign currency with another bank in a foreign country, it refers to this account as its *Nostro account* (nostro derives from the Latin word for "ours"). The flip side of this scenario is a *Vostro account* (vostro derives from the Latin word for "yours"), which is what a bank calls the bank accounts that it maintains in local currency for foreign banks.

While the presence of Nostro accounts is very beneficial to expediting payments in foreign currencies, it now presents a new point of reconciliation for the industry. With Continuous Linked Settlement (CLS) providing settlement in foreign currencies, banks need access to the status of their holdings around the world in real time as well. Banks that hold Nostro accounts must constantly reconcile their records with the records sent to them by their Nostro agents (providers of Nostro accounts) to check that cash movements were made correctly. This is the only way they will have a complete and accurate picture of their cash in all currencies globally at a given point in time, which is crucial for liquidity management.

Third-party vendor Cable and Wireless offers a Real Time Nostro (RTN) subscriber service that provides a way for financial institutions to view multi-bank, multi-currency Nostro account data in real time. It achieves this by getting information feeds from Nostro agents and then immediately streaming them to Nostro account holders using SWIFT's XML-based messages for cash reporting (part of SWIFT's SWIFTNet Cash Reporting service). Firms can reconcile data that they receive from Cable Wireless RTN with their own internal records, thereby helping them to manage their cash flows intraday and to predict their end-of-day cash balances more accurately. If there are any mismatches, they can be immediately addressed because reconciliation was performed during market hours, instead of after the market closes as was usually the case.

7.2.4 COLLATERAL RECONCILIATION

In order to mitigate credit risk—the risk that a counterparty will default on its obligation—firms have begun to use collateralization as insurance in an increasing number of transactions. Dynamic collateralization is particularly relevant for derivatives portfolios, which are more susceptible to credit defaults. More and more, firms now expect their counterparts to have collateral management systems that can handle arrangements that involve the giving and taking of collateral. These systems use predefined rules, based on historical credit history and current credit rating of counterparties, and the position and valuation of the transaction under question to calculate the collateral margin required at any given time. Collateral reconciliation is needed to identify any discrepancies—in position or in valuation—between a firm and its counterparty's calculations in order to avoid disputes on collateralization calls.

7.2.5 CASH MANAGEMENT

Along with collateral management and Nostro reconciliation, cash management is part of an overall *liquidity management* strategy to minimize operational risk and maximize market opportunities. When the front-office has access to real-time information on cash and collateral positions, it is better able to make better funding decisions.

Traditionally, cash balances were hard to predict because settlement information would come in end-of-day batches, and if there were any errors in the trade lifecycle, these would also be highlighted after the settlement had failed. This meant that after a transaction was made, there remained a great deal of uncertainty over when the payment would be credited or debited from the bank's account. This made investment decisions difficult because the front-office could never accurately predict its cash balances for the next day.

But now a number of firms use SWIFTNet Cash Reporting service to get transaction data from counterparties in real time. This allows financial institutions to reconcile their position records with their counterparties, making sure their counterparties have the correct records, and immediately raising issues with them on discrepancies. By moving quickly on real-time information using a built-in system or vendor product like the Sungard STeP Real-time Liquidity Management product, liquidity management has become a far more accurate science for financial institutions.

7.2.6   RECONCILIATION WITH PRIME BROKERS

Institutional investors, such as hedge funds, often use prime brokers, such as Morgan Stanley Prime Brokerage (MSPB), for their trading order and execution infrastructure, including clearing and settlement. Sometimes, they may even use more than one prime broker. Since all their trades are executed using the prime broker's systems, buy-side firms that utilize prime brokers must reconcile the trade, position, and cash data that they have on their own systems with those provided to them by the prime broker. Many prime brokers provide electronic interfaces through which institutional investors can retrieve data for automated intraday reconciliation of transactions.

7.2.7   RECONCILIATION WITH CUSTODIAN

Custodians are guardians of the assets managed by institutional investors. For instance, individual investors invest their assets—cash and securities—in a mutual fund. The fund's portfolio manager trades the assets to earn a return on them; however, the actual assets themselves are kept at a custodian bank or agent for safeguarding. Every time a portfolio manager trades assets from an individual account, messages are sent to the custodian bank so that it can take care of the payment and settlement of these transactions. Investment management firms need to reconcile their records with those of their custodians to ensure that messages were received accurately and in a timely manner. This reconciliation of transactions and updated positions reduces settlement risks.

A third-party solution, such as the Electra Information Systems STaARS (Securities Transaction and Asset Reconciliation System), can be used for automated reconciation. STaARS automatically reconciles the securities holding, transaction, and cash records between the systems of investement managers and their prime brokers.

7.2.8 RECONCILIATION WITH FUND ACCOUNTANTS

Investment managers also have to make their overall accounting public through fund accountants. A fund accountant keeps track of the fund's Net Asset Value (NAV), which equals the fund's assets minus its liabilities. For instance, in the case of a mutual fund, investors purchase mutual fund shares either from the fund, through a broker, or at a public marketplace, such as the New York Stock Exchange. They are always interested in a mutual fund's NAV because it allows them to value the fund and, more importantly, to calculate the price per share of the fund. This price is primarily calculated by dividing the fund's NAV by its outstanding shares. The SEC requires mutual funds to calculate the NAV once daily, which means that the fund must send its transaction reports to its accountant who then calculates the daily NAV. To ensure that the NAV was calculated correctly, funds reconcile their data with the data that the fund accountant holds in its database.

▋ 7.3 Reconciliation Engines

As shown in the last section, market players have to reconcile trade-related information with each other at multiple points in the trade lifecycle. The impetus for automated intraday reconciliation is the reduction of settlement risk and improvement of operational efficiency. In addition, recent regulations, such as Sarbanes-Oxley, have also put pressure on financial institutions to prove that their financial reporting is accurate, a goal whose achievement necessarily involves reconciliation of transaction data.

In an ideal STP environment, reconciliation is automated and real time, so that exceptions are identified immediately. Firms can either build an in-house reconciliation engine or use an off-the-shelf vendor product and tailor it to its specific needs. Regardless of how the engine is built, there are some standard features that must be included for streamlining operations and reducing settlement risk exposure. The following four attributes comprise the key features of a reconciliation engine.

7.3.1 INTRADAY AND REAL-TIME RECONCILIATION

The most important feature of reconciliation engines is that they must be set up to reconcile data as close to real time as possible. When a firm can reconcile intraday data, as opposed to the usual overnight batch reconciliations, it significantly reduces its risk exposure as transaction errors are identified immediately. This also holds true across multi-currency multi-asset scenarios.

7.3.2 ABILITY TO HANDLE MULTIPLE FEEDS AND MESSAGE FORMATS

In order for a reconciliation engine to be able to compare data from multiple feeds, internal or external to the firm, it must be equipped to accept messages in different formats. When it comes to interfirm communication, an industry standard such as FpML, FIX, or SWIFT is often used to carry transaction details. Increasingly, firms employ industry standards even in intrafirm communication. The engine should be flexible and scalable enough to handle feeds from new data sources.

7.3.3 RULES-BASED MATCHING

Most reconciliation engines are rules-based matching engines that compare the data in transaction records, flag exceptions when records are mismatched, and then direct generated exception messages to appropriate personnel for resolution. Rules range from very basic, such as matching trade identifiers, to complex, such as matching payment calculations for complex derivatives. The best engines are those that are flexible in allowing user-defined matching rules to be added through a user-friendly interface.

7.3.4 LINK TO INTEGRATED EXCEPTION MANAGEMENT SYSTEM AND OPERATIONS

When exceptions are flagged by the reconciliation engine, they are automatically sent to the firm's integrated exception management system, which is run by the Operations personnel of the firm. It is important that the system provides as much detail as possible concerning what constituted the reconciliation error. For example, a reconciliation error report should show exactly which fields did not match during the reconciliation exercise. This expedites the process of resolution, which should be carried out according to a standard set of procedures for addressing any kind of workflow exceptions raised in the firm.

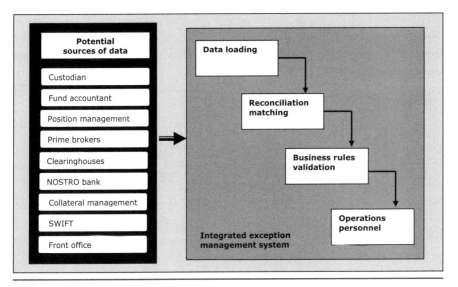

Figure 7-1 Integration exception management platform.

The next section explains how an integrated exception management system works toward providing a coherent framework for handling all kinds of exceptions, including reconciliation exceptions, in the enterprise. See Figure 7-1.

7.4   Exception Handling

Whenever the system fails to function as expected, resulting in a cessation of the business workflow, it is said to have had an exception. Reconciliation mismatches are just one type of exception. The notion of exceptions has been used in the software engineering community for many years, and refers to the time when systems do not behave as expected. In this chapter, exceptions are regarded more as *workflow exceptions* than system errors.

Traditionally, even though exceptions can occur at multiple points in the securities operations workflow, they have been identified only at the tail-end of the transaction cycle when the trade is near settlement. At that point, Operations is given the task of identifying and rectifying the problem as soon as possible. The result is that Operations scrambles to find root causes through a manual investigation—emails, phone conversations, and faxes. This ad hoc investigation and resolution of exception causes is a waste of time and resources.

What the organization needs is a *centralized integrated exception handling system* that is managed by a team of Operations personnel who have a sound understanding of the business, the workflows, and the systems involved in all aspects of the trade lifecycle. Any and all exceptions, including reconciliation errors, that are flagged anywhere in trading-related systems are directed to this integrated exception management platform. Such a centrally managed system has several advantages:

■ Elimination of redundant efforts by various teams in the organization to resolve the same error.

■ Institutionalization of a set of standard procedures for handling exception investigation and resolution.

■ Central workflow dashboard that keeps an audit trail of all the research conducted to resolve the error.

■ Creation of a knowledge base where experience and resolution with errors are documented.

At the end of the day, such a streamlined exception management system and team reduces the operational risks of the firm significantly. This section discusses some best practices to consider when setting up such an exception handling system.

7.4.1 AUTOMATED EXCEPTION IDENTIFICATION

It is imperative for an exception handling system to be set up globally throughout the enterprise and be prepared to receive confirmation or exception messages as the transaction moves through various stages. Transaction monitoring should be set up for the entire transaction lifecycle so that alerts can be sent out by the system if exceptions are identified. Usually, the system automates identification of exceptions by putting in validation rules based on business domain knowledge at key points in the operations workflow. There are three types of validation rules: *incorrect format*; *incomplete data*; and *business rule violation*.

7.4.1.1 Message Format

If a broker-dealer sends trade details via an FpML message to DTCC for clearing, the first thing that DTCC's receiving systems would do is to validate that the message is indeed an XML message. If the format expected is FpML, but it is mistakenly sent a SWIFT message, the system immediately rejects the message. Message format validation is the most basic level of system-to-system validation.

7.4.1.2 Completeness Check

If the message validates, then the next step is for DTCC to check whether all the mandatory information is contained in the message. For instance, the trade identifier is a mandatory data element in the message; if it is not present, the processing of the transaction cannot carry on. Thus, the second validation is to check for incompleteness.

7.4.1.3 Business Rule Violation

The final and most complicated validation stage is to check against business rules. For example, to validate that the CUSIP identifier has been correctly sent, the system uses a formula to see that the code is indeed a CUSIP identifier.

7.4.1.4 Exception Trigger Events

Exceptions are also triggered by unusual events that can affect the transaction, such as credit events, corporate actions, and overdue payments. These exceptions are directed as notification alerts to the appropriate users so that timely action can be taken. Depending on the nature of the exception, the system either generates a response or it is handled by Operations. However the exception is created, it is sent to the integrated exception management system, and automated alerts are sent over email, pager, and text to the Operations staff.

7.4.2 CATEGORIZING AND PRIORITIZING EXCEPTIONS

The rules engine can categorize and prioritize exceptions using business intelligence modules. In order to direct the Operations staff's attention toward exceptions that pose the highest risk, there must be a way for the exception processing system to flag exceptions that are a priority. Often, Operations will receive a whole set of exceptions, some of which are crucial to the trade lifecycle and some of which are not. Without any flagging of the priority of these exceptions, precious time is wasted investigating exceptions that are not crucial for settlement. Good exception handling systems flag business rules with priority numbers, so that when a validation rule for that business rule is violated, an associated number is sent to the Operations team that helps place it in the priority queue.

7.4.3 WORKFLOW TOOLS FOR OPERATIONS STAFF

The Operations staff is a centralized team that is given a workflow application tool and a clear set of guidelines to help it investigate the root cause of an exception.

This application is the central exception-processing hub of the enterprise, and receives exception notifications from exceptions raised by systems throughout the firm.

It has an easy-to-use graphical interface, and authorized users must log on to this system to take steps to repair errors, or send messages to relevant parties for help. This is the only way to prevent ad hoc manual resolution of exceptions (emails, phone calls, and conversations), which will just make the enterprise more vulnerable to errors in the long run. One example of a resolution may be collaborating with the counterparty to provide all the trade details that have resulted in reconciliation errors. A knowledge base is created of the resolution techniques, and notes are taken in case a similar situation arises again.

If an exception is outstanding for a time, it is automatically escalated by the system to senior management, depending on its priority number. Finally, depending on the priority assigned to the exception, if it is not resolved within a predefined time period, the exception is escalated and a note is automatically sent to senior management. Depending on the priority set for the exception, this message may be sent as an email or as a text message for immediate notification.

7.4.3 IDENTIFYING PATTERNS

Often, the problem causing the exception will continue to cause similar exceptions until the issue is resolved. Identifying exception patterns is important in understanding the cause of a recurring exception. In this respect, exception handling is not just about removing random errors, but resolving classes of exceptions permanently by fixing the root problems. This is the only way future errors can be prevented. The attitude should be to understand the problem, and to mitigate it as a holistic operational risk, rather than just seeing it as a one-time isolated problem to be solved.

7.4.4 MIS REPORTING

Detailed reports and statistics are gathered on the number and kind of exceptions that have been generated and have been resolved or remain as open items. These reports are then used by senior management to monitor the operational risk and efforts to mitigate it in the firm. It is imperative that even when exceptions are resolved manually, the system automatically keeps an audit trail and generates reports in standard formats daily or at preset intervals.

RECOMMENDATIONS

An integrated and centralized exception handling platform enables identification and resolution of exceptions that occur when the workflow does not proceed as expected. If reconciliation errors, which are one kind of exception, are caught early in the trade lifecycle, risks can be lowered significantly and loss of revenue due to unsettled trades can be prevented.

1. Reconciliation should happen continually at all stages of the trade lifecycle.
2. Reconciliation engines should use automated business rules to match data sets.
3. A central exception handling platform should be forwarded all exceptions, including reconciliation errors.
4. Best practices for building an exception handling framework should be utilized.
5. Operations personnel must document their investigations.

7.5 Summary

This chapter illustrates the importance of reconciliation and exception handling systems to identify and resolve exceptions during the trade lifecycle and beyond. Market players are increasing their efforts to establish good exception handling practices in order to automate business flows and find exceptions as early as possible. In order to optimize workflows, transaction flows must be monitored in real time and industry standards should be used to facilitate ease of matching and comparing data sets.

Chapter 8

Regulatory Compliance

8.1 Introduction

As markets evolve in complexity, interdependencies, participants, and diversity of products offered, the government often steps in with regulations to monitor and mitigate the risk that such evolution poses. Compliance is the process of meeting laws related to financial operations that must be followed by market participants in order to avoid disciplinary consequences from the government. Often, complying with these regulations involves enhancement of business processes, including the technology operations that support these processes. This chapter builds a framework for creating a straight through processing (STP) environment that is flexible enough to accommodate the regular influx of regulations that affect firms. It also reviews five major regulations that the securities industry is currently facing: Sarbanes-Oxley, Basel II, MiFID, Regulation NMS, and the Patriot Act's Anti-Money Laundering Provision.

By its nature, an STP environment creates an infrastructure that is automated and less prone to human error. But it relies heavily on the fact that the systems that have been built are flawless in transmitting, representing, processing, and storing vital information related to financial transactions. This is, of course, not the case as software, written code, encoded business processes, and so forth, are all prone to human error as they have been written by humans. The risks related to operational errors can be as severe as market and credit risks. Operational risk, however, has traditionally been downplayed by firms that, after having spent a great deal of money on automating systems, seem to place a degree of trust in them that defies reason. The government, recognizing that firms do not want to spend time and money on governing IT, has started demanding IT controls and audit trails for technology-related processes. Section 8.2 discusses the concept of operational risk, which is especially addressed in Sarbanes-Oxley and Basel II.

Regulations, in general, aim to create markets that are transparent and efficient. Thus, some regulations, such as MiFID and Reg NMS, require the expansion of technological infrastructure to achieve these goals, while others, such as Sarbanes-Oxley and Basel II, also include monitoring of technology systems themselves. Sections 8.3 through 8.7 discuss the five regulations—Sarbanes-Oxley, Basel II, MiFID, Regulation NMS, and the Patriot Act—and their impact on technology operations and systems. Finally, Section 8.8 attempts to find symbiosis between the technology requirements across all these regulations, pointing out how managers can build an STP infrastructure that is flexible and can accommodate multiple regulatory laws under one framework.

8.2 Regulatory Laws and Operational Risk

Before delving into regulatory laws for financial markets, it is a worthwhile exercise to understand the general principles on which regulations are based. Usually, regulations are set forth by the government to achieve three things: protection of investors, creation of fair markets, and prevention of systemic risk.

8.2.0.1 The Protection of Investors—Individual, Retail and Institutional

Financial markets are venues where people can invest their savings by providing capital to businesses that will use that money to build and expand their enterprises.

Individual investors buy and sell stocks on their own behalf in markets. Retail and institutional investors, on the other hand, are individual investors that come together to invest via a collective such as a mutual fund. More often than not, a number of investors use this money for their retirement savings. It is crucial to the government that these individuals, whether they come on their own or through a retail enterprise, feel confident that their interests are protected, and they will not suffer financial loss due to fraudulent, careless, or erroneous activities in the market.

8.2.1.2   The Creation of a Market that Is Fair, Efficient, and Transparent

Markets can be fraught with inefficiencies that lead to unfair pricing of products and layers that hide fraud, deficiencies in due diligence, and a general apathy to stream-lining the creation of a fair market. The government will often provide disclosure standards, which forces firms to publicly attest to their efforts to mitigate risk and inefficiencies in their processes. By helping prod market participants to perform better corporate governance and benchmark their performance, the government provides the base for a more efficient market.

8.2.1.3   The Reduction of All Kinds of Risk, Especially Systemic Risk

Systemic risk is the likelihood of the entire financial system collapsing, as opposed to just one market participant. When securities firms expose themselves to a great deal of risk, whether it is market, credit, or operational risk, they often put all other participants involved in the lifecycle of their transactions at risk as well. As the impact of the collapse of one system spreads through the market, it results in a general breakdown of the entire financial system. This is the worst kind of disaster that can occur in a financial market, and the government acts as the guardian of the interests of the industry as a whole; firms are more likely to act only in self-interest, oblivious to the impact of their mistakes on the larger economy.

It is with these objectives in mind that each of the regulations discussed in this chapter are mandated. The next section discusses operational risk, which is the most recent area in which governments and laws are focusing, and which is particularly related to technology operations.

8.2.1   OPERATIONAL RISK

Operational risk refers to the risks inherent in all operations across the firm. As more and more business operations in financial firms depend on technology to some degree, it is natural that the notion of operational risk becomes pertinent to technology operations as well. Operational risk is a fairly new concept, with firms traditionally being more focused on market and credit risk. But at the end of the 20th century, regulators began to emphasize other risks to the enterprise, such as those caused by employee errors, systems failures, fraud, and disasters, all under the collective heading of operational risk.

It was really in the Basel II regulations that the concept of operational risk became formalized. Operational risk was defined by the Basel Committee in 2004 as "the risk of loss resulting from inadequate or failed internal processes, people, and systems, or from external events." Operational risk can be divided broadly into preventable risk hazards, which are discussed in this section, and unexpected hazards. IT controls and regulations relevant to preventable risks are outlined in Sarbanes-Oxley and Basel II. Unexpected emergencies, such as terrorist attacks and earthquakes, fall under the heading of business continuity planning. This is the subject of the next chapter, Chapter 9, Business Continuity.

Usually, risks were identified by specific departments when they came across issues. For instance, systems personnel would provide a list of common risks faced in connectivity and networking, and back-office personnel would point to the most likely issues that will cause delays in payments and settlement. It became evident over time, however, that it was necessary to consolidate all this information, and to think of preventive strategies as part of the overall risk management of the firm.

IT governance and procedures to monitor technology operations become important in countering operational risk. In order to understand the weak links in the chain that result in financial loss and errors, academics and industry experts are trying to come up with a variety of ways and metrics for measuring operational risk. As yet, there is no clearly established industrywide approach. Modeling potential loss events requires keeping data, such as failed transactions due to incorrect data input, over a period of several years. Until a systematic approach to defining and capturing losses due to operational risk is created, firms rely on qualitative ways of mitigating this risk, mostly through interviews and by reviewing error logs. The important point to take away from this discussion is that operational risk is becoming more and more prominent in regulatory laws and one can expect governments to become stricter about enforcing IT controls related to such risks. It would be beneficial for IT managers to keep an eye out for the latest techniques for measuring and controlling operational risk.

8.3 Sarbanes-Oxley

The Sarbanes-Oxley Act of 2002 is a regulation that was instituted by the US government to ensure proper financial and accounting disclosure by firms. It was passed in response to a series of corporate accounting scandals, headlined by the Enron scandal of 2001 that resulted in a decline of public trust and confidence in public financial accounting reports.

In less then two decades, Enron, an energy company based in Houston, grew to become the seventh largest company in the US. It was the proud employer of 21,000 people in more than 40 countries and one of the most successful energy companies in the world. Investors flocked to its never-ceasing good luck in raking in profits. *Fortune* magazine called Enron America's Most Innovative Company for six years from 1995 through 2000. However, in 2001, it came to light that Enron had lied about its profits and had hidden its debt in offshore companies. As more and more came out in public, investors and creditors both began to panic and detracted their investments in the company. The firm eventually filed for Chapter 11 bankruptcy in December 2001, and a criminal inquiry was started by the Securities and Exchange Commission (SEC). Investors were outraged that a company could so blatantly publish fraudulent accounts in annual reports. That this creative and systematic fraud was assisted by its accountant, the auditing giant Arthur Andersen, further put faith in the whole system at risk.

The government immediately recognized that this loss of investor confidence could lead to a general loss of faith in publicly traded companies. It, therefore, enacted Sarbanes-Oxley, which established new regulations to govern the management of publicly held companies, particularly in regard to their accounting disclosures. Sarbanes-Oxley contains eleven sections outlining responsibilities, regulations, and penalties associated with noncompliance. It places the SEC in charge of implementing rulings on requirements to comply with the law. There is a close connection between the tenets of the regulation and the issues that were raised in the Enron scandal. In essence, Sarbanes-Oxley was formulated to restore confidence in equity markets and in the integrity and accuracy of financial reporting. The most important provisions are listed below.

1. The Public Company Accounting Oversight Board (PCAOB) was established to oversee the auditors of public companies.

2. It became mandatory that all public companies examine and disclose the effectiveness of their internal controls vis-à-vis financial reporting. Independent auditors were then to attest that the disclosure by this method was correct.

3. All financial reports published by a firm were to be certified by the chief executive officers and chief financial officers, thereby making them ultimately responsible for the veracity of the report.

4. The independence of the auditor became of primary importance, with bans on involvement of the auditor with the firm for non-audit work. In fact, another

requirement of Sarbanes-Oxley was that companies listed on stock exchanges have independent audit committees that oversee the relationship between the company and its auditor.

5. Penalties for violations of securities laws were increased significantly in terms of both fines and jail sentences.

Section 404, developed by the SEC, is closely related to IT functions because it addresses "management assessment of internal controls" and requires corporations to provide evidence on the methodologies, processes, and controls they have placed to ensure the validity and accuracy of their financial reporting numbers. In particular, these financial reports refer to the annual 10-K and quarterly 10-Q filings companies. Almost all processes related to financial data involve information systems. The data and calculations used for financial reporting are stored and processed by software systems that have been built either internally or bought off-the-shelf. Thus, a technology audit to monitor and test the accuracy of these systems became a natural corollary to any management audit concerning accounting and financial reporting. In fact, PCAOB's Auditing Standard No. 2 explicitly states that "The nature and characteristics of a company's use of information technology in its information system affect the company's internal control over financial reporting." Since CEOs, CIOs, and CFOs had to sign off on financial reports, they started taking a keen interest in documenting audit trails for calculations, reporting, data sources, and in general, the accuracy and integrity of data presented on public financial reports. This meant that the IT systems and associated controls for these systems came into focus for top management in every financial services firm.

The first set of filings under Sarbanes-Oxley was done in July 2004. The benefits versus costs of compliance with Sarbanes-Oxley debate has attracted a great deal of attention, with people feeling very strongly about the law being beneficial or completely detrimental to efficient operation of the financial sector. Costs in general associated with SOX 404 (as Section 404 of the Sarbanes-Oxley Act has come to be known) have been significant. Updating information systems to include IT controls, better document management, superior auditing of data sources, storage, and calculation, and hiring of teams to implement all these controls has been very costly for companies. According to the Financial Executives International (FEI), in a survey of 217 companies with average revenue above $5 billion, the cost of compliance was an average of $4.36 million. However, this number is expected to decrease after the initial investment in systems has been made and companies move to maintenance phase. But the cost, according to some, has also been in the flight of IPOs from New York to London and Hong Kong, with companies finding the costs of meeting the regulation too prohibitive to be in the US. In December 2006, the SEC voted to lessen what Commissioner Paul Atkins called an "obsessive-compulsive mentality" in checking for lapses in controls, and to make the controls more "risk-based."[1] Regardless of how firms now scale down their efforts to implement Sarbanes-Oxley, a bare minimum of IT governance needs to be instituted and this is discussed in the next section.

8.3.1 IMPACT ON INFORMATION TECHNOLOGY

Sarbanes-Oxley Section 404 has two main tenets: (i) Reporting internal controls after having been assessed by senior management and attested by external auditors; and (ii) establishing a framework for internal controls. An internal control is any process that ensures that financial statements prepared for external purposes were produced reliably in accordance with accepted accounting principles and are accurate. These controls pertain to the maintenance, recording, and processing of data related to financial transactions, and the acquisition and use of assets (such as market data feeds) that would be considered "material" to reporting (for instance, for mark-to-market calculations). The SEC recommends the COSO (Committee of Sponsoring Organizations of the Treadway Commission) Internal Control Framework as one framework appropriate for Sarbanes-Oxley implementation.

COSO is a paradigm of how to establish integrated firmwide controls and standards in order to reduce incidence of fraudulent financial reporting. It bases its tenets on the philosophy that quality control is linked to process control, since output is produced by processes. Its goal is to create controlled processes that achieve the goals of the organization, while adhering to regulations and producing output that can be reported as correct and accurate to the public. COSO has seven components that comprise its Internal Control Framework: internal control environment, objective setting, event identification, risk assessment, control activities, information and communication, and monitoring. A phased project plan is put together by those in charge of implementing controls for those systems that participate in the generation of financial reporting. High-level requirements of the framework are as follows.

8.3.1.1 Control Environment

This is the core of the framework, the ethical foundation of establishing an environment where internal control—the discipline, structure, and integrity of business technology operations—is part of the culture of the organization. It requires senior management to set key environmental variables such as management's operating style, ethical values, and delegation of authority systems. In the case of a technology team, an IT steering committee can be set up to oversee the IT activities and make

---

[1]David M. Katz, *SEC Says Materiality Should Drive 404*, CFO.com, December 14, 2006.

sure they are aligned with business objectives. A clear hierarchy of roles and responsibilities is instituted for all technology projects: the chain of command prevents any one individual from deviating from the standards of a critical process.

8.3.1.2 Risk Assessment

Before any controls can be formulated, documented, and implemented, a thorough business analysis is required to assess the risks and sources of error that lie in the processes that are responsible for generating financial reports. This stage is called risk assessment, and the results of this study form the basis of the control activities that are put in place by management.

8.3.1.3 Control Activities

Control activities are the most important part of implementing IT controls, because these are the policies and procedures that the firm carries out to ensure that any risks to accounting errors are mitigated. They include the gamut of activities from approvals, reconciliations, and segregation of duties, all the way through the audit of operating procedures. Examples of important control activities are making sure that changes to applications are documented and conducted only under authorized supervision; all systems are secure and strict access controls are set up, including for user-developed programs such as Excel spreadsheets; and there must be extensive testing for all new applications, with test scripts documented for audit purposes. This is particularly important as changes to procedures are usually considered suspect and might be motivated by desire to hide or contort facts.

8.3.1.4 Information and Communication

Information is constantly used in producing all kinds of reports, and includes data that is generated within the organization and is gathered from sources external to it. All sources of information must be documented and must be communicated to the parties that need it for their business critical functions throughout the organization, especially if these data are involved in any financial reporting measures.

8.3.1.5 Monitoring

After internal controls have been established, they must be regularly audited and updated to ensure that they are achieving their goals and have incorporated any changes to the business. Deficiencies identified during monitoring activities must be reported to senior management, and corrective measures are implemented to bring the control processes back in line with the Sarbanes-Oxley goals. In addition, the SEC requires that such "material" weaknesses be included in the company's report on internal controls.

8.4 Basel II

Basel II, or The New Accord, is a set of regulations for risk management methodologies and capital requirements in banks. The Basel Committee on Bank Supervision (BCBS), made up of bank supervisors and central bankers from thirteen countries (Belgium, Canada, France, Germany, Italy, Japan, Luxembourg, the Netherlands, Spain, Sweden, Switzerland, the United Kingdom, and the United States), is responsible for establishing and publishing international standards for bank supervision worldwide. These regulations are implemented by the member countries through their domestic policies and laws. The Basel Accords specifically refer to capital adequacy requirements for risk management. Basel II is a revised and expanded version of Basel I, which was implemented in 1988; a revision was thought appropriate because Basel I was unable to provide recommendations in line with the varying degrees of risk faced by banks. For example, banks were expected to hold the same amount of capital, 8%, against both AAA-rated borrowers and BBB-rated borrowers. Basel II also asserts that risky assets should have 8% of minimum collateral against it. However, it gives banks more flexibility in using different credit and operational risk methodologies to weight the riskiness of an asset.[2] Basel II was published in 2004, with an updated version published in July 2006, and banks have until January 2008 to implement the framework in the US. Note that only the largest banks with a significant international presence have been deemed by US regulators subject to Basel II. This section discusses the salient points of Basel II and the impact that it will have on IT systems.

8.4.0.1 The First Pillar—Minimum Capital Requirements

The first pillar addresses the minimum requirements for keeping capital in reserve to cover assets that are lost due to bad loans and other such problems. It separates risk into three categories: market risk, credit risk, and operational risk. While market and credit risk management have been used by financial firms for some time, this is the first time that operational risk was given its own separate category. Market risk is the exposure of a portfolio of assets to a number of market movements, including changes in interest rates. Under Basel II, the requirements for calculating market risk can be found in the amendment to the capital accord to incorporate market risks published in November 2005.[3] Market risk has been on the radar for banks for many years, and many of them now have sophisticated systems that calculate Value-at-Risk (VaR) to estimate market risk. It is for credit and operational risk that new compliance checks are being recommended by the new Basel II Framework.[4]

[2]Randy Myers, *Basel's New Balance*, CFO Magazine, December 1, 2003.
[3]Amendment to the capital accord to incorporate market risks, November 2005.
[4]Basel II: International Convergence of Capital Measurement and Capital Standards: A Revised Framework, November 2005.

Credit risk is the risk that a counterparty may default on its contractual obligations. Basel II places a great deal of emphasis on calculating credit risk, including calling for a rating system that takes into account risk metrics such as probability of default and loss given default. This is known as the internal rating based (IRB) approach to credit risk. Before Basel II, there were no regulatory requirements for a framework for calculating credit risk. Operational risk is exposure to losses from deficient and inadequate internal processes. Although Basel II was insistent on separating operational risk as an important risk factor, it is vague on the measurement of this risk. This is understandable, however, given that operational risk is just coming to the forefront of risk discussions, and methodologies are still being debated on its measurement. It is expected that banks will assess these risks using quantifiable risk metrics, and then adjust their capital adequacy accordingly.

8.4.0.2   The Second Pillar — Supervisory Review Process

Supervisory review is undertaken to ensure that banks implement the frameworks for capital adequacy. It places responsibility on bank management and boards for monitoring the effective management of risk in its bank. This includes risks that were not covered under the First Pillar, such as liquidity risk. Status reports on this internal governance of the institution are then provided to a designated Supervisor. Central to the review will be a review of an Internal Capital Adequacy Assessment Process (ICAAP). For banks in the EU, Supervisors receive guidance from the Committee of European Banking Supervisors (CEBS).

8.4.0.3   The Third Pillar — Market Discipline

The third pillar increases the disclosure and reporting requirements for a bank so that regulators have a more accurate picture of the risk profile of the bank. This is particularly relevant now that banks have the option of using their own internal methodologies to estimate risk and consequent capital adequacy. Recommendations outlined in Basel include public disclosure of a bank's capital ratio and other consolidated capital adequacy figures, the bank's quantitative and qualitative strategies for managing risk exposure, and information on its accounting policies. The idea is that if the market has good information about the bank's risk profile, then counterparties will be able to factor this into their deals with the bank. In an ideal world, perfect information will lead to a perfectly competitive market.

The most important of these three pillars is the first pillar, which involves improving and expanding risk management, and this will require the most changes to current IT infrastructure in financial services firms. If there were one way to describe the technology requirements that arise from Basel II, it could perhaps be encapsulated in the phrase, "integrated risk management and reporting." In other words, across all the lines of business of a firm, risk is calculated and aggregated into an enterprise risk calculation along each of the dimensions—market, credit, and operational—and then both the methodology and the results are presented in a report. The majority of costs related to Basel II compliance will most likely be related to enhancing IT systems and integrating data across disparate systems to calculate enterprise risk metrics. Aggregating, enriching, and sourcing data from both internal and external sources is thus one of the most important IT investments that will be made as part of the Basel II undertaking.

8.4.1 IMPACT ON INFORMATION TECHNOLOGY

8.4.1.1 Data Aggregation and Consolidation

Data regarding transactions is kept in different silos across the firm. Each department often calculates its risk exposure using its own databases with data relevant to the department. To calculate risk exposure across the firm means that data across asset classes has to be aggregated and consolidated.

8.4.1.2 Counterparty Reference Data

To correctly estimate credit exposure, the bank needs correct, complete, and current counterparty reference data. This includes the hierarchy of parent/subsidiary relationship and links to positions, transactions, and credit ratings. Many banks have incomplete legal entity data and will need to enrich their data sets to meet Basel II requirements.

8.4.3.2 Integrated Risk Management

A unified view of risk across all the lines of business in a firm is the key to understanding the total exposure a bank faces. The calculations for Probability of Default, Loss Given Default, and Expected EAD for all asset classes are often used to model credit risk. These calculations require internal position data, and current and historical market data from external sources that are used both for forecasting "what if" scenarios and for back testing and stress testing of strategies.

8.4.3.3 Corporate Transparency and Reporting

Transparency and audit is very important, which means that systems should allow easy drill-down to underlying source data functionality. This is also important when it comes to drilling down from the formulae for capital and risk measurement to methodologies and source data. These audit trails and documentation can be included

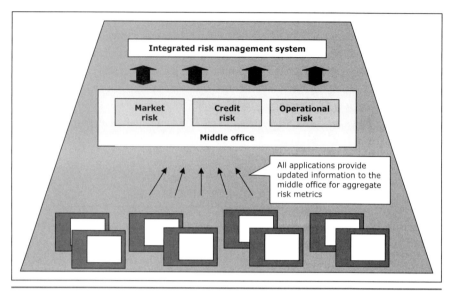

Figure 8-1 Basel II aims at having integrated risk management.

in reports to the supervisors of the bank, and in the more general public disclosure reports. See Figure 8-1.

▌ 8.5 MiFID

The Markets in Financial Instruments Directive (MiFID) is a set of regulations sanctioned by the European Commission to create a pan-European single capital market for trading financial securities, including equities, commodities, futures, fixed income, and derivatives. It aims to achieve two main goals: (i) to create a market where clients and providers have easier access to each other across Europe, thus allowing greater diversity of financial products and services for clients, and greater availability of and access to a wider variety of clients for service providers; and (ii) to ensure that this market is transparent and efficient, thereby assuring clients that they have the best price and service, and assuring service providers that their clients are legitimate. A number of different legislations have been stated under MiFID related to achieving these goals, and must be enforced by national financial regulators going forward from October 31, 2007. All financial services-related firms will be subject to MiFID regulations, including investment banks, stockbrokers, broker-dealers, portfolio managers, and exchanges. This section discusses the main features of MiFID and how the financial technology landscape will change as a result of it, including highlighting systems that will need to be overhauled and updated in order to comply with MiFID. The main features of MiFID are as follows.

8.5.0.1   Client Classification

The term "client" under MiFID covers a range of parties involved in a transaction, including professional clients, retail clients, individual clients, and other such eligible counterparties. MiFID places strict regulations on how clients are classified into each category and places responsibility on investment advisors to pay attention to client suitability for particular investment products. Clients should also be told what classification they fall under, and made aware of the level of protection that they have under MiFID.

8.5.0.2   Best Execution

MiFID has set requirements for advisors trading on behalf of their clients that they must choose the best execution for their trades, taking into account speed of execution, price, and transaction costs. The purpose of this regulation is to protect client interests and create a more efficient transparent market.

8.5.0.3   Cross-Border Passporting

Firms will be issued a MiFID passport after being authorized by the country in which they have registered their company. This MiFID passport will allow the firm to provide services to customers in all the EU member states.

8.5.0.4   Pre-/Post-Trade Transparency

Continuous order-matching systems must make the five best price levels on both the buy-side and sell-side available for everyone to see as part of pre-trade transparency. If it is a quote-driven market, then the best bids and offers of market makers must be disclosed. Once a trade has occurred, markets will have to publish the venue, time, volume, and price of share trades to the market not longer than three minutes for post-trade transparency.

8.5.0.5   Regulation of System Internalizers and MTFs

A Systematic Internalizer (SI) is a firm that holds securities on its own books and uses its vault to process orders for clients. MiFID treats these SIs as mini-exchanges and subjects them to the same pre-trade and post-trade transparency requirements as exchanges. In addition, multilateral trading facilities (MTFs) are also now under the jurisdiction of MiFID. This will create huge competition for traditional exchanges in the EU. See Figure 8-2.

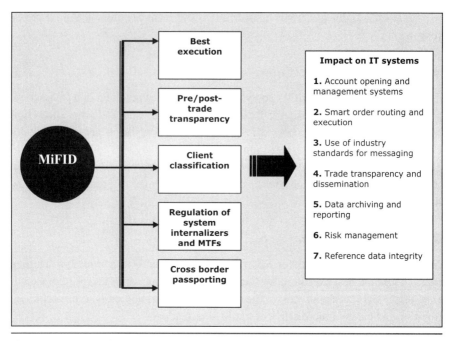

Figure 8-2 Impact of MiFID on IT systems.

8.5.1 IMPACT ON INFORMATION TECHNOLOGY

All the MiFID regulations will affect the internal systems in each of the affected financial services firms operating in Europe, but it will also affect the information and network infrastructure that these firms share. The changes will eventually lead to increased competition and lower transaction costs for financial firms aiming for a pan-Europe strategy. Thus, while initially implementation costs will be high, it represents a great opportunity for future growth and revenue for firms across Europe. This section reviews the systems and processes that will be affected by the tenets of MiFID.

8.5.1.1 Account Opening and Management Systems

Since an investment firm will have to document minimum necessary information to assess *investor suitability*, the account opening and management systems will have to be updated and streamlined. There is more focus on the client's profile and his or her experience of the relevant product or service. The impetus is to protect investor interests by forcing service providers to assess the suitability of a client for a particular product and service more thoroughly. This matching of client with product is part of the *appropriateness test* under MiFID. It first classifies clients into different categories based on initial information gathered upon account opening and then uses this information as a basis for evaluating whether a product or service is appropriate for a client. All clients will have to be informed of their classification under MiFID, and this agreement will have to be documented in the account management system.

8.5.1.2   Smart Order Routing and Best Execution

Investment firms will have to create policies that ensure that they choose the best routing and execution of client orders. They will have to share these policies with regulatory authorities as proof that they are following the MiFID directive. Best execution for the client means that effort is made to get the best price, cost, speed, likelihood of execution, and order size for the client. This will force investment firms to build order-routing systems that apply this optimization business rule after scanning all possible trade venues for the best deal. Passporting means that order-routing systems must have combined books that run across different venues and countries to take advantage of the right to do business across the EU. Algorithmic systems that have smart order-routing systems embedded in them are probably the best way to go for this regulation.

8.5.1.3   Industry Standards for Messaging

Industry protocols, such as FIX, SWIFT, and FpML, must be used for electronically communicating market and order data between systems. Systems will need to be updated to be able to accept, process, and transmit messages written in industry protocols.

8.5.1.4   Pre-/Post-Trade Data Dissemination

It is common for some firms to engage in trading between their clients, or from their own books when a client places an order, without the involvement of regulated exchanges. These SIs, for the first time under MiFID, will now have the same stature as exchanges and be subject to the same regulations. One of these regulations is making pre-trade bid/offer prices public on a continuous and regular basis. These quotes will have to be sent to an exchange for public viewing. Post-trade transparency is also now mandatory for all firms, including SIs, that must make this information (price, volume, time, etc.) public continually through public venues such as exchanges, MTFs, and data service providers. Choosing how to publish this post-trade information will be an important decision for business and technology managers.

8.5.1.5 Data Archiving and Reporting

Investment firms are required to store transaction and quote data. Transaction data must be maintained for at least five years. The enormous volume of data that must be tracked, stored, and maintained will increase exponentially for all firms that fall under MiFID's jurisdiction. Systems will have to be built to accommodate this new functionality, and, also, tools and GUIs must be built to retrieve, display, and analyze this data. Given that the data infrastructure will have to be ramped up, it is also important that redundancy and failover be kept in mind.

8.5.1.6 Risk Management

Most firms that fall under the jurisdiction of MiFID will also have to comply with the new Capital Requirements Directive (CRD) or Solvency 2. The CRD sets requirements for the regulatory capital that a firm must hold for better risk management. This means that sophisticated risk management systems need to be implemented.

8.5.1.7 Reference Data

Unique identifiers for securities that will be valid throughout the EU are required as one centralized dictionary will now be used.

8.6 Regulation NMS

The SEC has adopted Regulation NMS (National Market System), which is a set of four interrelated proposals to improve and modernize the US equity market. NMS consists of nine market centers trading over 5,000 listed securities with a market capitalization of $14 trillion. Many believe that this regulation will revolutionize US equity markets, replacing floor-based trading with electronic trading and STP. The incentive for the regulation was to address problems such as inaccessible markets, lack of price transparency, and inefficient execution. Different portions of particular rules have varying deadlines, but the deadline for completion of all phases of Reg NMS is October 8, 2007. The SEC estimates that while it will cost market centers $144 million initially to comply with Reg NMS and an additional $22 million annually, benefits to investors will be around $320 million per year.

8.6.0.1 Order Protection Rule

This rule is aimed at obtaining the best price for investors when that price is immediately accessible and can be automatically executed. It was mandated to protect investors from execution of their orders at inferior prices compared to those available in the market. *Trading centers* are therefore required to establish policies that prevent execution of orders at inferior prices (prices that are not the best bid or offer) displayed in that security in another trading center. Trading centers are exchanges, SROs, and Alternative Trading Systems (i.e., ECNs, OTC marketmakers, and any broker-dealer internal crossing network that has over 5% of the market in terms of average daily volume).

8.6.0.2   Inter-Market Access Rule

This rule facilitates uniform market access to the best prices in the market by establishment of three tenets.

■ It allows accessing quotes through private linkages rather than mandating that a centralized market infrastructure, such as ITS (Intermarket Trading System), be used. The SEC established this rule because it believes that leaving the market to create its own linkages will result in more efficiency and newer technology than depending on a bureaucratic centralized system.

■ It levels the pricing of quotations across trading centers by limiting the fee that a trading center can charge for access to its quotations. This fee is capped at $0.003 per share.

■ The rule also requires SROs to enforce practices that disallow members from displaying quotations that lock or cross the protected quotations of other centers.

8.6.0.3   Sub-Penny Pricing Rule

This rule prevents market participants from accepting or displaying orders in pricing increments smaller than a penny, unless the price of the stock is less than one dollar. This rule is meant to address the practice of stepping ahead of market prices by making the bid or ask prices more favorable in miniscule increments. The ability to step ahead gave investors who have electronic access to markets execution priority by trumping orders through sub-penny increments, which created market confusion through flickering quotes. This rule has generally been very favorably received by the market.

8.6.0.4   Market Data Rules and Plan Amendments

The Market Data Rules and Plan Amendments are amendments to the current plan that aims to increase price transparency in the market.

■ It achieves this by reallocating revenues to SROs that participate in market data dissemination plans and instituting clauses that reward those SROs that provide the most useful data (i.e., the best price quotes) to investors. Right now, the plan distorts behavior by allocating commissions primarily on the basis of number of trades, no matter how small, rather than the value of those trades. This kind of formula creates an environment for manipulative trading such as wash sales and trade shredding. A *wash sale* is the selling of a security at a loss and then repurchase of it quickly, generating revenue from two reports of quotes. *Tape shredding* occurs when a participant breaks up a large trade and reports it in smaller quotes to get commissions for a greater number of quotes.

■ The rule also broadens the participation in the governance of the market data consolidation plans with the creation of advisory committees composed of non-SRO representatives for effective monitoring of the plan.

■ Finally, the rules also give marketplaces and their members liberty to distribute market quotes themselves and gives them permission to charge fees if they wish for this service. Note, however, that market centers still have to report core data through a Securities Information Processor (SIP), such as NASDAQ. The rule also allows data to be unbundled, for instance, so that investors can choose to pay only for the depth of market data that they need.

8.6.1   IMPACT ON INFORMATION TECHNOLOGY

The technological impact of Reg NMS will primarily be felt by broker-dealers and exchanges, and not so much by buy-side firms that depend on broker-dealers and vendors to provide the technology for routing their orders to a best-execution venue. The emphasis on efficient electronic trading under Reg NMS will put smaller players that are not tech-savvy at a distinct disadvantage. In the world of marketplaces, Electronic Communication Networks (ECNs) have a lead in the ability to succeed in the Reg NMS world. However, exchanges are either buying ECNs or building their own to ramp up their ability to automate electronic trading.

8.6.1.1   Order Management and Routing Systems

Broker-dealers will need to update their order management systems to route orders to multiple market places in order to implement the Order Protection Rule. This rule requires that every system should have direct access to markets and smart order routing that executes only at best execution prices. Broker-dealers who do not have private linkages, either directly or through an extranet, will have to establish these to access protected quotes and build FIX connectivity to marketplaces if required. Order management systems must also be reworked to reject sub-penny orders.

8.6.1.2 Compliance Monitoring

All broker-dealers will have to implement systems that are equipped for real-time monitoring so that they can prove to both their clients and the government that they are providing best execution prices.

8.6.1.3 Algorithmic Trading Applications

Algorithmic trading applications will have to be adjusted to implement the sub-penny rule.

8.6.1.4 Ability to Handle High-Frequency Market Data

Broker-dealers have to build their data management systems to handle the explosion in market quote and order data that will result from Reg NMS. This means not only having the ability to store large amounts of data, including tick data, but also to ensure low-latency data access; that is, data must be acquired and processed at high speed. Market data, order status, and execution reports must also be stored in order to reconstruct the transaction if need be for audit purposes. See Figure 8-3.

8.6.1.5 Development of Private Linkages

The Access Rule requires private linkages between investors, broker-dealers, and marketplaces. All market participants will have to create linkages to multiple

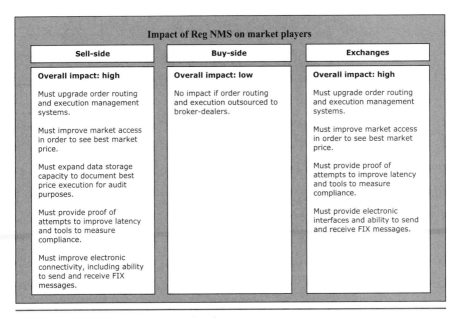

Figure 8-3 Impact of reg NMS on market players.

marketplaces. While a lot of broker-dealers already have connections to marketplaces, some of them will have to create these through outsourcing to extranets, such as Radianz and NYFIX (see Chapter 5 for details on connectivity options).

8.7   USA Patriot Act

The USA Patriot Act (officially called "Uniting and Strengthening America by Providing Appropriate Tools Required to Intercept and Obstruct Terrorism (USA PATRIOT) Act of 2001") was enacted as a response to the September 11, 2001 terrorist attacks in New York. In particular, Title III: International Money Laundering Abatement and Financial Anti-Terrorism Act of 2001, which is part of the Patriot Act, was enacted to monitor and investigate any suspicious activities that may point to money laundering and the financing of international terrorism. It was motivated by the discovery that a number of terrorist funds were laundered through banks in the US. Money laundering is the process of transforming money from illegal sources into legal and acceptable form. This is achieved through a series of financial transactions that slowly but increasingly distance the source from the funds. The IMF estimates that up to $3 trillion are laundered in the world every year. The Patriot Act is the most comprehensive regulation up to the present to prevent, detect, and prosecute any money laundering activities, especially those that may be related to terrorism.

In the US, the Bank Secrecy Act (BSA) passed by Congress in 1970 was the first legislation aimed at fighting money laundering in the country. It required that businesses keep and report records of transactions that may be deemed suspicious, such as filing Form 8300 with the IRS to report any cash payments from one buyer of over $10,000 as a result of a single transaction or two or more related transactions. In 1986, the Money Laundering Act further strengthened the law against money laundering by making it a Federal criminal offense. The Patriot Act significantly amended portions of the Bank Secrecy Act and the Money Laundering Act by adding further requirements, such as a more detailed customer identification process. It therefore placed new demands on IT systems to store more data regarding customers and their transactions, coding business rules that would send red alert flags if any suspicious financial activity occurred in a client's account, and providing regular training modules to employees to discern money laundering activities.

8.7.0.1   Anti-Money Laundering (AML) Program

Firms are expected to develop anti-money laundering (AML) programs that must include at a minimum: the creation of the post of compliance officer; ongoing employee training; the establishment of policies and controls to counter money laundering; and regular independent audits that attest to the efficacy of these policies.

8.7.0.2 Know Your Customer (KYC)

Firms must institute procedures that help them verify the identity of their customers at the time of account opening. In other words, reasonable due diligence must be performed on each and every customer to rule out identify theft fraud, money laundering, and terrorist financing. Apart from having a standard questionnaire that helps the firm identify the customer, the firm must also check that the customer is not on any published list of known terrorists, money launderers, or fraudsters as published by the Office of Foreign Assets Control's (OFAC) Specially Designated Nationals list. These lists are updated at least once a month by OFAC. Audit trails of all documentation gathered and checked for customer verification must be maintained by the firm.

8.7.0.3 Suspicious Activity Reports (SARs)

Once the customer has been included as a client, his or her transactions must be recorded and monitored and any suspicious activity reported to the authorities. Suspicious activity reports (SARs), as they are known, are reported to the Financial Crimes Enforcement Network (FinCEN), a subsidiary of the Department of the Treasury.

8.7.1 IMPACT ON INFORMATION TECHNOLOGY

8.7.1.1 Account Management

Customer account management will become relevant in two ways: due diligence before an individual is accepted as a client, and account monitoring if the individual is added on as a client. The account management system will have to verify customer identity, whether corporate or individual, using public and private databases. In particular, the data provided by the customer must be checked against the watch lists provided by regulatory agencies such as OFAC.

8.7.1.2 Transaction Monitoring

All transactions must be monitored and alerts set off based on preestablished business rules. This surveillance of accounts could be as simple as reporting a high sum of cash entering or leaving the customer's account; or as complex as reporting sudden changes in how the customer is conducting his or her business with the firm.

8.7.1.3 Online Training Modules

Regular training of all employees in the anti-money laundering laws of the country, and how to detect and report fraud, is mandated by the law. Firms will have to build online training modules with reminders sent to employees if laws have been updated and must be reviewed by them.

8.8 Synergies Between Compliance Requirements

In Section 8.2, earlier in this chapter, we discussed common objectives that government regulations and guidelines share. Unfortunately, as regulations are published with sometimes stringent deadlines, firms get overwhelmed and begin to develop IT procedures and systems for compliance in silos. The result is that time, resources, and staff are being used redundantly and operating across the firm working toward essentially the same goals. This duplication of effort and activities is a direct result of not recognizing the similarities and potential for economies of scale that come from realizing that all regulations have the same objectives more or less. This section examines how to step back and to see synergies in complying with different regulations, and in leveraging one system to meet several regulatory requirements.

To recapitulate, governments have three aims when mandating regulations for financial markets:

1. The protection of investors, individual, retail, and institutional.
2. The creation of a market that is fair, efficient, and transparent.
3. The reduction of all kinds of risk, especially systemic risk.

The business technology requirements that result from most regulations based on these objectives can be broadly put into five business categories:

8.8.0.1 Data Aggregation and Dissemination

Data is perhaps the most important part of government regulations, because it is the best way for them to monitor compliance. Thus, not only is data production important, but also the quality of data produced, and accessibility of this data by the public, are just as important to regulatory goals. Examples of data used for monitoring include more client data as required by the Patriot Act, while examples of data for market efficiency include display of all the best bid/ask quotes at any given time as required by Reg NMS and MiFID.

Applicable To: Patriot Act; Reg NMS; MiFID

8.8.0.2   Market Connectivity

Connectivity between market participants is becoming crucial to achieve better market efficiency. Nowhere is this more evident than in Reg NMS and MiFID, both of which are pushing for automated access to prices, exchanges, and pools of liquidity. Connectivity at all points of contact in the trade lifecycle is also one of the highlights of an STP environment.

Applicable To: Reg NMS; MiFID

8.8.0.3   Integrated Risk Management

One of the most important tenets of financial market regulation is to prevent risk exposure that one firm takes from threatening the stability of the entire industry. This kind of systemic risk can be the result of market, credit, or operational risk. Since financial risk is inherent in all the transactions undertaken by a financial entity, it is only when *enterprise* risk management is done that the overall risk exposure of a firm can truly be calculated. This calls for integration of transaction data across all lines of business and market data sources, which are then processed in risk management engines and produce risk metrics. Basel II's capital adequacy requirements are based on how much risk a firm has undertaken at the institutional level, that is, aggregated across all the departments in the firm.

Applicable To: Basel II

8.8.0.4   IT Governance

Operational risk management, especially as it relates to IT processes and governance, has also become a prominent factor in regulatory laws. This has come after government and industry experts have realized how every single business operation in financial services is now dependent on IT in some way or another. In essence, IT capability is no longer considered a black box that only IT personnel are responsible for; given its importance in business calculations and process flows, all the stakeholders, including senior management, are interested in and responsible for putting in adequate procedures for IT governance.

Applicable To: Sarbanes-Oxley; Basel II

8.8.0.5   Transaction Monitoring and Reporting

Better monitoring and reporting of transactions, including client data, prices, quantities, and accounting methodologies, is a running theme among almost all of the regulations. Firms have to expand their current systems to generate and store more data, and more importantly, develop reporting systems that capture the data necessary for complying with a particular regulation. If the system is built with flexibility, it can quite easily create different reports from the same set of data, depending on the requirements of the report. Not only is reporting on business-as-usual important, but one of the reports that is crucial is the one generated when unusual activity occurs. Especially relevant for tracking suspicious activities, this means that business rule engines have to be attached to each business process in the securities lifecycle, so that problems and exceptions are immediately logged, stored, and included in a report.

Applicable To: Sarbanes-Oxley; Basel II; Patriot Act; MiFID

RECOMMENDATIONS

All STP-related technology initiatives must include an analysis of current regulatory laws and how to build software systems that comply with them. Five major regulations currently affect securities operations: Sarbanes-Oxley, Basel II, MiFID, Reg NMS, and the Patriot Act.

1. Regulations are mandated to increase market transparency and efficiency, and to protect investor interests.
2. It is recommended that technology solutions be leveraged across regulatory requirements.
3. The main areas affected by current regulations are:
   A. Transparency in trade-related data
   B. Industrywide connectivity
   C. IT governance
   D. Integrated risk management
   E. Transaction monitoring

▌ 8.9 Summary

This chapter has gone over the major regulatory laws facing financial firms and intermediaries in the US and in Europe. Similar regulations to monitor and mitigate the risk in markets are being enforced in other financial centers across the world. Five main laws are discussed—Sarbanes-Oxley, Basel II, MiFID, the Patriot Act, and Reg NMS—along with their implications for technology systems; it is emphasized that compliance must always be considered when building any part of an STP system. The chapter ends with a framework for evaluating the similarities between regulations and leveraging technologies to create an infrastructure that is flexible and resilient in being compliant for multiple IT regulations.

Chapter 9

Business Continuity

▌ 9.1 Introduction

Building an integrated straight through processing environment, both inside a firm and throughout the industry, demands an infrastructure that is resilient to unforeseen disasters. A disaster can be anything from a power disruption to an earthquake to a terrorist attack. *Business continuity* and *disaster recovery*, or the ability to recover and continue critical business functions soon after the occurrence of a disaster, are crucial aspects of an STP infrastructure. After the terrorist attack of September 11, 2001 in New York, financial services firms have been focusing on building business continuity plans. They are encouraged by the government, which is keenly aware of the impact of a disruption in financial markets on the general economy. This chapter provides a detailed overview of the importance of *business continuity planning (BCP)* and provides a framework for planning quick recovery from unexpected disasters in an STP environment.

In Section 9.2, the impact of the September 11, 2001 terrorist attack in New York is discussed as an example of a disaster that exposed deep vulnerabilities in financial markets. Section 9.3 outlines how a particular firm can devise a business continuity and disaster recovery strategy for itself. While planning should be done in all departments in the firm, this chapter will focus on financial technology systems in particular. All the major milestones of creating and maintaining a business continuity plan are discussed in this section, including business impact analysis, audit checklists, service-level agreements, and testing.

While it is crucial for each firm to have its own business continuity plan, it is just as important for the industry as a whole to protect its infrastructure, since systems of each firm are intricately linked together in an STP environment. Section 9.4 examines the steps being taken by the industry as a whole to build a robust financial technology infrastructure, and how market interlinking is increasing exponentially around the world. Finally, continual testing and reevaluation of systems and plans are necessary to any business continuity plan.

9.2 Impact of Disasters on Business

After the terrorist attacks of September 11, 2001, the US equity markets were closed for four days; bond trading, including government securities trading, was disrupted for two days; and there were breakdowns and issues in the clearing and settlement mechanisms for government securities, repurchase agreements, and commercial paper. Operational failures such as these can cause liquidity bottlenecks and severely undermine confidence in financial markets. They are the result of telecommunications breakdowns, infrastructure meltdown, loss of crucial data and connectivity, and lack of a solid plan for quick disaster recovery. More than anything else, they point to the increasing interconnectivity between all participants in the marketplace, and the need for an industry-level business continuity plan as well as a firm specific plan. The SEC conducted a thorough analysis of the impact of the attacks of September 11, 2001 on the financial sector, and published a discussion note called *Summary of "Lessons Learned" from Events of September 11 and Implications for Business Continuity.*[1] This section presents some of the findings in this

---

[1] US Securities & Exchange Commission, *Summary of "Lessons Learned" from Events of September 11 and Implications for Business Continuity*, February 13, 2002.

Major disasters in recent years

Year	Incident
2001	Almost 3000 people die in the terrorist attacks on September 11th on the United States. New York's financial district is especially hard hit.
2002	SARS (Severe acute respiratory syndrome) epidemic breaks out in China and affects over 8000 people.
2003	The North East Blackout causes massive disruption as whole parts of northeastern United States plunge into darkness due to a power outage.
2004	The Asian Tsunami causes catastrophic loss of lives and infrastructure in South and South East Asia.
2005	On July 7th, a series of bomb blasts explode that are aimed at paralyzing London's public transport system.
2005	Hurricane Katrina causes large-scale devastation along the Gulf Coast of the United States, especially in New Orleans.
2007	Estonia's servers are attacked in waves by cyber-terrorists, rendering the commercial, personal, and government sites unable to function properly.

Figure 9-1   Major disasters in recent years.

and other reports regarding the impact of disasters on critical business functioning.

Given the importance of the financial services sector in New York and for the economy in general, it was considered imperative that vulnerabilities be identified and mitigated. Both the SEC discussion note and a report by consulting firm McKinsey & Co[2] point to several vulnerabilities in the current infrastructure, which were exposed in the September 11 disaster. The prominent breakdowns are briefly described below:

1. *Breakdown in payments systems*—Clearing and payments are vital to smooth running of financial markets. Overall, the payment systems worked fairly well. However, the clearinghouses suffered major disruptions, and this resulted in liquidity bottlenecks for many days, especially in the clearing of Treasury securities, which had to be suspended briefly. The Federal Reserve, along with other payment systems, stayed open for longer than usual to help facilitate the exchange of funds, allowing banks to borrow from the central bank discount window to maintain liquidity. In fact, according to the SEC, the Federal Reserve pumped $80 billion of liquidity into the market to prevent a market failure. Commercial

---

[2]McKinsey & Co., *Impact of Attack on New York Financial Services*, November 2001.

paper, a fundamental pillar of corporate credit markets, also suffered breakdowns in clearing, and the fear of illiquidity made some corporations keep high cash balances for precautionary reasons, and this, of course, further exacerbated the bottlenecks in the market.

2. *Reconciliation issues*—Reconciliation, as discussed in Chapter 7, is a crucial factor in building trust, reliability, and automation in the financial market. Some transaction records were lost; others could not be confirmed, causing distortions in balance sheets and credit disruptions across institutions in the market. Often, transactions had to be reconstructed because of the physical damage to the computers holding the information, leading to a laborious and sometimes inaccurate process.

3. *Markets closed*—Several markets remained closed for days due to the physical damage to the buildings that housed the exchanges. These included commodities and foreign exchange markets, and equity markets, all of which were closed for four days. The fact that the foreign exchange market was closed meant that foreign banks were unable to borrow US dollars from US banks, causing ripple effects in the country's balance sheet. The Federal Reserve Bank arranged for $90 billion in foreign exchange to meet this shortfall.

The three major breakdowns discussed above caused severe problems in the normal workings of financial markets in the US, with effects echoing around the world. They exposed the financial system's vulnerability to unexpected disasters. In particular, it showed that the areas below were weak spots in the way business was conducted in the market currently.

■ *Lack of business continuity planning (BCP)*—The lack of sound business continuity and disaster recovery planning was painfully obvious in the aftermath of September 11, 2001. Financial firms had quite clearly never imagined a wide-area disaster, severe physical damage to their infrastructure, and loss or inaccessibility of critical staff members. More often than not, BCP was done for breakdowns in individual systems and disasters such as fires in buildings. In fact, many firms had backups to their primary systems in nearby buildings, or even when they were located in faraway sites, the firms depended on the ability of staff to quickly travel to the backup site. With rows upon rows of buildings destroyed, all transportation systems shut down, and the whole city in a state of emergency, these BCP steps were not a feasible solution for a disaster of the magnitude of September 11. The result was that several firms were unable to get their backup systems up and running, because the backups were also destroyed, or due to the disruption in transportation, it was impossible for staff to get to alternate sites.

■ *Concentrated operations*—The concentration of operations geographically was one of the major reasons that financial systems failed after September 11. Here, the reference is to primary sites, where the majority of critical business functions were being conducted by a staff on systems in close proximity to each other. This proximity, clearly leading to efficiencies before technological advancements in telecommunications, now is not only unnecessary but also results in hazard zones. This was not only true in individual banks, but also in clearinghouses and settlement houses. Finally, as discussed in the last section, this is especially problematic when backup sites are also close to the primary sites.

■ *Interlinked and interdependent systems*—The third most important feature of the financial system that made it vulnerable to disasters was the increasing interlinking and interdependence of financial systems. Connectivity between banks, broker-dealers, exchanges, custodians, clearinghouses, and other market participants is becoming more and more common, especially as the entire industry moves towards a more STP environment. But the very fact that an STP infrastructure is being built demands attention to the vulnerability it is allowing to seep into the system with its deep interlinking and connectivity. This was obvious in the aftermath of September 11 when many financial participants suffered even when their own systems were all right, because their critical business functions depended on other systems that they were connected to in the industry.

■ *Special choke points*—The McKinsey report very appropriately pointed out that a few critical links in the financial system, special choke points, needed to be given special consideration when planning for business continuity and disaster recovery. Given the increasing interdependence of the different systems in the lifecycle of securities trading and settlement, these choke points include exchanges, clearing firms, and inter-dealer brokers. The spillover effects of a disruption in the normal workings of these links is particularly devastating for the health of the system overall.

The first step to addressing the vulnerabilities and weaknesses in the financial system is to build both an internal and an industrywide BCP, which is the subject of Sections 9.3 and 9.4 that follow. See Figure 9-2.

9.3 Firm-Level Business Continuity Planning

BCP is a methodology for planning how to deal with unforeseen disruptions in financial business processes. These disruptions are expected to be of a large scale, such as the disaster of September 11, only 5% of the time; more often than not, disruptions are minor and on a much smaller scale. These smaller disruptions may

Business continuity	
Type of risk	Unexpected event causing significant disruption in business operations.
Scope	To protect all parts of the business: personnel, physical infrastructure, IT systems, data, and business operations.
Scale	Potential negative impact of a disaster is much larger than a failure in business-as-usual operations due to minor system failure. Business continuity applies both to large-scale and small-scale disruptions.
Strategy	Business Continuity Plan (BCP) based on Business Impact Analysis.

Figure 9-2   Business continuity.

be due to short-term power outages, fires, disk drive failures, or computer viruses. Regardless, the firm must make a plan based on a thorough analysis of all scenarios that may affect its normal working, and create and test contingency and recovery measures for such situations. This section discusses what constitutes BCP for a financial services firm, focusing on financial technology systems in an STP environment. Barring concern for personnel safety and physical infrastructure, the two most important assets in an STP environment are *business workflows* and *data*. Systems throughout an organization are interconnected, constantly updating and processing information that is stored in databases. A breakdown in any process or loss of any vital data can result in loss of revenue and profits at a minimum.

There are three main dimensions to a business that are vulnerable to disasters: connectivity, data, and expertise. Businesses cannot afford to have any downtime in these three aspects of providing services to their clients. In fact, in a world where businesses need to operate 24 hours a day, the disruption of services can be fatal to a business. The goal is to provide seamless business-as-usual processing even when, behind the scenes, unforeseen circumstances have caused the regular infrastructure to break down. Solutions are therefore needed for data protection and high availability at all times, which means organized disaster recovery and graceful transition to backup systems if disaster occurs.

9.3.1   BUSINESS CONTINUITY MODELS

Traditionally, business continuity models depended on an active operating site with an associated backup site. This includes technological backup for both data processing and business operations. Because it was focused on hardware and software, it required staff to be able to move from the active to the backup site easily in order to operate from the backup servers. It limited geographic separation to allow staff to quickly access the backup sites for recovery of business-as-usual processes. As September 11 showed, this kind of geographic concentration of active/backup sites can be problematic in the case of a wide area disaster, especially if transportation systems are affected negatively. Thus, while this model is the most cost-effective, it is not appropriate for the kind of disasters firms now find themselves facing.

A business model that has recently been emerging as the model of choice is the *split operations* model. This involves nationwide or global operations, where both the technology and the staff are dispersed over a wide area, and are equally equipped real-time to pick up process functionality. It is also known as an active/active model because each site can absorb the operational responsibility for a department or for the entire firm. After September 11, a number of firms separated their technology staff to different buildings across New York and New Jersey to reduce the impact of concentrated vulnerabilities. Again, data is continually updated in real time as are software updates, and testing is done on a regular basis to make sure that both sites are always current.

Even as firms have improved their ability to have IT systems and staff dispersed over a wide area, the business staff is still usually concentrated in one area. This is true of senior management, which often all sits in one building, and also of front-office trading staff, which usually sits close to each other.

9.3.2 MAKING A BUSINESS CONTINUITY PLAN

Making a BCP for a firm can be divided into ten steps as shown below, based on the framework provided by the Business Continuity Institute.[3] Each of these steps is discussed in detail in this section. See Figure 9-3.

1. Initiation and management
2. Business impact analysis
3. Risk evaluation and control
4. Developing business continuity management strategies
5. Emergency response and operations
6. Developing and implementing business continuity plans

---

[3]The Business Continuity Institute, *10 Standards of Professional Competence,* August 2003.

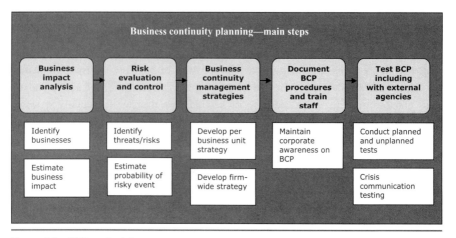

Figure 9-3   BCP methodology.

7. Awareness and training programs

8. Maintaining and exercising business continuity plans

9. Crisis communications

10. Coordination with external agencies

BCP is essentially a written collection of procedures that are developed through thorough analysis, development, and extensive testing, to prepare a firm for emergencies or disasters. It is also sometimes referred to as a *disaster recovery plan (DRP)*. Once a BCP has been developed and published, both employees and shareholders have confidence in the firm's ability to continue business with a safe and orderly recovery with an emergency management team in the face of unexpected disasters. This means that there will be minimal potential economic loss, legal liability, and loss of leadership if critical staff members are cut off from the rest of the firm. It is also important for satisfying regulatory compliance requirements for such circumstances, and in doing so, lowers insurance premiums for the firm.

The exercise of developing the BCP is headed by a team put together specifically for this purpose. The process itself involves a number of participants headed by the *project management office (PMO)*, including IT managers who manage IT operations, system administrators who are responsible for maintaining daily IT operations, the staff (Information System Security Officers) responsible for maintaining the firm's IT security activities, and the users who need the systems to conduct their job functions. In addition, one of the results of BCP will be the assignment of an emergency team that will coordinate contingency operations to remedy disruptions due to unforeseen circumstances.

9.3.2.1 Initiation and Management

A policy statement forces the planners to clearly state their vision, goals, and objectives in making a BCP. It also establishes stakeholders and sets out responsibilities among staff members for developing, implementing, and testing the plan. A BCP must really be approached the same as any financial technology project, which requires a vision statement with scope specifics, analysis, implementation, testing, and maintenance. This statement can range from one to a few pages and is really a lighthouse to make sure the project is implemented on time and on budget.

9.3.2.2 Business Impact Analysis

Business impact analysis or BIA is essential for putting a dollar value on how much it would cost a business if processes were disrupted or shut down for an hour, or a day, or a week due to any of the risks identified in the last section. It identifies the processes that are most essential and costly to lose, and in doing so, gives them highest priority when determining level of protection in a BCP. Many consider this to be the most important step of the entire business continuity exercise, as it determines all the focus of the plan.

Usually, the risk assessment stage consists of the following eight steps:

1. Establish and agree on terms of reference and scope of work with stakeholders.
2. Identify and describe key critical business processes in the firm.
3. Determine, through interviews and analysis, how the impact of disruption of business critical processes could negatively affect the firm's assets, reputation, or financial position.
4. Determine the *minimum service level (MSL)*, that is, the level to which a process must be recovered for service expectations to be met, and the resources required to achieve this level of performance.
5. Determine the *recovery time objective (RTO)* for each process, that is, the time by which the process must be recovered to its minimum service level.
6. Determine *recovery point objective (RPO)*, that is, the point to which information must be restored for business objectives to be met for each process.
7. Identify the dependencies between these business processes.
8. Summarize and present findings to senior management in a business impact analysis report.

9.3.2.3 Risk Evaluation and Control

The first step in any business continuity exercise is to do a risk analysis study, which means identifying the range of threats that the business faces. For each of these threats, a business impact analysis is conducted that calculates the cost to the business of losing operational functionality due to the realization of risk. Risk assessment not only documents all the threats that a business faces, but also does an assessment of the likelihood of each threat occurring. BCP falls under the general rubric of risk management, along the lines of credit, market, and operational risk in terms of importance. However, unlike operational risk, which is the result of systemic errors in the process flows or systems, business continuity is for disruption risk management. The controls instituted as part of BCP can be thought to be protection against three classifications of threats:

1. *Natural*—This includes natural disasters such as floods, fires, hurricanes, and earthquakes.
2. *Human*—This includes malicious computer viruses, terrorist attacks, and sabotage.
3. *Environmental*—This includes hardware and other related infrastructure problems, such as telecommunications outage, power failures, and equipment failures.

Usually, the risk assessment stage consists of the following five steps:

1. Establish and agree on terms of reference and scope of work with stakeholders.
2. Identify, through interviews and analysis, all potential internal and external threats to the firm.
3. Estimate the probability of each of these threats occurring.
4. Identify risk reduction and mitigation alternatives.
5. Summarize and present findings to senior management in a risk assessment report.

9.3.2.4 Developing Business Continuity Strategies

After the initial analysis on critical business functions and threats to these functions, the most important and extensive part of BCP begins. This is the stage where the strategies for disaster recovery are developed and documented. There are six main steps in this stage.

1. Understand the available recovery strategies and the advantages, disadvantages, and cost of each alternative.

2. Identify the recovery strategy for each business functional area.
3. Consolidate all the strategies into one document.
4. Identify off-site and alternative facilities.
5. Develop business unit strategies.
6. Obtain sign-off and commitment from management for suggested and developed strategies.

9.3.2.5 Emergency Operations and Response

Business continuity has to incorporate emergency response requirements as well. These are additional operations that will be incorporated into the BCP that are specifically responses to emergency situations, such as fire and hazardous materials leaks. These are more related to immediate threat to lives of personnel and not just mere disruption of business functions. Emergency actions can include evacuation, medical care, firefighting, and other such actions. Again, the BCP sets out clear roles and responsibilities for the individuals who will take over as Emergency Operations management and implement the procedures set out in the Emergency Response and Operation part of the BCP.

9.3.2.6 Implementing the Business Continuity Plan

Once the documentation of the plan has been completed, it must be implemented; that is, the analysis, strategies, and suggestions must now be organized into a clear set of action plans, checklists, procedures, and databases.

9.3.2.7 Awareness and Training Programs

A BCP is of little use if everyone is not made aware of it, and if the appropriate people responsible in case of emergency are not trained in their roles and responsibilities. Preparing a program to create and maintain corporate awareness is part of the BCP. There are several ways in which training can be given to employees, including computer based, classroom, scenario based, and instructional guides. Ideally, business continuity instruction would be a part of new employee orientation and current employee refresher programs.

9.3.2.8 Testing and Maintaining Business Continuity Plans

Once a plan has been completed, it must be tested, maintained, and updated with regular exercises that monitor its effectiveness and identify strengths and weaknesses. For exercises to be useful, exercise objectives and success criteria must be established. Types of exercises that would require a run-through of the BCP based on realistic scenarios include: walk-throughs, simulations, functional tests across specific lines of business, planned tests, and unannounced tests. Regular testing is a key part of a BCP and should be scheduled throughout the year. Feedback and results should be documented and kept as part of audit and control.

It is very useful as the business expands that external threats and their business impact are also reevaluated. Whenever changes are made to the plan, change control procedures must be used to make sure that changes to the published criteria are done in a logical order and then announced to all relevant parties.

9.3.2.9 Crisis Communications

While often neglected, developing an efficient plan for communicating during a crisis with employees, management, customers, shareholders, and external agencies such as local government and the media, is crucial as part of reassuring all people and agencies affected about the status of the firm's response to a crisis. Again, all essential crisis communication procedures must be clearly laid out in the BCP with members of the emergency team assigned as part of their task list.

9.3.2.10 Coordination with External Agencies

It is imperative that the BCP team also outline any procedures necessary for coordinating continuity activities with external agencies, whether government—local, state, national, or defense—or other participants in the network to which the firm is connected. The next section discusses in detail how the financial industry in the US and across the world is working on business continuity management tests and guidelines for the industry as a whole. As far as the government is concerned, this is especially relevant in large-scale disasters such as terrorist attacks and earthquakes, where the lives of citizens are at stake. In fact, there are many laws and regulations that are applicable to such situations, and the BCP team must be aware of and include these regulations in their plans. Finally, coordination with external agencies involves communication and exercises to test coordinated plans to counter disruptions in business continuity.

9.4 Industrywide Business Continuity Planning

The operations of all the participants in financial markets are now deeply intertwined. This will be particularly true as STP becomes more a reality not just internally in the firm, but also externally across all the participants in the market. Institutions coordinate everything from live data feeds to order routing, to trade matching and clearing, payment and settlement, to collateral and asset management. Such coordination means that the resilience of the entire financial system as a whole must be strengthened because failure or disruption at one link in the chain of events can adversely affect the entire lifecycle of a transaction. With the realization that financial systems are more interlinked and interdependent, industry organizations across the world, including the US, England, and Singapore, have been conducting industrywide exercises to test business continuity planning for the entire financial market.

The aim of industrywide business continuity exercises is to answer the following questions:

- How resilient is a country's financial sector; that is, how quickly can the sector recover from major operation disruption?
- Do firms across the industry plan and prepare effectively for disasters?
- What are the dependencies between firms that make it more vulnerable to a domino effect of disruption in one area?
- How can the sector improve its recovery capability overall?

Usually, a scenario is provided to the market participants with a date and time, and then everyone goes into emergency response mode. The test results are evaluated, and a report created that documents answers to the questions listed above. This section will review the major industrywide business continuity tests conducted in Singapore, the United Kingdom, and the United States, and discuss the lessons learned. However, before going to the case studies, it is useful to discuss at an abstract level the key vulnerabilities in a financial sector that is deeply interconnected.

Just as internal business functions can be divided across three dimensions, across the industry there are also the same three dimensions to business-as-usual processing:

1. *Connectivity*—all major participants are connected via a myriad of connections which, as discussed in Chapter 5, require servers and networks.

2. *Data*—without data, processes cannot be recreated by reestablishing connectivity under expert staff.

3. *Staff*—although processes are increasingly automated, expert staff, both IT and business, is needed for emergency and extraordinary circumstances.

For each of these dimensions, the critical operational components of the entire financial system that uses them must be identified. Each institution contributes to the industry infrastructure and business continuity uniquely, and an industry organization with representatives from all market participants must examine and document the role of individual firms for disaster recovery coordination. Of course, expectations will be highest for institutions whose activity affects the highest number of processes. This includes major clearing and settlement entities, such as Depository Trust and Clearing Corporation (DTCC), and other utilities that provide payment infrastructure across the industry, such as the SWIFT network. In addition, companies outside the financial services sector on which key business processes depend must also be consulted and included in an industrywide BCP. These are civil and commercial authorities such as those providing health care, telecommunications networks, and transport. Clearly, an industrywide plan is far more involved and requires more coordination and effort, but is ultimately the key to the entire sector functioning smoothly through an emergency.

Along with dividing the key dimensions of business processes among institutions, they must also be categorized according to business function. Operations that require the highest level of operational resilience because of their importance must be considered first when developing a line of defense against disasters. Thus trading, brokering, clearing, settlement, and custody will be placed higher than any other reporting communication between firms, for instance. See Figure 9-4.

Figure 9-4 shows that the trade lifecycle, as discussed in Chapter 2, touches many market participants including inter-broker dealers, exchanges, clearinghouses, and data vendors. Each of these participants is linked by a web of networks, and a collapse in any one of these due to viruses, fire, server destruction, and so forth, can break the business-as-usual processes. Data integrity and preservation is also extremely important, for this is what the connectivity is being used for in the first place. Data changes as it goes through processes, and at any given point, a snapshot of the data must be saved in case the data is lost due to any unexpected hazards.

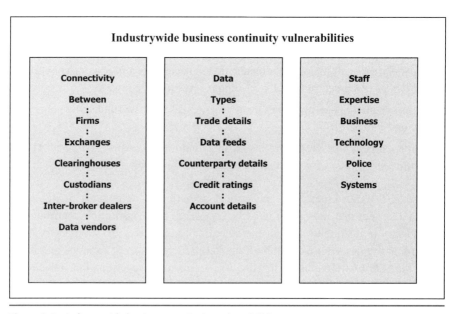

Figure 9-4   Industrywide business continuity vulnerabilities.

This means that participants immediately switch to their backup data servers if needed. Information such as account details, counterparty details, and trade transaction details are all part of important data fields that are exchanged between market participants in a trade lifecycle. Finally, while automation is the mantra of STP, a staff that is expert in finance, technology, systems, and business continuity is necessary to the normal business functionality of any industry, mainly because unexpected extraordinary circumstances sometimes occur.

All these vulnerabilities were kept in mind, and the sector's resilience to them in case of unexpected disasters was examined in the case studies discussed next.

CASE STUDY: SINGAPORE

On May 9, 2006, the Association of Banks in Singapore (ABS) conducted a large-scale real-time industrywide business continuity exercise. Singapore is considered by many to be the financial hub of East Asia and therefore a terrorist target. The scenario was as follows:

> On Tuesday 8th May, Singapore's financial industry was rocked by a major terrorist attack. Reports of explosions began filtering through at around 2:15 PM. Evacuation and cordons were set up by police and transport was halted. Key financial indices plummeted in response.

The exercise scenario was delivered in real time through news broadcast and websites as well as telephone injects simulating a broad range of customers, regulators, media, and security issues.

According to ABS, Exercise Raffles, as it was called, saw the participation of more than 170 major financial institutions in the financial sector of Singapore, including banks, the Singapore Exchange (SGX), the Monetary Authority of Singapore (MAS), as well as providers such as SWIFT and the Singapore Automated Clearinghouse. The exercise lasted from 2:00 PM to 5:30 PM and tested the resilience and coordination of participants in recovering business critical processes both internally and externally in conjunction with other firms, in the face of a terrorist attack. It was also an opportunity for firms to test their own internal BCPs.

Overall, the test was deemed successful, with the general market conditions restored to business-as-usual quickly. The Singapore Exchange Ltd., which operates the city's securities and derivatives market, did not suspend stock trading, and the Monetary Authority of Singapore, which also took part in the drill, provided S$2.2 billion in response "to demand for liquidity by the banks."[4]

---

[4]Bloomberg, *Singapore Stages Anti-Terror Drill for Financial Industry*, May 10, 2006.

CASE STUDY: UNITED KINGDOM

The UK has three financial authorities, known as UK's Tripartite Authorities: these are HM Treasury, the Bank of England, and the Financial Services Authority, and they work together to ensure the smooth, efficient, and effective running of the UK's economy and the financial sector. Recently, they have been working to ensure that there are procedures in place that will facilitate the resilience of the financial sector against an industrywide operational disruption. Together, they have established the Financial Sector Continuity website (http://www.fsc.gov.uk/), which provides information on business continuity for the UK financial sector. While the Authorities had been conducting business continuity tests, the terrorist bombings of July 7, 2005 in London pushed the government and industry into a more proactive state vis-à-vis disaster recovery planning. In 2005, the Tripartite Authorities conducted the largest industrywide business continuity test in the world and published its findings. In November 2006, the Authorities conducted another six-week test; this time the scenario was that of a flu pandemic.

Large-Scale Disaster Scenario: Over 3,000 people from 70 organizations participated in the Marketwide Exercise of 2005. A major disruption due to a terrorist attack was simulated to test the response, communications, decision-making, and coordinated recovery of the sector. Every dimension from financial markets and systems to civil contingency responses and media was under examination in the test. Planning the scenario under the sponsorship of the Tripartite Authorities involved the consulting firms KPMG and Crisis Solutions Ltd., and representatives from all the key financial and civil organizations in the country. As in Singapore, which incidentally based its scenario on this exercise, the scenario was broadcast via websites and media to participants who then had to react to the situation in an organized manner. The Authorities deemed the test was a success in that the market was able to continue functioning, with participants putting all their business continuity plans into action and the civil authorities such as Transport for London also implementing their emergency strategies. In a post-test questionnaire,[5] 90% of the participants stated that the exercise increased or validated their understanding of the marketwide response process. The exercise reinforced the importance of industrywide tests in strengthening the financial sector against unexpected disasters.

Flu Pandemic Scenario: Around 70 firms participated in the November 2006 test, including key infrastructure providers such as payments, clearing and settlement, and the main exchanges. The scenario simulated the first five months of a flu pandemic, and participants assessed how they would cope as the pandemic worsened. Of course,

---

[5] KPMG LLP (UK), *UK Financial Sector Market-wide Exercise 2005*, 2006.

the most obvious disruption would be caused by rising levels of absenteeism among employees in this case. Early results indicated that overall, the financial sector had controls in place for such an event that would allow it to be able to sustain its core services. However, it was highlighted that considerations such as key staff members working from home needed to be incorporated into business continuity planning.[6]

HEDGE FUNDS

Studies estimate that the number of hedge funds in the US is over 9,000. Even though these hedge funds manage large sums of money, most of them lack the IT infrastructures of large securities firms. The question of who is managing the disaster recovery of the mission critical data and systems of hedge funds has traditionally been neglected.

However, large hedge funds have become aware of the importance of BCP and are paying more attention to their infrastructure and process resiliency. Of course, this applies to funds that have over $1 billion under management; note that most hedge funds are much smaller and will continue to pose a threat to industrywide business continuity unless they are pressed to make disaster recovery plans.

CASE STUDY: UNITED STATES

Large-Scale Disaster Scenario: Just as the UK has the Tripartite Authorities looking after the general safety and health of the financial sector, the four associations—The Securities Industry Association (SIA), the Bond Market Association (TBMA), the Futures Industry Association (FIA), and the Financial Information Forum (FIF)—have together been working on building the resilience of the US financial sector against disasters. On October 14, 2006, a second annual industrywide business continuity test was conducted, this time on a larger scale than the one the previous year, involving more participants and more business processes. Again, the aim of the test was to evaluate the ability of primary security market participants to operate during a significant emergency of some kind. It involved more than 250 firms, including buy-side and sell-side firms, exchanges, service bureaus, clearinghouses, and other industry utility providers, each of which demonstrated that it could continue functioning by switching to backup sites and using business continuity communication and recovery

[6]The Financial Services Authority, *Resilience Benchmarking Project*, Discussion Paper, December 2005.

procedures. Product groups and business processes covered included components for equities, fixed-income, options, futures, settlements, and money markets.

In the test, which simulated over 80% of normal market trading volume, all the firms and infrastructure providers were able to connect simultaneously when the emergency was announced by utilizing backup data centers, alternative trading sites, and emergency management teams. In doing so, they were able to continue business-as-usual and to place test orders, receive executions, and conduct settlement and payment interactions. According to the report published after the test, the test achieved a 95% overall success rate.

Pandemic Scenario: In March, 2007, the Government Accountability Office (GAO) released a report[7] based on a year-long study of the resilience of financial markets in the US to disasters. The GAO study concluded that the country's seven critical exchanges, clearing organizations, and payment processors had taken steps to improve their ability to recover from unexpected disasters. These included steps such as increasing the distance between primary and backup sites for operations and clearing. However, it found that these organizations were ill-equipped to handle a major pandemic in which there would be a great deal of pressure on telecommunications infrastructures. It urged financial services firms to increase their efforts to create business continuity plans and conduct disaster recovery tests particular to pandemic scenarios.

RECOMMENDATIONS

The development of a comprehensive BCP is important to ensure operations are not significantly disrupted in case of a disaster such as a terrorist attack or pandemic. As far as possible, operations—including staff, IT systems, and databases—should be dispersed over multiple sites covering a wide geographical area.

1. A solid BCP must be prepared based on:
   a. Estimation of probability of a disaster
   b. Business impact of the disaster
   c. Recovery strategy from the disaster
2. Staff must be educated and trained in BCP procedures.
3. Firms must participate in industrywide disaster recovery tests as systems in different organizations are interlinked.

---

[7]United States Government Accountability Office (GAO), *Financial Market Preparedness*, March 2007.

9.5   Summary

This chapter discusses the salient parts of a BCP, which constitutes a strategy for recovering from sudden and unexpected disruption of critical business functionalities. Business continuity and disaster recovery became more important after the occurrence of the September 11, 2001 terrorist attacks in New York, which led to widespread failure in financial systems. Developing a business continuity and disaster recovery plan requires setting aside resources and treating the development of the plan as a project for the firm. Once the analysis has been conducted, and strategies have been formulated, the plan must be tested using simulated emergency scenarios. These scenarios are also important when it comes to industrywide testing, which has become more of a focus recently as firms in financial sectors across the world become more deeply interlinked.

Chapter 10

Virtualization and Grid Computing

10.1   Introduction

Virtualization and grid computing are twin technologies that are fast becoming the most watched technologies in the securities industry. This book has discussed how STP is achievable within the framework of SOA. But today's competitive market environment calls not just for automation, but automation that is scalable, flexible, and able to perform at high speed and performance. The answer lies in virtualization and grid computing, which can turn an SOA infrastructure into a powerhouse that can handle the demands of a 24/7 business that spans markets across the globe. This chapter focuses on how to extend the capabilities of a firm's internal STP infrastructure with virtualization and grid computing.

Virtualization is the decoupling of all application logic from the hardware on which this logic resides. It treats the representation of a hardware resource like an infrastructure resource, much as SOA treats application logic like a software service. Now several virtual servers can exist in one physical server box, serving multiple applications, resulting in significant cost savings for an organization. Virtualization allows this separation of workloads on one machine very effectively and is probably the most popular use of the technology. Grid computing takes this notion of virtualization and abstraction of infrastructure resources further, and applies it to spread computing needs over several disparate machines to meet one business goal. So instead of one server being shared by several applications, grid computing is about having one application run over several different servers. The basic idea is the same: using the virtual layer that exists between applications and hardware resources to intelligently allocate resources. Grid computing distributes the computing requirements of a particular application over a set of computer nodes throughout the enterprise. It achieves this by coordinating the parsing and reassembling of a program's computational needs through a master coordinator program. There has been much debate over the differences between virtualization and grid computing. However, at a fundamental level, the two technologies are similar in their approach and their value. In fact, this book treats grid computing as an extension of the virtualization concept.

Section 10.2 introduces the basic concepts of virtualization and grid computing, including its synergies with SOA. Section 10.3 describes how firms in the securities industry can specifically benefit from the power of virtualization and grid computing. Finally, while the benefits are enormous, the costs and ease of implementation of these technologies must be considered, and are reviewed in Section 10.4.

▊ 10.2   Virtualization and Grid Computing Basics

Virtualization enables the optimization of IT infrastructure. By decoupling the hardware from the operating systems on which applications are run, virtualization allows more efficient use of IT resources. It was first introduced in the 1960s to partition mainframe computers, which were a scarce resource and users wanted to utilize as much of the hardware as possible. However, with the introduction of smaller computers, such as PCs and servers, the need for virtualization was not felt as strongly and its use fell off significantly in the 1980s. In recent years, IT management has again begun to see the value of this technology as issues of underutilization and mismanagement of resources have come to the forefront. The trend toward virtualization was helped when vendors such as VMware, Xen, and DataSynapse began to bring products to the mainstream market that helped firms implement virtualization across the enterprise.

The addition of a virtual layer between applications and hardware resources has two immediate benefits:

- More efficient use of resources as multiple applications can be served by one machine. This combats the traditional problem of *server sprawl*, where new machines are added every time new system development takes place. By consolidating multiple servers in one machine, organizations can reduce costs by as much as 30%.

- Better framework for business continuity as the technology allows quick switching of back-end hardware without disruption of the client interface. This is because virtualization can reduce all the information on a server to a set of files that can be restored quickly on any other machine.

10.2.1 LEVELS OF VIRTUALIZATION

Virtualization is the abstraction and encapsulation of infrastructure resources into logical units that can be accessed via a virtual layer. This section discusses the six main levels of virtualization that are used in different ways to pool resources and create a scalable, flexible infrastructure for quick and efficient access to services.

10.2.1.1 *Server Virtualization*

Business applications usually have servers dedicated to them. The existence of these silo servers results in servers being grossly underutilized because most applications rarely use the entire capacity of the server. Server virtualization allows several servers to exist on one machine by enabling multiple virtual operating systems to run on a single physical machine. This is done by partitioning the server into multiple virtual servers. In essence, the client applications always get the sense of a single large server, whether this means that several servers exist on one machine or on separate machines at the back end.

10.2.1.2 *Operating System Virtualization*

Virtualization of operating systems allows a single computer to accommodate several different operating systems, such as Windows, Mac, Linux, and so forth, each running in isolation. This kind of flexibility on a single machine requires partitioning of the hardware. A virtual machine monitor or hypervisor is needed to ensure that all the virtual machines that are hosted on a machine are running efficiently and do not adversely affect each other. The open source Xen is one such virtual machine monitor which is quite popular for OS virtualization, and which along with VMWare and Microsoft Virtual Server are the three leading vendors for this technology.

10.2.1.3 Storage Virtualization

Storage virtualization is one of the most commonly used virtualization categories. It allows several storage devices to be perceived as one single unit. Behind the scenes, the storage is parsed out efficiently and effectively among storage facilities. This kind of virtualization is usually employed in what is known as a storage area network (SAN), which is a complex network of storage devices with files that have to be archived and backed up. The virtual console simplifies the work of the storage administrator by abstracting away the details of the complexity of the SAN.

10.2.1.4 Network Virtualization

Virtual networks, such as VLANS (Virtual Local Area Networks), have been making the monitoring and management of all the servers across a network easier and more efficient. A VLAN is a network of computers that appear to be connected and are treated as one resource pool when, in fact, the computers may be physically connected to different parts of a LAN. These parts of the LAN can be configured and managed via a central console using an abstract virtual layer over the network. This makes it far easier to manage the network and to move computers around physical locations.

10.2.1.5 Application Virtualization

A natural extension to the hierarchy of virtualizations would be application virtualization, which is essentially the standard Web Services paradigm. This book discusses the idea of services that are packaged as on-demand services, which can be invoked via standard messages, in Chapter 3, Service-Oriented Architecture. Application virtualization takes the notion of Web Services communicating across an Enterprise Bus, or virtualization layer, and couples it with server virtualization and other kinds of virtualization, making it into a completely flexible global virtual IT architecture. Vendors such as Data Synapse provide this kind of cohesive coherent framework for virtualization at several levels from hardware to application software.

10.2.1.6 Data Virtualization

Data is a pervasive and vital commodity across all lines of business for a firm. Data virtualization is the creation of a virtual access layer to a whole set of different database management systems (DBMS) which allow an application to access a myriad variety of data. This kind of information virtualization is invaluable as data usually exists in silos across the enterprise, resulting in redundant storage of the same data. It can also provide a unified interface to several different central data warehouses that store market reference data.

10.2.2   GRID COMPUTING

Grid computing enables and enhances virtualization by using the virtual layer to combine infrastructure resources across disparate platforms to serve one business goal. Virtualization is the separation of a resource from the underlying physical infrastructure. It is *hardware-independent*, putting a layer of abstraction—a virtual layer—between the hardware and the resources and services that use it. This is applicable to the gamut of hardware infrastructures—servers, networks, desktops, laptops, and so forth. This insertion of a virtual layer or decoupling of hardware and software is carried out behind the scenes and therefore never causes any disruption at the client interface. The user experience remains the same, but at the server side, the IT manager is able to partition or pool different hardware resources for the application service needs.

In a grid environment, applications are separated into smaller programs that are parsed out to different resources on a network of computing resources (also known as *nodes* on the grid). Then, they are reassembled from all the nodes into one coherent result. This entails a master system that allocates and tracks resources continually, optimizing resource utilization and matching demand and supply of resources. In grid computing, this method of communication between the master coordinator and the other individual nodes commonly uses Web Services. Thus, the grid is responsible for intelligently and dynamically matching application demands with available hardware resources. The result is the creation of a virtual environment, where services are accessible and executable everywhere, enabling ubiquitous processing.

The grid can leverage any resource for processing power—idle desktops, underutilized servers, and so forth. Now applications have all the computing resources of the firm at their disposal, whether that resource is the computer sitting idle in the next-door office or in the Tokyo office thousands of miles away. Either way, the process is completely invisible to the user. In using the grid, the company is able to utilize unused resources immediately, adding power, speed, and scalability to applications. See Figures 10-1 and 10-2.

Until recently, it was too costly to implement virtualization and grid computing that would match demand and supply for resources across the enterprise, but now, virtualization has come to the mass market. In fact, banks have been leveraging this

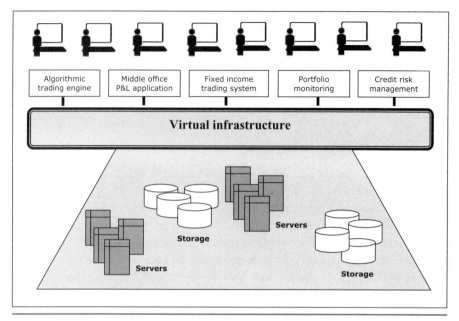

Figure 10-1 The virtualization infrastructure.

technology for a few years now, and are extremely pleased with both the cost efficiencies and increased computing power that virtualization has brought them. In addition, the shared infrastructure is very useful for business continuity and disaster recovery, because resources have been set up to be shared and easily switched from one point to another in the entire network.

The advantages of grid computing can therefore be summarized as follows:

- *Simplification*—Complex networks are simplified through a virtual layer that directs resources for data, server, and application management across the entire network.

- *Computing power*—Computations are faster given the additional power that comes from leveraging servers throughout the firm.

- *Scalability*—By decoupling lines of business from specific IT resources, virtualization allows idle resources to be utilized so that a firm can quickly and effectively expand operations without having to buy or build new infrastructures.

- *Cost efficiency*—There are significant cost advantages to pooling all the resources across the enterprise.

10.3   Applications for the Securities Industry

There are many business problems and goals faced by the securities industry today that are effectively solved and met, respectively, by using virtualization and grid computing. This section highlights some of the most relevant applications of virtualization in the current market environment.

10.3.1   HIGH PERFORMANCE COMPUTING (HPC)

Banks are constantly pricing, forecasting, optimizing, and managing the risk of assets in their portfolios. Often, these mathematical calculations are computationally intensive tasks. In the industry, this is referred to as supercomputing or high performance computing (HPC). A large investment bank, for instance, computes several hundred thousand derivatives trades each day, calculating profit/loss and risk for thousands of market scenarios. Usually, Monte Carlo simulations are used for this analysis, which is a brute force way of data mining and then predicting and forecasting metrics. Without this kind of analysis on a continual basis, the bank would not have the knowledge to calculate its risk exposure.

Monte Carlo simulations, used by almost all securities firms in one way or another, are a very common pricing and risk management technique deployed by the middle office. A Monte Carlo simulation is essentially a randomized scenario analysis. By looking at historical data, a distribution of prices is constructed and different parameters, such as interest rates, that may be causing or correlated with the changes in price, are discerned. Then, by shifting these parameters up or down, traders and risk managers look for extreme or tail events that may raise the exposure of the portfolio to unacceptable levels. But to do this correctly, the simulation involves tens of thousands of evaluations to get enough data to build a curve.

Banks have become used to running these simulations serially on a server. Sometimes, these simulations are run in overnight batch processes. However, given that these computations are vital for traders to make on the spot decisions on buying and selling securities, by the time these reports come through, they are outdated for the original purpose of having them. There is a need across all large sell-side firms to have a faster way of performing these computation-heavy analytics. Getting analytics on prices and risk exposure within minutes can be worth millions of dollars to a firm. However, these analytics are often so computation heavy that they can take up to hours, rendering themselves almost useless in a high pressure competitive environment where every second counts.

Banks have been employing grid computing successfully in areas of complex equity, currency, and fixed income derivatives products to speed up the results (sometimes up to hundreds of times faster) of mathematically intensive calculations. Using grid computing is a good option for running computation-heavy programs, such as Monte Carlo simulations, since these simulations can be spread over several nodes in a grid. This speeds up the computation as simulations occur in parallel instead of one server processing all the simulation scenarios. In addition, this is a more cost-effective way for the bank to run computational programs, because adding on cheap small servers is far cheaper than buying a larger, more expensive server. In fact, all the initial success of grid computing was really due to its ability to enhance the computational power of analytics engines in banks.

Banks that have successfully used grid technologies to improve their computing power for derivatives pricing and analytics significantly include BNP Paribas, which deployed DataSynapse's Grid Server to support the complex pricing and risk models in its UK structured-credit department. Across the board, the response by senior management in these banks has been that their computing needs were met more than adequately with virtualization. But it is not just the fact that the current infrastructure can do this computational heavy-lifting now, but that the improvements in speed are astronomical. Merrill Lynch found that installing a grid infrastructure in 2005 resulted in a 200% increase in the speed by which exotics are priced.[1] In fact, Merrill Lynch was so pleased with improvements in performance due to virtualization that in 2006, it set up a Grid Computing Center of Excellence to provide firmwide guidance and vision for virtualization across the board in the enterprise.

10.3.2   EFFICIENT USE OF RESOURCES

A large investment bank can have up to 30,000 desktops, almost 10,000 servers, and over 50 offices worldwide. Usually, when personnel go home, these resources are lying idle until the next morning. More often than not, IT resources are utilized only up to one-third of their capacity. Senior management feels frustrated that it keeps adding hardware and IT infrastructure whenever new requirements come up, but it is unable to effectively leverage the IT investments it has already made. Thus, better use of existing resources by efficiently using IT investments to the full extent is a concern among banks, which are trying to cut costs as competition in the market increases and squeezes profits.

JP Morgan proved a leader in implementing virtualization technology with the Compute Backbone (CBB) project that it set up in 2002.[2] This grid infrastructure

---

[1]Tim Clark, *Merrill Lynch Drives Efficiency Through Grid Computing*, Wall Street & Technology, May 15, 2006.

[2]Paul Allen, *Banks Take Their Places on the Grid*, Wall Street & Technology, May 15, 2006.

is installed in London, Asia, and New York, and supports multiple applications across various lines of business, including global risk management and derivatives pricing analytics. When JP Morgan started the Computing Backbone project, it was impressed with, among other benefits, the fact that hardware utilization went up significantly, from an average of about 15% before the project was started to almost 70% within a year.[3] This meant that the service charge to the business was being cut in half. Service charges are calculated per month on a per CPU basis, and the reduction in service charges translated into millions of dollars of savings per line of business. These cost efficiencies are a direct result of better utilization of resources across the firm. Grid computing, according to some estimates, can improve server utilization from 15% to up to 90%. This means that rather than spending millions of dollars on expanding server capacity when new products and services are developed in a bank, the CIO can rely on getting the same requirements fulfilled in-house using existing resources. Not only is this cost-efficient, but management sees greater returns on the original investments in any technology infrastructure, and shorter time to production when existing resources are used for new services. Finally, virtualization and grid computing have found a way to use the thousands of desktops that sit idle when personnel switch off the lights to go home for the night. Just by using the CPU capacity of these idle desktops at night, the bank can increase transaction speed and enhance the computing power and reporting requirements of the firm.

The question arises on how different lines of business will pay for their use of a virtual infrastructure. The metric to assess costs is known as *total cost of ownership (TCO)*. TCO reflects all aspects of purchase, utilization, and maintenance costs associated with any investment in computer software and hardware. This depends on their service level agreement (SLA) for that shared resource.

10.3.2.1 Prioritizing Computing Requests

As requests for high-performance computing rush toward the grid from all directions in the bank, the question arises of how the grid can prioritize the requests coming to it. Wachovia has developed a methodology of allocating computing resources depending on the value-added in revenue or risk mitigation that the requesting application provides to the bank.[4] If, for instance, a request comes from a highly mission critical application that affects the bank's bottom line, it will be immediately directed by a service management module to a server that provides higher throughput. The Azul server is an example of the kind of high-end server that processes requests at incredibly high speed.

---

[3]Paul Allen, *Banks Take Their Places on the Grid*, Wall Street & Technology, May 15, 2006.
[4]Penny Crosman, *Wachovia Delivers High-Performance Computing Through a Services-Oriented "Utility,"* Wall Street & Technology, March 19, 2007.

10.3.3   DATA VIRTUALIZATION

Chapter 6, Data Management, discussed the many challenges that face all players in the securities markets today. Organizations have to find a way to manage and store larger volumes of market and trade data from multiple sources. In addition, they also have to create an architecture in which this data can be accessed quickly by applications across the enterprise. One way to achieve this low-latency data infrastructure is by using data virtualization. Data virtualization is the creation of a middle-tier *data layer* that virtualizes all the disparate data sources and data types (e.g., XML, relational data). Such a middle-tier data access layer is called an Enterprise Data Fabric (EDF), and includes building multiple interfaces (data abstractions) for data access and data caching for low-latency data access. It extends the SOA framework to data resources and delivers a distributed data infrastructure that enables real-time delivery. One of the leading vendors used by some securities firms in this space is GemStone Systems.

10.3.4   BUSINESS CONTINUITY

The fact that resources can be quickly moved through a central system monitoring resource availability means that as soon as there is a problem with one server or data center, the virtualization infrastructure easily moves the application to the next available resource. This is obviously very helpful in complying with business continuity requirements that demand high availability and graceful failover at all times. When the Chicago Stock Exchange implemented grid technology, it found that availability was one of the advantages that it had along with cost savings and more processing power. Alongside the ability to leverage relatively inexpensive hardware, with the cost savings and scalability potential that produces, availability also is an advantage.[5] Now, the stock exchange can easily replace one server for another behind the network interface, without clients ever feeling any impact of network difficulty.

10.3.5   SCALABILITY FOR GLOBALIZATION

A large bank can have trillions of assets that are managed by offices in dozens of countries; its needs are constantly increasing as it offers new products and services to clients, and it faces new compliance requirements from the governments in every location. Facing significant growth rates in certain lines of business, banks are deciding to use virtualization to achieve scalability. With the introduction of more

---

[5]Paul Allen, *Banks Take Their Places on the Grid*, Wall Street & Technology, May 15, 2006.

interconnected networks both within a country, such as the United States, or between countries, as in the European Union, firms now have an unprecedented opportunity to reach a higher volume of clients. However, this means that they must be able to scale their operations quickly to meet expanding demand. Given the current tendency of firms to utilize their resources in silos, this essentially means throwing a lot of money at additional hardware, which is costly. The idea of virtualization creating a grid of resources that spreads over products, services, and locations, the notion of a *global* infrastructure, is very attractive to firms that are expanding into Asia and the European Union.

10.4   Cost, Implementation, and Issues

While the last section established the business value of using virtualization and grid computing, the only way to establish whether an investment in the technology is worth the money is to do a cost benefit analysis. This section attempts to do a back of the envelope cost benefit analysis by examining the advantages and issues that face a virtualization implementation.

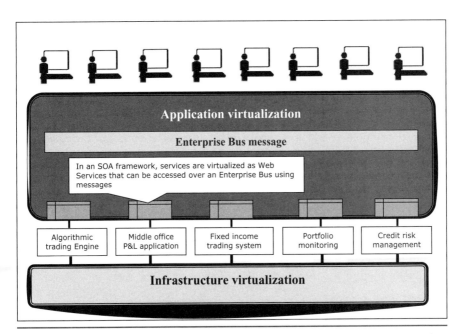

Figure 10-2   Applications are virtualized as services that can be accessed via a WSDL interface using SOAP messages sent over an Enterprise Bus message.

10.4.1 IMPLEMENTATION AND COST SAVINGS

10.4.1.1 Quality Vendor Solutions

For the first time, virtualization has become an option for everyone in financial services because the technology has become mainstream with a number of vendors offering high-quality solutions. Firms can choose to invest as much as several million dollars or as little as a few hundred thousand dollars, and have vendors cater to their requirements and budget. Not only are there more grid vendors available, but integration between grid and software vendors has improved over time as well. HSBC found, for instance, that integration between its credit trading platform Calypso and grid technology DataSynapse was relatively easy.[6] Leading vendors for virtualization include VMWare and Xen, while DataSynapse and Platform Computing are leaders in grid computing software.

10.4.1.2 Compatibility with SOA

One of the great advantages of virtualization and grid technologies is that it is perfectly compatible with SOA, which is the recommended architecture for implementing an STP system. Application virtualization, as discussed in Section 10.2, is very similar in concept to Web Services in SOA, that is, packaged discrete services that can be invoked via interfaces defined in a virtual layer or enterprise bus. Firms are currently looking into Open Grid Services Architecture (OGSA), which describes an architecture for grid computing that can be used in the context of an SOA framework, especially Web Services technologies.

10.4.1.3 Power Savings

One of the costs associated with having hundreds of servers is the electricity bill from air-conditioning, which is needed 24/7 during summer to cool the equipment. As servers are virtualized and serve multiple applications, the number of servers used can decrease dramatically, leading to significant reduction in electricity costs. Saving on power bills has become an important issue for Wall Street, as management begins to assess the computational capacity of a server per kilowatt of power. A whole new generation of servers have emerged that not only process more per unit of energy, but also have mechanisms of cooling down that reduce the cost of air-conditioning in data and storage centers. Vendors such as Verari tout the combination of superior performance and savings that these new servers and server racks provide (see the "Data Centers" gray box for the definition of server racks).

---

[6]Olivier Laurent, *Networks: A Wider Grid*, Waters, March 1, 2006.

10.4.1.3.1 The Green Grid

There has been a general push toward energy savings given the recent worldwide focus on environmental concerns. Server makers, such as VMWare have joined a nonprofit organization called The Green Grid (http://www.thegreengrid.org/), which aims at improving how efficiently energy is consumed at data centers. Large banks are contributing to energy savings, perhaps more motivated by cost savings than the green revolution, by increasing their use of virtualization software that allows one server to be used for multiple applications.

DATA CENTERS

The majority of large organizations keep their servers in a *data center*; in fact, for business continuity, one organization may have more than one data center. A data center, therefore, is a physical location—ranging from one room to an entire building—where mission critical computer systems are located.

Servers in a data center are usually kept in an equipment framework known as a *rack*, by securing each server in one of the many mounting slots in the rack. Racks are thus designed to hold multiple computer servers. The advantage of using a rack is that it allows consolidation of network resources for multiple servers and provides an organized way to store servers.

Because so many power-dissipating servers are physically located close to each other when in a rack, data centers must install air-conditioning to cool the atmosphere. Without the cooling, the electronic equipment would begin to malfunction because of excessive heat and humidity.

The market saw the emergence of *blade servers*, which are successful in allaying this problem of excessive power consumption per unit of processing capacity. A blade server is essentially an electronic circuit board that can function fully as a computer and includes processors, network connections, and memory. Several blade servers can slide into existing servers, providing a more cost-efficient form of the traditional server box.

10.4.1.4 Cost Trade-Offs

There are enormous cost advantages to implementing a grid technology. A 20-node grid is substantially cheaper than a 20-CPU single machine, which would be far more expensive—up to four to ten times as expensive. However, do note that the single machine will probably have greater speed than the 20-grid node, but this difference may not be large enough to justify the extra cost of a single high-cost large server. For example, grid software may cost up to $100,000 a year to license, while a 20-CPU machine can cost up to one million dollars.

10.4.2 ISSUES

10.4.2.1 Security

Authentication and security is a leading concern for lines of businesses that agree to come on board to a global virtual infrastructure in which resources can be shared. Whenever equipment, data, and CPU power is pooled, the question of who will manage and administer the master system that choreographs resource allocation is always of concern to everyone who participates in the technology. In addition, authentication now needs to be conducted at multiple nodes in the grid.

10.4.2.2 Lack of Standards

The lack of industry standards for everything from an industry definition of a grid to data provisioning protocols is proving problematic for universal adoption of virtualization technology. In fact, a report by Celent calls the lack of standards the biggest obstacle to further spread of grid computing in the industry.[7] Two industry standard bodies, the Global Grid Forum and Enterprise Grid Alliance, merged in June 2006, and it is expected that this merger will push the establishment of standards within a year or two. Both groups are consortiums of vendors and customers working to set standards for accelerated adoption of grid technologies in commercial data centers. With specifications becoming public and standard, one expects grid technologies to become more interoperable and overall costs of projects to go down.

10.4.2.3 Organizational Resistance

10.4.2.3.1 Sharing Resources

It is often difficult to convince departments to share resources in organizations that are used to having resources allocated solely for their IT needs. Server virtualization, for instance, partitions one physical server into several virtual servers that can be utilized by a myriad of applications, and dynamically reallocates resources to applications that need it at a given time. But people used to having servers dedicated just to their operational needs get very nervous at this, and fear that their applications will suffer from this sharing of resources. One way of convincing them is to educate personnel about virtualization and have a contractual service level agreement that always ensures minimum computing capability to be channeled to their applications. This way, wary managers know that, if anything, they will benefit from virtualization by getting more computing power, not ever less, than what they already have.

Similar issues arise when business units' are faced with the idea of data virtualization, which creates a layer of abstraction between physical data servers and the

---

[7]Celent, *Grid Computing: A Guide for Financial Services Firms*, February 2006.

applications that access them. Internal politics makes individual units careful about relinquishing control of data, CPU, or any other IT infrastructure that they have invested in to other departments in the firm.

10.4.2.3.2 Assigning Costs

The question of return on investment brings the interesting and relevant question of how different departments will be charged for resources given that now everyone shares a global resource infrastructure. Given that the bonuses of staff depend on profits that are calculated after subtracting costs from revenues, the question of assigning costs to particular departments will continue to be a touchy subject, and one that will have to be negotiated carefully between all the users of a virtualization infrastructure.

10.4.2.3.3 A New Computing Paradigm

The impact on the development and technology team itself cannot be underestimated. A significant shift in skill sets will have to occur as administrators and programmers are trained in the technology of grid computing. Often, a bank will face resistance by the IT team that prefers to leverage its current skills rather than learn new computing paradigms. It will be up to technical managers to arrange workshops for employees to learn about virtualization, and get them to feel comfortable working with the new vendor solutions and technologies.

RECOMMENDATIONS

The needs of today's global 24/7 trading environment, such as high-speed high-computing algorithms, puts great pressure on firms to increase their computing resources. Virtualization and grid computing are the recommended technologies to improve and efficiently utilize the physical infrastructure of the firm.

1. Compatible with SOA.
2. Particularly relevant for:
   A. High-performance computing
   B. Resource utilization
   C. Scalability
   D. Business continuity
3. Proven to significantly improve computing power and increase efficiency.
4. Can be implemented in just one department or across the firm.
5. Availability of quality vendor solutions in the market.

10.5 Summary

Virtualization and grid computing are becoming increasingly popular on Wall Street, which is struggling to expand computing power and curtail costs at the same time. In fact, many banks have successfully implemented various levels of virtualization in their IT infrastructure. The combination of virtualization and grid computing serves three business uses: (i) it makes the general IT infrastructure more *flexible* and simple, by creating access to software and hardware resources through user-friendly interfaces, regardless of where these resources may reside (this is in line with the SOA and Web Services paradigm); (ii) it *utilizes resources* that are lying idle for processing that needs more power, such as simulations for Monte Carlo analysis in risk calculations; and finally, (iii) by its abstract flexible architecture, it allows firms to *scale* their processes as transaction volumes, clients, products, and connectivity between firms rise.

This chapter reviews basic concepts and levels of virtualization, and shows, with examples of implementations, how virtualization and grid computing have met the requirements in banks. Finally, the chapter ends with an overview of the cost and ease of implementation of adding a virtual layer onto existing infrastructures, pointing out the synergies between SOA and virtualization. There will be an increasing use of virtualization across all participants in the industry. Eventually, some predict, the industry will see a virtual grid of resources and applications linking all the players in the market, where each player can buy resources from the grid as required. This would very much resemble the power grid paradigm from which the term *grid computing* comes. While this may feel a little far-fetched, it does show that the partitioning of resources and reassembly into coherent service via a virtual layer is full of possibilities and cost and resource efficiencies.

Appendix

The Securities Industry

▌ A.1   Introduction

The securities industry is the name given to that part of the financial services industry that is responsible for the issuance and trading of securities. A security is a contract that is tradable and has financial value. Securities are sometimes also referred to as financial instruments, financial assets, or just assets. Examples of securities include stocks, bonds, and options. Many different types of players participate in the securities industry. The general public traditionally views the securities industry as consisting primarily of investment banks and exchanges, such as Goldman Sachs and the New York Stock Exchange. But utility companies such as the Depository Trust and

Clearing Corporation (DTCC), market data vendors such as Bloomberg, and institutional investors such as American International Group, also participate in the industry. The government too plays a role in the industry as the overseer and guardian of public interest.

The core of this industry is the securities themselves—financial instruments that are created and traded to provide value to the firms' clients and to generate revenue for the firms. *Straight through processing (STP)* is a term used to describe an infrastructure, both within a market participant and across the industry, that facilitates automated trading and settlement of securities. Any discussion of STP first necessitates familiarity with the industry, the trade lifecycle, and the market conditions driving the need for an STP solution. This appendix provides an overview of the securities industry—the products and the major players—and is useful background material for the discussions in the book.

A.2   The US Securities Industry

The securities industry is one of the most important industries in the US. To understand why there is so much attention paid to automating processes in this industry, it is helpful to have an appreciation for its economic value and size. The Securities Industry Association (SIA) points to key statistics such as the following to provide an insight into the role of the industry in the general economy.

1. *Contributes to GDP*—According to the US Bureau of Economic Analysis (BEA), the US Gross Domestic Product (GDP) was almost $12.5 trillion in 2005. Of these, finance and insurance-related activities contributed nearly $957 billion or 8% of GDP.[1] The BEA defines the Finance & Insurance category as being composed of the following classes:
   1. Federal Reserve banks, credit intermediation, and related activities
   2. Securities, commodity contracts, and investments
   3. Funds, trusts, and other financial vehicles
   4. Insurance carriers and related activities

   The diagram in Figure A-1 shows how much each class contributes within the Finance & Insurance category.

   Put another way, if the value added to the GDP by the finance and insurance sector were a country's entire GDP, it would be the equal of the 11th largest country in the world by GDP. As Figure A-2 shows, IMF estimates for the 2005 GDP of countries in the world, this would be greater than the GDP of Brazil, India, and Russia.

---

[1] US Bureau of Economic Analysis (BEA) Statistics by Industry.

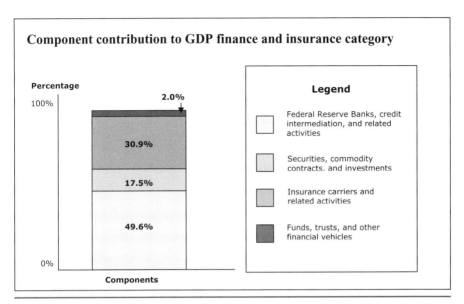

Figure A-1 Components of GDP Finance and Insurance category. Source: US Bureau of Economic Analysis (BEA) Statistics by Industry.

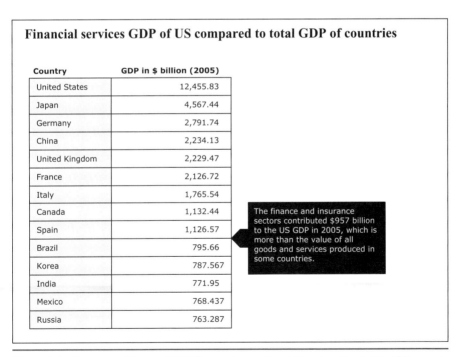

Figure A-2 Country ranking by GDP. Source: International Monetary Fund, World Economic Outlook Database, September 2006.

2. *Provides employment*—The finance and insurance sectors were responsible for the employment of over 6 million people in 2005, providing employment to 4% of all full-time and part-time workers in the country.[2] Of these, the US securities industry in particular employed 822,000 people, which is almost equal to the entire population of the state of Delaware, 841,000, or the city of Detroit, 886,000.[3]

3. *Raises capital for business and government*—The securities industry is crucial in raising money for large and small businesses in the US. The main purpose of financial markets is to bring together those who need to borrow money with those who have savings they want to lend to borrowers. Companies are constantly looking to raise funds to expand their businesses, and the securities market provides a venue for them to find investors who can provide these funds. According to an SIA Research Report,[4] the US securities industry raised a record $3.23 trillion of capital for American businesses through corporate underwriting, including equity and debt issuance and Initial Public Offerings (IPOs). In fact, another SIA report estimates that the industry raised $14.0 trillion for US businesses through overall underwriting activity in the five years 2002–2005, a number that is nearly equal to the $14.2 trillion it raised in the prior thirty-year period 1971–2000.[5] Like corporations, federal and local governments also look to raise funds to finance their activities. In 2006, local governments raised $381 billion through municipal bond issuance.[6]

4. *Is a vehicle for household savings*—According to the SIA/ICI 2005 report *Equity Ownership in America, 2005*, the number of households that own equity has more than tripled since the early 1980s.[7] In 2005, 57 million or nearly half of all US households owned stock directly or through a mutual fund. In 1983, only one-fifth of all US households had channeled their investment to the stock market (see Figure A-3). This increase in household participation in financial markets has been largely driven by contribution retirement plans such as the 401(k). Equivalently, over 99 million people, or almost one in three individuals in the US, have invested in the stock market.

The average investor is college-educated, 51 years old, married or has a partner, and employed with a salary of $65 K and about $125 K savings in financial assets. The biggest impetus for saving for this investor is to have post-retirement income. Given

[2]US Bureau of Economic Analysis (BEA) Statistics by Industry.
[3]US Census 2005 Estimates.
[4]SIFMA Research Report, January 29, 2007, Vol. II, No. 1.
[5]Fernandez, Delalex, Toto, *The Year in Review, The Year Ahead*, SIA Research Reports Vol. VI, No. 12.
[6]SIFMA Research Report, January 29, 2007, Vol. II, No. 1.
[7]Investment Company Institute and Securities Industry Association, *Equity Ownership in America, 2005*.

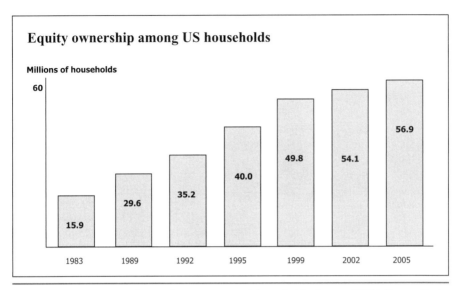

Equity ownership among US households

Millions of households

Figure **A-3** Equity ownership on the rise among US households. Source: ICI/SIA Report, Equity Ownership in America, 2005.

the large numbers of savings, especially those that the baby boomer generation has poured into retirement funds, that the securities industry holds, it is clear that the vitality of the industry is important to citizens.

Since the securities industry has an enormous impact on the economy, it is taken very seriously by the government. The government mandates better risk management and encourages more efficient transaction processing. These directives show the government's awareness that the risks posed by technological inefficiencies may result in loss of investor confidence, jeopardizing the health of the entire financial market and pushing the economy into a possible recession.

No discussion about the US securities industry would be complete without showing how it far outstrips by revenue the securities industries of other countries. The global industry earned over an estimated $712 billion in 2006, an increase of 22% over 2005; over half of this revenue ($414 billion) was generated by the US securities industry. The European Union (excluding the United Kingdom) was second in line with an estimated $121 billion in revenue, followed by the United Kingdom with an estimated $51.1 billion in revenue in 2006. But while the industries of the United Kingdom and other countries, such as Japan, are far smaller than the US securities industry, they are following a similar trend of growth and expansion.[8]

[8]SIFMA, Research Report, November 2006, *Securities Industry & Financial Markets Fact Book Global Addendum 2006.*

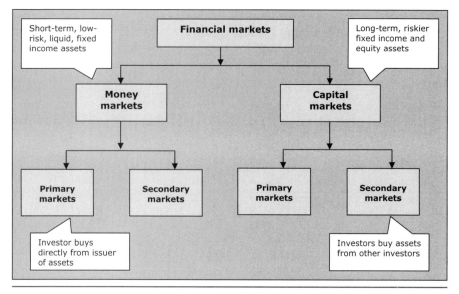

Figure A-4 Financial markets.

A.3 Securities Markets

Financial markets exist to bring together those who have funds to invest and those who need those funds. There are two main kinds of sub-markets in the financial industry: *money markets* and *capital markets*. For short-term financing, borrowers go to money markets, where lenders who can temporarily lend their funds provide financing. For long-term financing, borrowers go to capital markets, where lenders who can afford to provide funds for longer periods are available. See Figure A-4.

Money markets, therefore, consist of short term, highly *liquid* low-risk debt securities, such as Treasury bills and commercial paper. A liquid security is an asset that can be easily bought or sold in the market. Capital markets, contrary to money markets, consist of longer term riskier financial instruments, such as equities, bonds, and derivatives. The fact that the financial instrument is held for a longer period makes it a riskier investment as more uncertainty prevails in the long run.

A.3.1 MONEY MARKETS

Money market securities are issued by the government and by corporations. They are characterized by four things:

- They are *fixed-income* securities; that is, they are securities that yield a periodic or regular return on investment.

- They are short-term securities, and their maturity period is less than one year.

- They are considered low-risk investments. However, precisely because of the low risk factor, these securities offer fairly low rates of return. A *rate of return* is the ratio of money gained or lost in an investment relative to the initial investment in the asset. For instance, if an instrument pays quarterly interest, that interest is part of the yield or return on that investment.

- They are very liquid, which means that a large market exists for trading money market instruments.

Money market instruments are usually traded in large denominations, making it difficult for the individual investor to buy them. The best way for an individual investor to buy a security in the money market is to invest in a money market mutual fund through a money market bank account or to buy treasury bills. There are seven main types of securities in money markets:

- Treasury bills
- Commercial paper
- Certificates of deposit
- Bankers' acceptance
- Repurchase agreements
- Eurodollars
- Federal funds

A.3.1.1   Treasury Bills

Treasury bills, also known as T-bills, are the most liquid of all money market instruments. They are issued by the US federal government to raise money for government projects. A T-bill is like a bond in that it is a loan that an investor provides (in this case to the government) in exchange for a predetermined interest. This interest is reprised by the investor in the following way: T-bills are sold at an auction at a *discount*, and at the time of maturity, the investor can reprise the *par value* of the T-bill. For

A *liquid asset* is one that can be easily bought and sold or *liquidated* in the market. In other words, there are a large number of buyers and sellers in the market who are willing and able to trade the security near the price at which it is quoted anytime during market hours. This means that the bid-ask spread will not be wide for a liquid asset.

The *bid-ask spread* is the amount by which the price at which a seller wants to sell an asset exceeds the price at which buyer wants to buy the asset. In a liquid market, the bid-ask spreads are thin because a seller can always find a buyer in the market at or near the asking price.

Liquidity in an asset is often measured by its trading volume, that is, how often that asset has been bought or sold in a given period of time.

A *bond*, also known as a fixed-income or debt security, is a contract or IOU in which an investor agrees to lend money to a government or a corporation in exchange for a predetermined interest rate.

The principal, face value, or *par value* of the bond is the value of the bond listed on the bond certificate. It is the amount that will be returned to the investor on the maturity date.

The *coupon rate* of the bond is the annual rate of interest payable on a bond. Most bonds pay coupons semiannually to their investors.

The investor receives regular interest payments on the par value until the bond reaches its *maturity date,* which is the date the issuer of the bond repays the par value of the bond to the investor.

Example: A company issues a $40,000 10-year bond with a 5% coupon rate. Each year, the owner receives $2,000 (5% of $40,000), paid in two semiannual installments of $1,000 each.

Par value = $40,000
Maturity = 10 years
Coupon rate = 5%

instance, if an investor buys a 3 month T-bill whose par value is $100, the investor can buy it at the discounted price of $97. At the end of 3 months, he or she can exchange the bill for $100. The government pays the investor interest equal to the difference between the price at which he or she bought the T-bill and the par value that he or she received at the time of maturity.

Since T-bills are issued by the government, they are considered free of default risk, and thus offer low returns. They are also exempt from state and local taxes. Maturities of T-bills are 3, 6, and 9 months.

A.3.1.2 Commercial Paper

Commercial paper is often issued as short-term debt securities by large companies that want to avoid taking a large loan from a bank. Instead, they issue notes called commercial paper, which are often backed by a bank line of credit. This means that if the issuer needs to repay the debt, it can access cash from the bank. Maturities for commercial paper run up to 270 days and are issued in multiples of $100,000. Commercial paper is available for small investors. They are considered safe investments, because investors can reasonably guess the creditworthiness of a firm over the coming few months.

A.3.1.3 Certificates of Deposit

A certificate of deposit, or CD, is a time deposit with a bank, which means that the money cannot be withdrawn on demand by the investor. CDs are issued by a bank, and can be bought through a brokerage firm. Maturities of CDs run from 3 months to 5 years. They offer a slightly higher rate of return than T-bills because a bank has a slim chance of defaulting as opposed to the negligible chance of default for a government. In general, they are considered safe investments, and the interest on a CD varies according to the denomination (currency), bank issuer, and maturity.

A.3.1.4 Bankers' Acceptances

A bankers' acceptance (BA) is a short-term investment issued by a corporation and guaranteed by a bank. It is akin to a bank check with a specific date on which it can be cashed. BAs are particularly popular in international trades. Companies are often hesitant to conduct business in countries where counterparty credit histories are unknown. Counterparties from these countries have a draft made out in the name of a bank. Once the bank *accepts* the draft, in effect certifying it, any holder of the draft can then cash it at the bank. Counterparties that issue these bank drafts thus substitute their credit standing for that of the bank, making business with them a more attractive proposition. Like T-bills, BAs are sold at a discount and then can be retrieved at par value.

A.3.1.5 Repurchase Agreements

Repurchase agreements or *repos* are short-term collateralized loans at a given interest rate. A firm sells securities to another firm, with the agreement that it will repurchase the securities for a specific price at a following date. The securities act as collateral for the loan, and the repurchase price includes the interest that the borrower must pay the lender. This implicit rate is known as the *repo rate*. Any kind of security can be used as collateral, including T-bills, stocks, and corporate bonds.

A.3.1.6 Eurodollars

Eurodollar deposits, unlike what the name suggests, have nothing to do with the Euro. In fact, they are purely dollar deposits, and the reason they are called Eurodollars is because these dollars are held in banks outside the US. Originally, most of these dollar-denominated accounts were held in Europe, which is why the Euro prefix remained on these securities, even though they are applicable to any country outside the US. The biggest advantage of having Eurodollar accounts is that this money is not subject to the US Federal Reserve laws. Note that Eurodollar deposits are time deposits and the Eurodollar rate is the interest that a bank pays to another bank that holds this money in a country outside the US for it. On average, a Eurodollar deposit is quite large (in the millions), and its maturity is up to 6 months.

A.3.1.7   Federal Funds

In the US, the Federal Reserve requires all banks to keep a minimum percent (currently 10% of all transaction deposits) of their customer deposits in reserve at the Federal Reserve. This ensures that the bank can always meet its withdrawal demands. As money moves back and forth from the Federal Reserve, there are times when some banks have excess reserves. These reserves can then be lent as overnight credit between banks. The rate at which banks lend each other this money is known as the *federal funds rate*.

A.3.2   CAPITAL MARKETS

Capital markets are markets where corporations, institutions, and the government raise finances for *long-term investments*. Since the maturity of securities issued in capital markets can sometimes extend over years, there is more uncertainty related to the value of these securities. Because of this higher uncertainty and consequent risk, these securities offer higher returns to investors compared to securities issued in money markets. The following are the main types of securities issued and traded in capital markets:

- Equities
- Bonds
- Derivatives
- Alternative investments
- Structured products

This book addresses the STP requirements of the industry when trading equities, bonds, and derivatives.

A.3.2.1   Equities

A stock is a contract of ownership or *equity* in a corporation. Corporations sell shares in their businesses as a way of raising money to invest in future growth. When corporations decide to open ownership of their business to the public, they approach investment banks to organize an initial public offering (IPO). An IPO is the first time that stocks issued by the firm are available in the market to all investors. The dollar value of all the outstanding shares of a company in the public is known as the *market capitalization* of that company. Stocks are tradable assets: once the shares have been issued, they can then be traded in the secondary markets. If the value of the stock rises after the purchase of the security, the owner's net worth increases, and this is known as capital gain. The reverse is called a capital loss.

There are two main types of equities: common stocks and preferred stocks.

A.3.2.1.1   Common Stocks

Common stocks represent ownership in a corporation. They are characterized by three things: voting rights, residual claim, and limited liability.

- Stockholders have voting rights on matters of corporate governance that are discussed at the annual shareholders meeting of the corporation.

- If the corporation experiences bankruptcy, the debt-holders of the company are repaid first, and then any residual assets are divided among the owners or stock-holders of the company. That is why equity owners are said to have residual claim on the assets of the firm.

- Finally, stocks are unique in that the owners have limited liability in case of bankruptcy or legal law-suits against the firm. This means that unlike the owners of private corporations, they are not liable for any debt or legal entanglements of the firms in which they own stocks.

Firms commonly pay periodic *dividends* to stock owners. Dividends are a percent of the profits of a company and are distributed among the stockholders. They are not mandatory upon the management to distribute, and if the management decides that the dividends are better reserved for future investment or other expenses, profits are not shared with the stock owners.

A.3.2.1.2   Preferred Stocks

Preferred stocks are similar to common stocks with a few important differences. On the positive side, preferred stocks are given preference over

A *stock market index*, such as the Dow Jones Industrial Average (DJIA) or Standard & Poor's (S&P) 500, is a statistic that tracks the average performance of a specific basket of stocks. This basket could consist of stocks from companies from a particular industry, or those traded on a particular exchange, or of a particular market capitalization.

The DJIA is an average of the 30 largest industrial companies in the US, while the S&P 500 is an index of 500 stocks of companies with high market capitalization (also called *large-cap*) companies.

Indices such as these are useful not only in gauging the strength of the market, but also in comparing the performance of a portfolio to the stock market. In fact, many index funds shadow the performance of indices like the S&P 500 by holding the same mix of stocks in their portfolios.

common stocks when it comes to distribution of assets in case of bankruptcy. This means they are second in line after debt to have a claim over the firm's assets.

In addition, dividends on preferred stocks are usually fixed, unlike those on common stocks, and owners of preferred stocks receive their dividends before the owners of common stocks. However, it is not mandatory that dividends will be paid in any given year; dividend distribution is dependent on the financial vitality of the firm.

On the negative side, owners of preferred stocks do not have the voting rights of common stock owners. They do, however, have certain special voting rights to approve extraordinary events, such as a merger or acquisition.

A.3.2.2 Fixed Income Securities

Both corporations and government agencies raise capital through another type of security known as a fixed income security. Fixed income securities allow firms to take a loan from investors (distinct from equities where firms actually give investors ownership of their businesses). Fixed income securities are also known as debt instruments. Say an investor lends $1000 to IBM so that IBM can build a new factory in Mumbai. IBM will give the investor an IOU that stipulates that IBM will return the $100 in 3 years, and will pay an interest of 5% per year on this loan for that period. This IOU is referred to as a bond, the par value of which is $1000 with a coupon rate of 5% and a maturity of 3 years. Bonds are the most common type of fixed income securities.

In general, most fixed income securities share the following attributes:

- *Issuer*—the entity, government or corporation, that issues the security.
- *Par value*—the value of the security at which it can be redeemed at maturity.
- *Coupon rate*—the interest that the security pays periodically.
- *Maturity*—the length of time after which the security holder can redeem the par value.
- *Credit rating*—the metric by which the creditworthiness or the issuer's ability to repay is measured.
- *Price*—the price at which the security is traded, which can be above or below the par value. Bond valuation methods are beyond the scope of this chapter, but available in most fixed income textbooks.

A.3.2.2.1 Treasury Notes and Bonds

Like Treasury bills, Treasury notes and bonds are also issued by the government. However, notes and bonds have longer maturity than T-bills and are generally coupon-bearing instruments. Treasury notes have maturities from 2 to 10 years, while Treasury bonds have maturities exceeding 10 years. Since the government is the issuer, these securities are considered very low-risk instruments.

A.3.2.2.2 Municipal Bonds

Just as the federal government issues Treasury notes and bonds, the state and local governments also issue bonds to finance public works, such as bridges and parks. These bonds, known as municipal bonds or *munis*, provide resources besides taxes to local governments. Municipal bonds are exempt from state and local taxes in the state where they are issued.

A.3.2.2.3 Corporate Bonds

Large corporations regularly issue corporate bonds to raise money to finance growth, including venturing into new markets and products. These bonds are considered riskier than those issued by the government and government agencies. Credit rating agencies, such as Standard & Poor's (S&P) and Moody's, provide ratings for the bonds issued by corporations to indicate the level of default risk for the bond. For example, if Moody's gives a bond a rating of AAA, the market values the bond as very safe and refers to such a high-rated bond as "gilt edged."

A.3.2.2.4 Mortgage Backed Securities

Banks and other institutions that give out loans sometimes pool these loans and issue securities on them (a process known as *securitization*). For example, if a bank has given out a thousand mortgages, it can pool these mortgages and use the interest and principal payments on them as coupon and par payments in a mortgage backed security (MBS). Mortgage backed securities are thus issued as bonds with periodic coupon payments, just like regular bonds. If the bonds are securitized using student loans or other assets as collateral, then these bonds are known as *asset backed securities*.

A.3.2.3 Derivatives

Derivatives are financial assets whose value is *derived* from the value of some other underlying asset. This underlying asset can be any kind of security, or combination of securities, such as a stock, a bond, or a basket of stocks.

Say an investor thinks that the price of Google stock will increase; he or she might buy the option to purchase Google stock at a price lower than the expected future price. This *option* costs money and derives its value from the price of the underlying stock, in this case Google. If the market believes that the price of Google stock will go up significantly, then the option to buy it at a lower price at some particular date in the future is going to be costly; if the market believes the reverse, then this option will be quite cheap.

This is just one example of an option; hundreds of different kinds of derivatives now exist in the market. In fact, the growth of the derivatives market has been one of the major developments in the securities industry in recent years. For example, according to the Bank of International Settlements (BIS), the notional amounts of derivatives (i.e., the face value of derivatives based on stocks, bonds, currencies, interest rates, and commodities) rose to $370 million in the first half of 2006, which amounted to a 24% increase over the previous six months.[9] This phenomenal growth was primarily driven by the proliferation of credit derivatives in the market.

Derivatives are either standard contracts that are traded over an exchange (known as exchange-traded or listed derivatives) or privately negotiated contracts that are traded *over the counter (OTC)*. They can be used with a wide variety of underlying assets, including equity, fixed income, currency (FX), commodities (such as copper, tin, and aluminum), and energy (such as oil, power, and natural gas).

There are three types of derivative products:

- Forwards
- Futures
- Options

A.3.2.3.1 Forwards

A forward agreement is an *obligatory* contract between two parties, one of which agrees to buy and the other agrees to sell an asset at a particular price on a specified date. Forward contracts are privately negotiated and traded OTC. Forward contracts are commonly used to *hedge risk*. To hedge risk is to mitigate or cancel risk in an investment through some financial strategy or product. For example, a farmer may believe that a boom in global wheat production will increase supply and therefore reduce wheat prices. In order to protect himself or herself from the risk of having to sell the wheat harvest for a lower price, the farmer might enter a forward contract with a buyer who promises to buy the farmer's wheat in the future at some mutually agreed upon price. This price is called the *forward price*.

A.3.2.3.2 Futures

A futures agreement is an *obligatory* contract that is quite similar to a forward contract. In other words, it is the agreement to buy or sell an underlying asset for a particular price (*futures price*) on some predetermined future date (*delivery date*). However, unlike forwards, futures are standardized contracts that are always traded on a futures exchange.

---

[9]BIS, *OTC derivatives market activity in the first half of 2006,* November 17, 2006.

An advantage of trading through exchanges is that the clearinghouse associated with the exchange guarantees that the trade obligations will be met by both parties. The concept of a clearinghouse is discussed in Section 1.4. For now, it is important to understand that the clearinghouse helps remove the credit risk that traders often face in forward contracts. To implement this credit-risk-free environment, the exchange vets traders who are allowed to trade on the exchange thoroughly, requiring them to always hold a certain reserve of cash in margin to make sure they can meet their obligations even if the market changes unfavorably for them. The Chicago Mercantile Exchange is a financial exchange based in Chicago that has one of the largest volumes of futures trading in the world.

A.3.2.3.3   Options
An option is different from forwards and futures in that it is a contract between two parties, which allows one party the *option* to sell or buy a certain asset at a particular price (*strike price*) on a specified date (*exercise date*). The seller of the option is obligated to honor the contract if the buyer decides to exercise the option, but the buyer must pay a *premium* or price for this option. The buyer of an option is said to have a *long position*, whereas the seller of an option is said to have a *short position*. Options can be traded over an exchange or privately negotiated and traded over the counter.

- *Types of options*—The simplest options are put and call options, which give the buyer the right to sell and buy a security at a given price and a given maturity, respectively. Options can be created on any number of assets, including baskets of assets. Common examples of derivatives are equity options and interest rate derivatives.
- *Exercise styles*—Options can be exercised in three ways depending on their maturity dates. If an option can be exercised at any point before the maturity date, it is known as an American Option. If it can be exercised only on the maturity date, it is known as a European Option. And finally, if it can be exercised at discrete dates before the maturity date, it is known as a Bermudan Option.
- *Pricing options*—European options can be priced using the famous Black-Scholes formula. American and Bermudan options are more complicated to price as they have more options for an exercise date. They are often priced using numerical methods such as binomial trees and Monte Carlo simulations.

A.3.2.4   Structured Products

Structured products are *synthetic* investment instruments that are created to meet the specific needs of an investor. They are nonstandard instruments that are usually composed of some form of derivative contract and that are not generally available in the market. They are created as direct investments to meet the unique requirements of a high net worth investor, or the particular risk and return specifications of a company offering them as a retail offering. Usually, a structured product offers investors a degree of capital protection, combined with the potential to make some return based on an underlying asset. These kinds of structured products are also known as *principal protected investments*. One example of such a structured product is an *equity-linked note (ELN)*.

An ELN is structured like a bond, except that its principal is typically protected and its final payout is linked to the returns on an underlying asset such as a stock. ELNs do not, therefore, have any regular coupon payments, but provide a final payout at the time of maturity. For example, at the maturity date, the investor reprises 100% of the par value of the note along with any gain in the value of the underlying basket of stocks (according to some predetermined formula).

ELNs are just one type of structured products. There are hundreds of variations of these kinds of products, each specifically tailored to either the investor or the issuer. Since structured products are *bespoke* or tailored products, especially customized to meet the needs of clients, automating their trading and settlement is a challenge.[10]

A.3.2.5 *Alternative Investments*

A whole slew of alternative investments are also available to investors, whether institutional or individual. One kind of alternative investment that has recently garnered a lot of public attention is the *private equity fund*. Private equity funds allow high net worth individuals and institutional investors, such as mutual funds, to invest in private equity investments. A private equity fund uses its capital, partly financed by investor capital, to buy out a majority stake in a company. If the company is public, the shareholders are usually paid off and the company is taken private. While the company remains under the management of the private equity fund, it is restructured, and management and operations are streamlined. At this point, the valuation of the company increases significantly, and the company is taken public again, usually generating a great deal of profits for its original investors. Leading private equity companies are Blackstone and KKR.

A.3.3 PRIMARY AND SECONDARY MARKETS

One important distinction to make when considering money and capital markets is the distinction between primary and secondary markets. *Primary markets* are the

---

[10]*The straight through challenge*, Structured Products, July/August 2006.

markets where the security is issued, and the *investor buys the security directly from the issuer,* whereas *secondary markets* are markets where the security is traded and the *investor buys the security from other investors.* So if an investor buys Treasury bills at the auction of the bills by the government, he or she has bought the bills in the primary market. On the other hand, if the investor buys the T-bill at an exchange from another investor, he or she will have bought it in the secondary market.

▌ A.4   Industry Participants

The securities industry is made up of many players who work together to facilitate the trading of securities discussed in the last section. Broker-dealers, institutional investors, exchanges, and custodians are just some of the participants that exert influence in the industry. From an STP perspective, the flow of execution and information for a particular trade touches each of these participants, and it is important to understand the role each category of participant plays. Participant roles fall into these general categories:

- *Issuer*—Securities are issued by the government and corporations using a variety of mechanisms, including holding an auction and using an investment bank as an advisor.
- *Participant*—Investors buy and sell securities, and are often represented by investment managers or broker-dealers in the market.
- *Facilitator*—Many service providers, including utility firms, software, and data providers facilitate and streamline transaction operations between market participants.
- *Regulator*—The government and its appointed agencies, such as the Securities and Exchange Commission (SEC), oversee and regulate activity in the financial services sector to protect investor interests. See Figure A-5.

A.4.1   ISSUERS

Stocks, bonds, and derivatives are all issued in the primary market. Investment banks are often involved in the issuance either as advisors or structurers of the security itself. Usually, when a company wants to go public, it hires one or a group of investment banks, called the underwriters, that both advise it on the terms and conditions of the offering, and also market the securities for the firm. It is common for the underwriters to buy the securities from the firm at a discount and make a commission

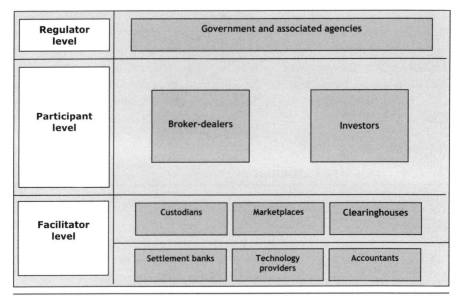

Figure A-5 Securities industry participants.

on the spread between the price they pay and the price that they sell it to the public. Selling the securities to the general public in this manner is known as an IPO. Sometimes the investment bank sells the shares directly to a small group of wealthy institutions and individuals. This kind of primary issuance is known as private placement and is rarer than doing it through an IPO.

An alternative way for a company to go public is to do it through a Dutch auction, in which investors submit a price for a given number of shares. The shares are eventually sold at the highest price that will result in all the shares being sold to the public. This is a fairly new way of issuing securities, and a very small percent of the market is traded using this method. However, the fact that Google used a Dutch auction to offer its securities to the public brought the method into prominence.

Similar to the process of an IPO, an investment bank helps set the terms and conditions of new bonds, and bring them to the market. The government directly auctions off Treasury bills, bonds, and notes periodically.

Derivatives such as futures, forwards, and options are structured by financial institutions in two ways: standard contracts and structured derivatives. Standard contracts, such as futures contracts, can be traded on an exchange and are not specific to a particular arrangement between two parties. However, structured derivatives, which are traded in OTC markets, are formulated specific to the needs of the two parties.

A.4.1.1   *Investment Banks*

Banks are corporations that are licensed to advise and manage the financial assets of their clients. There are two main types of banks, commercial banks and investment banks. This book is particularly concerned with the investment banking arm of a bank, which issues securities, and the sales and trading arm of a bank, which advises clients and trades securities on their behalf.

Investment banks are financial institutions that cater to the needs of large companies and high net worth individuals. Examples of investment banks include Goldman Sachs, JP Morgan, and UBS. The investment bank can be divided into two main sections: Investment Banking and Sales and Trading (see Figure A-6). *Consumer banks*, on the other hand, are financial institutions that cater to individual investors and small businesses. Examples of consumer banks include Chase, Commerce, and Bank of America. These banks also give out small business loans, credit cards, and provide mortgage finance for consumers.

Traditionally, investment and consumer banks used to be one and the same thing. However, after the Stock Market Crash of 1929, the government prohibited banks

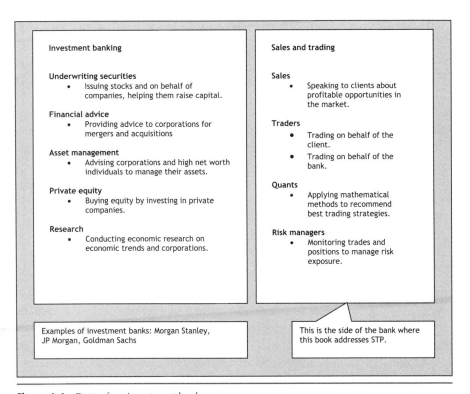

Figure A-6   Parts of an investment bank.

from both accepting deposits and underwriting securities under the law called the *Glass-Steagall Act*. The reason for this act was to avoid recklessness by the traders when it comes to spending all the money that innocent consumers have deposited in the consumer bank. However, in 1998, the Act was repealed, and you began to see a lot of mergers between commercial and investment banks. One example is the merger of the consumer bank Chase and the investment bank JP Morgan, resulting in the current JP Morgan Chase bank.

A.4.2 MARKET PARTICIPANTS

The market consists of two main categories of players: the sell-side and the buy-side. The sell-side consists of large broker-dealers that act as middlemen in trade execution and as advisors that provide research on best investment and execution options. The buy-side consists of large institutional investors that trade the financial assets of large groups of investors.

A.4.2.1 Broker-Dealers

Brokerage firms execute trades on behalf of their clients. Full service brokerage firms, such as investment banks, provide research and advice to their clients as well as execute trades on behalf of clients. This makes them significantly more expensive than traditional brokers. Often investment banks that provide brokerage services are called *broker-dealers*.

There is a slight difference between brokers and dealers, although one institution can act as both: brokers, such as E*Trade, just match buyers and sellers for a commission, whereas dealers, such as Merrill Lynch, can trade out of their own inventories as well if needed.

Marketmakers are a type of broker-dealers who are required to trade to keep the market moving smoothly. Marketmakers profit through commissions and the bid-ask spread on the securities they hold and then sell in the market.

Brokerage firms are also known as *securities* or *sell-side firms*.

A.4.2.2 Individual Investors

The individual investor is someone who buys and sells securities with his or her own money. He or she may be using online trading applications, such as TradeWeb, or working with the sales representative in a large bank, such as Morgan Stanley's Private Wealth Management Group. Traditionally, individual investors relied on middlemen, such as stockbrokers, for advice, but with the proliferation of information on the web, many investors are making their own investment decisions after consulting relevant sites.

A.4.2.3 *Institutional Investors*

Institutional investors include pension funds, hedge funds, mutual funds, and charities and trusts. They are also known as *buy-side firms*. These companies are often advised by top investment banks that provide recommendations to buy-side firms on where and how much to invest. Institutional investors make up the majority of the investment market in terms of capital invested, and their managers require efficient and high throughput of their investments. In terms of STP, banks have to cater to the needs of institutional investors in particular.

A.4.2.3.1 Pension Funds

Companies that offer pensions post-retirement regularly take a part of the employee's salary over the course of his or her employment at the firm. This money is either kept at a bank where it earns interest, or more likely, is invested in different financial assets to secure higher returns than can be offered by a savings account in a bank. Pension fund managers are usually risk-averse since they cannot afford to have market volatility drastically affect the money that will be used by pensioners. The easiest way to ensure risk minimization is diversifying the types of assets in the pool.

A.4.2.3.2 Insurance Companies

Insurance companies, such as American International Group, have large quantities of capital in the form of premiums that they receive on a variety of insurance contracts, such as life, car, and health insurance. They can go on to invest these premiums in various financial assets, hoping to earn a high return on this money.

A.4.2.3.3 Hedge Funds

Hedge funds are funded by high net worth individuals who are interested in putting their wealth in a fund that invests in different strategies and markets across the globe. These private investment funds are not regulated by the government. Hedge funds are traditionally risk-takers and take positions that have a high upside. In recent years, the number of hedge funds has exploded to over 9,000 around the US. A *fund of hedge funds* is an investment company that invests in hedge funds.

A.4.2.3.4 Mutual Funds

Sometimes individual investors put money into mutual funds, because they trust the expertise of mutual fund managers to make educated and calculated investments that will bring high returns. Funds often offer a variety of types of investments, such as US Motor Industry, to meet the preferences and risk appetites of their clients.

A.4.2.3.5 Charities and Trusts

Like all the other institutions mentioned earlier, charities and trusts also have capital to invest and a desire to earn high returns on it. Often, these institutions will hire an investment manager such as US Trust to manage their assets.

A.4.3 THE FACILITATORS

Several market participants play the role of facilitators in a trade transaction. They neither buy nor sell the security; however, without them, the trade lifecycle would not proceed as smoothly as it currently does in the industry. Industry utility providers such as exchanges and clearinghouses are important for matching buyers and sellers, and for settling trades. From a financial technology and STP perspective, the technology service and solution providers are crucial facilitators.

A.4.3.1 Marketplaces

A marketplace is a venue where buyers and sellers can exchange securities. Recent years have seen the creation of electronic marketplaces and the proliferation of venues other than traditional stock exchanges.

A.4.3.1.1 Exchanges

An exchange is a corporation that creates a market in which financial securities, such as equities, options and futures, can be traded. Examples of exchanges include the NYSE, NASDAQ, and Amex. Only members can trade in an exchange, and a member, whether an individual or an institution, is approved by the exchange through a rigorous application process.

A.4.3.1.2 Alternative Trading Systems (ATS)

Alternative trading systems are electronic networks approved by the SEC as marketplaces that provide liquidity and are alternatives to traditional exchanges. They include electronic communications networks (ECNs) and crossing networks.

In 1998, the SEC approved the formation of ECNs, which are electronic marketplaces for trading securities. It was revolutionary in connecting traders directly with brokerage houses, eliminating the need of a specialist in the exchange to act as a middleman. ECNs are registered with the SEC as an exchange or as a broker. A *crossing network* is a private marketplace internal to broker-dealers where buy and sell orders are matched or crossed from the requests of their clients, before they are sent to a public marketplace (i.e., an exchange). Examples of crossing networks include Liquidnet and ITG's Posit. Another type of marketplace that is becoming popular is known as *dark books*, which are also nontransparent and restricted-access marketplaces for buyers and sellers. Because they are hidden from the public, these marketplaces are essentially dark. Examples of broker-dealer dark books are Goldman Sachs' Sigma X and Credit Suisse's CrossFinder. According to the TABB Group, crossing networks and dark pools of liquidity had captured almost 10% of the total equity market in 2006, executing an average of 420 million shares per day, a number that is expected to rise further in the coming years.[11]

A.4.3.2   Clearinghouses

Clearinghouses provide clearing and settlement services for securities transactions. *Clearing* is the process of calculating the payments that are due, and *settlement* is a process by which the exchange of money for securities occurs. Clearinghouses act as *central counterparties*, which means that they become the counterparty in every transaction, thus transferring all credit risk to themselves. This process is called *novation* and reduces counterparty risk in the market. Of course, only accredited parties can use a clearinghouse, after having shown that it is safe for the clearinghouse to substitute itself for them in a contract, and also requires all participating parties to keep collateral margins with the clearinghouse as insurance. Some exchanges have clearinghouses associated with them, and these clearinghouses are the reason that these exchanges can guarantee that all obligations will be met in a trade. For example, the Chicago Board Options Exchange (CBOE) uses the Options Clearing Corporation (OCC) to clear its options contracts.

A.4.3.3   Settlement Banks and Payment Systems

At the time of settlement, investors direct their banks to transfer money to their counterparties. The two main payment networks for interbank funds transfer are Fedwire Funds Service (which is operated by the Federal Reserve Bank) and the Clearinghouse Interbank Payments System (CHIPS). Banks find that transactions that involve foreign exchange can be risky because the trades are settled separately in different time zones and currencies. In 2002, the leading banks in the world came together to form *Continuous Linked Settlement (CLS)*, a bank created specifically to eliminate the settlement risk involved in foreign exchange transactions by creating a mechanism to settle these trades on a *payment-versus-payment basis* (i.e., payments are exchanged simultaneously instead of at different times).

A.4.3.4   Custodians

Custodians are responsible for safeguarding cash and securities on behalf of financial institutions. In this capacity, they manage the settlement of securities by allocating

---

[11]Jeromee Johnson and Larry Tabb, *Groping in the Dark: Navigating Crossing Networks and Other Dark Pools of Liquidity*, January 2007, The TABB Group.

them to the correct client account and by providing reports on the status of the account. This is one way of ensuring that the exchange of securities and cash is done correctly, and that both the buy-side and the sell-side are assured that the integrity of the contract is maintained. Custodians, therefore, play quite an important role in the transaction, and they charge a fee for their services. Many banks will act as custodians for a transaction between two other financial services institutions. For instance JP Morgan may act as a custodian for a transaction between Goldman Sachs and BNP Paribas. The custodian network consists of a network of global and sub-custodians, which together do business in different financial centers around the world.

A.4.3.5   Prime Brokers

Prime brokers are large brokerage firms, such as Goldman Sachs, which provide the technology, operations, and business support for hedge funds and traders when they cannot afford to set up such an infrastructure themselves. A prime broker can provide a number of services including:

- *Clearance and settlement* of all trades that are made using the prime brokerage infrastructure.
- *Technology infrastructure* for portfolio management, trade execution, and consolidated reporting on position and transaction data.
- *Securities lending* and exclusive borrowing arrangements at competitive prices.
- *Capital introduction,* which means introduction to potential high net worth clients of the brokerage firm who are looking to invest in a hedge fund.

A.4.3.6   Technology Providers

Technology service and solution providers can be categorized along four dimensions: connectivity infrastructure, software platforms, data, and personnel.

- *Infrastructure*—Connectivity between the different participants involved in the trade lifecycle is the first step towards building a seamless trade lifecycle process, and requires a robust, scalable, and flexible technology infrastructure. This infrastructure can either be outsourced to a third party, such as SWIFT, or built in-house.
- *Software applications*—Companies such as IBM are providers of software applications such as application servers and databases that are used to create an STP system infrastructure for trading and managing securities.

- *Data feeds*—Data vendors such as Bloomberg and Reuters provide electronic real-time feeds of key market reference data including market prices, corporate actions updates, credit ratings, and security attributes, all of which are useful in pricing securities and managing portfolio risks.

- *Consulting services*—Technology systems must be put together by skilled personnel. Most banks put together in-house technology teams to create their trading and risk management systems. However, increasingly, many are also using consulting firms, especially cheaper ones based in India, to provide either individual or project-based consulting.

A.4.4 THE REGULATORS

Regulatory authorities such as the government and self-regulatory organizations (SROs) work together to ensure that securities markets are fair, transparent, and efficient.

A.4.4.1 Government Agencies

In the US, the *Securities and Exchange Commission (SEC)* is the primary overseer of the securities industry. It was created by Congress in 1934 as a federal government agency after the Stock Market Crash of 1929 when thousands of small investors lost their savings. The SEC was conceived with the mandate to protect investors against fraudulent and manipulative practices, and to investigate firms that do not provide full disclosure. In this vein, the SEC requires all public companies to submit quarterly and annual financial reports to the SEC in order to review the authenticity of the information given to investors. It also monitors the activities of key market participants including broker-dealers and investment managers such as mutual funds. The power of the SEC resides in its ability to enforce its authority. Each year, the SEC identifies and brings to court hundreds of cases of violations of securities laws, such as insider trading. It is responsible for enforcing a number of regulations, including the Sarbanes-Oxley Act and the Regulation National Market System (Reg NMS). These laws are discussed in detail in Chapter 8, Regulatory Compliance.

A.4.4.2 Self-Regulatory Organizations

Self-regulatory organizations (SRO) are nongovernmental organizations that have the authority to regulate activities in their sector in order to promote fair and ethical practices. In some cases, SROs are also delegated responsibilities by the government to create and enforce industry regulations that protect investor interests and maintain market integrity. For example, in the US, the SEC has delegated authority to

NASD, Inc. (formerly known as National Association of Securities Dealers) and exchanges such as New York Stock Exchange (NYSE) to help regulate the industry. NASD is the primary private-sector regulator of the US securities industry and oversees the activity of over 5,000 brokerage firms, which includes admitting firms to the industry, examining them for regulatory compliance, and overseeing the trading of equities, corporate bonds, futures, and options.

A.5 Summary

The securities industry is crucial to the economic well-being of a country and its citizens. It is used to provide a vehicle for investor savings and a venue for raising funds for businesses. Securities issued in capital markets, particularly equities, fixed income, and derivatives, and how they are traded are the subject of this book. STP is the creation of an end-to-end automated trade lifecycle in which there is minimal human intervention.

Bibliography

Chapter 1: The Trade Lifecycle

Bliss, Robert, R., and Robert S. Steigerwald. 2006. Derivatives clearing and settlement: A comparison of central counterparties and alternative structures. *Economic Perspectives,* vol. 30, no. 4.

Citigroup's real-time, web-based answer to pre-trade analytics. 2005. *Windows in Financial Services: The Magazine for Microsoft in the Financial Enterprise.*

Concept Release: Securities Transactions Settlement. 12/21/2004. SEC.

Dipping into dark pools of liquidity. 2006 *Wall Street & Technology,* May 17.

Forman, Michael. 2006. Under pressure, compliance starts earlier than ever. *Securities Industry News,* May 23, 2005.

HSBC Securities services implements CheckFree eVent(TM) for corporate actions automation. 2007. CNN Money. January 15.

Execution Quality Statistics: How to find information on order execution and routing practices. 2007. Securities and Exchange Commission (SEC).

Massaro, Kerry. 2006. Highway to liquidity. *Wall Street & Technology,* August 7.

Mehta, Nina. 2006. Goldman's REDIPlus opens doors to outside brokers. *Traders Magazine,* October 30.

Moskow, Michael H. 2006. Public policy and central counterparty clearing. Speech delivered at the European Central Bank and Federal Reserve Bank of Chicago Joint Conference. *Issues Related to Central Counterparty Clearing, Frankfurt, Germany,* April 4.

Ramachandra, Prema Aiyer, and Santosh Padhi. 2006. Role of custodians in OTC derivatives—A critical analysis. *TATA Consultancy Services,* December 20.

Schmerken, Ivy. 2005. Pre-trade analysis. *Wall Street & Analytics,* February 4.

Schmerken, Ivy. 2006. Crossing over. *Wall Street & Technology,* March 31.

Schmerken, Ivy. 2006. Time to swap your OMS. *Wall Street & Technology,* September 26.

Spending on credit derivatives technology to hit $500m in 2006. 2006. Finextra.

Tabb, Larry. 2004. Efficient markets: Measuring and monitoring efficiency in today's global markets. New York: The Tabb Group/Omgeo.

Spat, Chester S. 2006.Volatility, price discovery and markets. Speech given by Chief Economist and Director, Office of Economic Analysis U.S. Securities and Exchange Commission, Keynote Address at the Wilton Park Conference on Capital Flows and the Safety of Markets Wilton Park, England, November 10.

Chapter 2: The Business Case for STP

Anderson, Jenny. 2006. Big bonuses seen again for Wall St. *New York Times,* November 7.

Anderson, Jenny. 2006. "Bonus heaven" at Goldman Sachs after record year. *International Herald Tribune,* December 13.

Anderson, Jenny. 2006. Huge bonuses on Wall Street fuel luxury spending. *International Herald Tribune,* December 25.

Bank of America lays off more NYSE floor staff. 2007. *Finextra*, February 15. http://www.finextra.com/fullstory.asp?id=16522.

Division of market regulation: Order directing the exchanges and NASD to submit a decimalization implementation plan. 2000. *Securities and Exchange Commission (SEC),* Release No. 34-42360/January 28.

Cresswell, Anthony M. 2004. Return on investment in information technology: A guide for managers. *Center for Technology in Government.*

Equity Ownership in America, 2005. 2005. Investment Company Institute and Securities Industry Association.

Fernandez, Frank A., Isabelle Delalex, and Grace Toto. 2005. The year in review, the year ahead. *SIA Research Reports,* vol. VI, no. 12, December 20.

The Impact of Decimalization on the NASDAQ Stock Market. 2001. Final Report to the SEC. NASDAQ Stock Market, Inc. June 11.

Manchester, Philip. 2002. Powerful incentives for trading in 'real time.' *Financial Times*, April 2.

Pittman, Mark, and Caroline Salas. 2006. Bond traders lose $1 million incomes on transparency. *Bloomberg*, October 24.

Pittman, Mark, and Caroline Salas. 2006. "Bond Traders lose $1 million incomes as transparency cuts jobs. *BondsOnline*, October 24.

Tabb, Larry. 2006. What's up with exchanges? *Advanced Trading*, September 26.

Ten critical business technology issues for the street. 2007. *Wall Street & Technology*, January 23.

Wall Street average paycheck near $300,000. 2006. *CNN Money,* October 17.

Bank for International Settlements, 2006. *Statistical Annex, BIS Quarterly Review*, December 11.

SIFMA, 2006. *Securities Industry & Financial Markets Fact (SIFMA) Book, Global Addendum.* SIFMA Research Report, vol. 1, no. 2, November.

SIFMA, 2007. *Self-Regulation in Financial Markets: Results of an Exploratory Survey*, SIFMA Research Report, vol. 2, no. 1, January 29.

Chapter 3: Service-Oriented Architecture

Albinus, Phil. 2006. Certoma floors it. *Waters*, June 1.

Cearley, David W., Jackie Fenn, Daryl C. Plummer. 2005. Gartner's positions on the five hottest IT topics and trends in 2005. May 12.

Deb, Manas, Johannes Helbig, Manfred Kroll, and Alexander Scherdin. 2005. Bringing SOA to life: The art and science of service discovery and design. *SOA World Magazine*, December 27.

Marguilus, David L. 2006. Banking on SOA. *InfoWorld*, July 13.

McKendrick, Joe. 2006. Ten companies where SOA made a difference in 2006. *ZDNet Blog,* December 17.

McKendrick, Joe. 2006. The information layer matters. *Database*, July.

Middlemiss, Jim. 2005. CIO Challenge—SOA. *Wall Street & Technology*, May 25.

Schneider, Ivy. 2006. Eight banks join SAP in development of service-oriented architecture. *Information Week*, January 3.

Chapter 4: Industry Standards

Allen, Paul. 2004. Slow, but powerful. *Wall Street & Technology*, October 25.

Daly, Bob. 2006. A simple approach. *Waters*, October 1.

Swift's securities efforts boosted by DTCC link. 2006. *Finextra*, October 10.

Chapter 5: Connectivity

Jaffe, Justin. 2002. Happy birthday, dear Internet. *Wired Magazine,* December 31.

McIntyre, Hal, and Pam Pecs Cytron. 2002. *The Summit Group surveys middleware for fifth year.* 2002 Middleware Survey.

Safarik, Dan. 2005. Direct Market Access—The Next Frontier. *Wall Street & Technology,* February 28.

W3Schools. 2006. Tutorial on TCP/IP.

2006. JP Morgan Chase leads open source messaging push. *Finextra,* June 20.

Chapter 6: Data Management

Allen, Paul. 2007. The NYSE focuses on improving data integrity. *Wall Street & Technology*, January 5.

Clark, Tim. 2007. Surging electronic trading volumes and Reg NMS require financial firms to enhance underlying technology infrastructures. *Wall Street & Technology*, January 24.

Crosman, Penny. 2007. The do-nothing costs of messy data architectures: Data management still takes a backseat at many financial firms. *Wall Street & Technology*, February 21.

MacSweeney, Greg. 2006. Citigroup names Bottega CDO. *Wall Street & Technology,* March 16.

Rothke, Ben. 2007. Weak enforcement of corporate governance and lax technical controls have enabled the illegal backdating of stock options. *Wall Street & Technology*, February 21.

Tabb, Larry. 2006. Is the increased speed of direct market data feeds worth the price? *Wall Street & Technology*, October 20.

MacSweeney, Greg. 2006. Citigroup Names Bottega CDO. *Wall Street & Technology*, March 16.

Chapter 7: Reconciliation and Exception Handling

Guerra, Anthony. 2002. Exception management: The safety net you've been looking for? *Wall Street & Technology*, September 4.

WS&T Staff, 2006. Reconciliation to grow steadily. *Wall Street & Technology*, April 14.

ISDA, 2006. Recommended practices for portfolio reconciliation. *ISDA*, February.

Chapter 8: Regulatory Compliance

Govardhan, Giridhar. *Regulation NMS and fast market.* White Paper. Bangalore, India: Wipro.

Levine, Cory. 2006. Inefficient efforts: Firms look to break down their isolated compliance processes. *FinanceTech*, November 21.

Mukandan, Rajeev. *MiFID: Impact on the European Securities Landscape.* White Paper. Bangalore, India: Wipro.

Roy, Indranath, Mahesh Sunderaman, and Shweta Joshi. *MiFID: A Systems Perspective.* White Paper. Bangalore, India: Wipro

2001. *Operational risk: Supporting Document to the New Basel Capital Accord.* Bank for International Settlements. January.

2004. *Guide to the Sarbanes-Oxley Act: Internal Control Reporting Requirements: Frequently Asked Questions Regarding Section 404,* 3rd ed. Protiviti Inc.

WS&T Staff, 2005. Reg NMS cheat sheet. *Wall Street & Technology,* February 3.

2005. *Planning for MiFID.* London, UK: Financial Services Authority (FSA). November.

2006. *Joint implementation plan for MiFID.* London, UK: HM Treasury and the FSA.

Chapter 9: Business Continuity

2007. Business continuity: Slow burn. *Waters,* February 1.

2002. Summary of "lessons learned" from events of September 11 and implications for business continuity. Washington, DC: SEC.

McKinsey & Company's Banking & Securities Practice 2001. *Impact of attack on New York financial services.* New York, USA: McKinsey & Co. November.

The Business Continuity Institute. 2003. *10 Standards of professional competence.* August.

2006. Singapore stages anti terror drill for financial industry, *Bloomberg,* May 10.

2006. *UK financial sector market-wide exercise 2005.* London, UK: KPMG LLP (UK).

2005. *Resilience benchmarking project.* Discussion Paper. London, UK: The Financial Services Authority.

2007. *Financial market preparedness.* United States Government Accountability Office (GAO).

2002. *Contingency planning guide for information technology systems.* National Institute of Standards & Technology. June.

Chapter 10: Virtualization and Grid Computing

Allen, Paul. 2006. Banks take their places on the grid. *Wall Street & Technology,* May 15.

Clark, Tim. 2006. Merrill Lynch drives efficiency through grid computing. *Wall Street & Technology,* May 15.

Dubie, Denise. 2006. Credit to the new data center. *Network World,* February 20.

Gillet, Frank E., and Galen Schreck. 2006. *Server virtualization goes mainstream.* Forrester Research, February 22.

Kramer, Leslie. 2006. Powering up the grid. *Wall Street & Technology,* January 6.

Laurent, Olivier. 2006. Networks: A wider grid. *Waters,* 1 March.

Maldonado, Martin F. 2006. *Virtualization in a nutshell: A pattern point of view.* IBM developerWorks, June 20.

McCrory, Anne. 2005. *Ten technologies to watch in 2006.* SearchCIO.com, October 27.

Middlemiss, Jim. 2004. Gearing up for grid. *Wall Street & Technology,* February 12.

Schmerken, Ivy. 2003. Girding for grid. *Wall Street & Technology,* March 12.

Rosen, Michele. 2004. Networks: CSFB on the Grid. *Waters*, July 1.

Hersh, Chad. 2006. *Grid computing: A guide for financial services firms*. Celent, February.

Making your business disaster ready with virtual infrastructure. White Paper. VMWare.

Virtualization overview. White Paper. VMWare.

Index